To Sri Aurobindo

Whose torch illumed the path

FOREWORD

This is the age of uncertainty. This is the time of emotional upset and nervous instability. This is the era when man, surveying the universe from atop the heap of his material accomplishments, sees his insignificance in comparison to the stars, understands how puny is his strength in comparison to atomic power. This is the time when man, in his headlong rush to master the elements and harness nature's energies, has come far enough to know that he treads the wrong path to his own security. For there is no security in machines or electricity or electronics or atomic power.

What am I? What caused me? Why am I here? Where am I going? These are the questions of the human soul that demand an answer. Their resounding echoes arc in the offices of our psychiatrists, in our penal institutions and our homes for the insane and depraved and wicked. Their anguished cries are on our battlefields, in our uprooted families, in every charred ember of every burned village and pillaged town that exists in the wake of the hordes of humanity who have cut off their ties from God and from hope and from divine reality.

For man is not an animal that exists upon the earth for a day, a freak of existence in a maelstrom of chaos. The human soul does not exist who at some cloistered moment has not reached out with timid fingers and touched God.

No circumstance or fact or event or thing exists that does not have a reason, and so it is with man. All harnessing of nature's elements and powers, all creation of material wealth and possessions are but passing fancies, things of the moment, for man enters into life naked, and naked he departs. The only thing, the single important thing that concerns his existence on earth, is the discovery of his soul.

For man is not body alone. No human being can bear to live who regards himself as only a freak occurrence in a freak circumstance. Man is spirit, clearly and without dispute. Man is the essence of the mighty intelligence that guides and controls the universe. Man lives in this intelligence; he is a part of it and the whole of it. He is as small as his temporal life and as great as his spiritual life, for the intelligence from which he comes is greater than all, greater than the far reaches of space, greater than the power that holds the planets in their courses. This intelligence is man's to use as he sees fit. It is God-given, a divine birthright, and is denied to no man except by himself.

In the pages of *The Key to Power,* you will learn of the unlimited power that is yours. You will learn how you can turn this power to work for you, here on earth, to make your life majestic and overflowing with good. *The Key to Power* is not a religion or a sect or a society. In its entirety it is a series of essays aimed at revealing to you your power over all things. You will learn that there is only one mover in all creation and that mover is thought. You will learn that there is only one creator and that creator is the Universal Subconscious Mind, or God. You will learn that this creator creates for you exactly what you think, and you will be shown how you can control your thoughts, not only to obtain answers to your problems but to create in your experience exactly what you desire.

You will not do this in a day or a week or even a month; but do it you will if you keep heart and keep faith. It requires only a few minutes of your time each day, a few minutes that will reward you with greater vistas in life, greater hope and promise than has ever been dreamed.

There is a cause! There is a reason! There is a power greater than you are, which you are a part of, which you can use to make your life good and great and vigorous and full of abundance!

If thou canst but believe; All things are possible to him who believes.

Chapter 1 - THE LOCK

O, raise up thine eyes to eternal sky
In thy bondage strike out to be free
Hush the whispering voice of the infinite why
With "I am and I was and I ever will be."

THE FORGING OF THE LOCK

Somewhere, in some city, town or hamlet, there is a child being born. Somewhere pure spirit is inspired into form. And even now the Lock takes shape. Mighty is the anvil that forges this Lock, for it is the memory of the Subconscious Mind. Light, sound, discomfort, pain, roughness, dampness, hunger, smells—all impinge on subconscious memory, forging the Lock that bars the door to the infinite.

There is something both sad and beautiful about this—sad because it seems sad to see spirit deny itself—beautiful because self-determination is beautiful. For this infant, wherever it is being born at this moment, is free, even as each member of the entire human race is born free—free to determine his destiny—free to discover the source of his being and the immensity of his power.

FALSE THOUGHT HABITS

Why is it, you may well ask yourself, that the great mass of humanity lead drab and colorless lives, concerned only with fear, frustration, and insecurity? What, you may well wonder, is the point of this scheme into which you have been drawn through no volition of your own and from which you will soon depart, a microbe in a microcosm, a pinpoint on a pinpoint, a flicker in a flash of light? These thoughts are products of your Conscious Mind, and it could not be otherwise. *For only the Conscious Mind remembers its beginning and looks forward to its end.*

The world, said Wordsworth, is too much with us. Circumstance shapes our destiny, and this should not be so. There is a resource which can raise the human soul above all circumstance, but how few people use it!

Do you know this man? John Jones was born in San Francisco in 1906. His parents were immigrants, and his father was a laborer. John grew up in modest circumstances and was a child during the first World War. His father was drafted and killed overseas, and the burden of support of his mother and two smaller brothers fell entirely on John's shoulders. Following the line of least resistance, John became a day laborer. Each week his paycheck went to his mother. Later, when his brothers were able to contribute to his mother's support, John continued at his job as a laborer. He was, as he thought, unable to do anything else, and the full blame for his lost future he laid at the doorstep of a cruel fate, personified in resentment towards his mother. When he was forty-two, John developed a brain tumor and spent the latter years of his life bedridden, partially paralyzed, dying at the age of forty-eight.

Does this sound like one of the children to whom, as Jesus put it, it is the Father's good pleasure to give the Kingdom? Does this sound like a free soul expanding into conscious cosmic power? It most certainly does not. Multiply John Jones by a million and a million times it does not. Yet John Jones was using the same power as Einstein, Homer, Plato, Lincoln, Emerson, Buddha, and Jesus.

Thought habits of the Conscious Mind shaped John Jones' life. He thought he was hemmed in by circumstance, and so he became; so that even when the circumstance dissipated of its own accord, he still could not stir away from his own conception of his position. He harbored a resentment toward his mother until it grew within him, in the form of a tumor, to end his life; even as he was wishing his life ended through his own attitudes of defeat.

Conceptual habits of the Conscious Mind are the greatest bar to man's discovery of himself.

THE SAME POWER BRINGS BOTH GOOD AND EVIL

If you have engaged in competitive athletics, you have seen a sign on the locker room wall that read, "A team that won't be beat, can't be beat." And you know that a team that understood the meaning of that sign was a winner.

If you are a business man, you have heard it said, "Think big, do big." And you know that the men who operate on this premise do big things.

If you are a member of a family, you have seen the power of faith work miracles—in an illness, in financial insecurity, in birth, in death, in all of life's events.

If you are a member of an organized religion, you have seen the tremendous power of prayer.

If you have ever in your life been faced with a crisis, you know the calm inner self you have turned to in a flash, which has rewarded you with an answer in an instant.

Everyone has experienced this power to some degree. It is not so securely locked away that each human being does not touch it during some period of his life. Yet, strange to say, the vast majority of humanity shrug it off as perhaps only a fortunate circumstance, a coincidence, a "piece of good luck."

It is important for you to remember—every day of your life—that the same power that brings you good fortune brings you bad fortune and it does so according to how you use it. The only reason it brings so little good fortune to the great mass of people is that they do not know it exists, use it but sparingly, and use it the wrong way. Their conceptions of themselves are *locked* in the Subconscious Mind. And just as surely as the earth rotates, their futures are mapped out according to these conceptions and thoughts. The *only* way they can become free to achieve success and happiness and health is to arrive at truth—unlock the Lock—discover the Key!

THE MIND THAT NEVER SLEEPS

Perhaps you do not know or truly understand that the mind of man is not alone memory and reason such as he exerts when in a conscious active state. There is in man a mind that never sleeps, that is constantly active, with untold reservoirs that have never yet been plumbed—a mind of such infinite capacity and power that it could not possibly belong to one man alone. This is the Subconscious Mind, as sharply delineated from the Conscious Mind.

The advent of psychiatry has told us a good deal about this Subconscious Mind. We know, for instance, that its memory is perfect—not just for important facts but for every shade and detail and scene ever experienced. The skilled psychiatrist can run back twenty years in a patient's Subconscious, eliciting a scene from him when he was six years old, and lo, the scene unfolds with color, sound, and detail such as could not be recorded on photographic film. A bird's song faint on the summer air, the soft rustle of maple leaves drying on the grass, the distant rumble of a train, the grimace of a countenance, the movement of a person, words, inflections—all exact even to emotional impact. *And yet here is a scene that the Conscious Mind had long forgotten.*

PROBING THE SUBCONSCIOUS

Psychiatry, concerned with restoring people to mental health, has run back along the time track of the Subconscious Mind, probing for emotional "sore spots," then exposing them to the patient's Conscious Mind so that he can rationally judge how trivial they are. Varying degrees of success have been achieved in the restoration of mental health by such methods, and certainly enough to have merited the procedure. Sometimes, alas, disaster has occasioned when a serious "rejection" of the Conscious Mind has been elicited from the Subconscious and submitted to the patient, who in terror at this exposure has lapsed into hysteria or a stony depression, so great have been the emotional conflicts aroused.

But this probing of the Subconscious Mind has unearthed a vast store of hitherto unknown material. Under deep hypnosis, patients have described noises and surroundings that could have been experienced only in the womb. In the same manner, there have been patients who have described scenes and times that it would have been impossible for them to know of or witness. A previous life? Some other person's life? Thought transference? Perhaps the psychiatrist has occasionally laid it to "static" on the time track of the Subconscious Mind, but the existence of such phenomena is indisputable.

What a powerful stupendous toy this Subconscious Mind is turning out to be! Games played in parlors are now assembling in the laboratory. The psychic who can foretell the future, the thought reader, the hypnotist are falling under the scrutiny of the microscope. Measured, numbered, weighed, counted, tabulated and cross-tabulated, they all add up to one thing: The Subconscious Mind is the most powerful creative instrument in the universe; it spans space and time, manifests form from substance, reaches out to all knowledge. *And it exists in every man!*

THE MASTER AND THE SERVANT

You might wonder why, with such an inexhaustible subject as this, we should concern ourselves with the Conscious Mind at all—the tiny, insignificant Conscious Mind, that only remembers a very few years, that only remembers a very few facts, that barely has learned the rudiments of thought, and indeed is scarcely capable of dealing with its immediate surroundings.

We are concerned because here we are dealing with master and servant, and startling as it may seem, the tiny, little Conscious Mind is the master!

It is like a button that works a switch, that works a lever, that starts an engine, that generates electricity, that moves the world!

The Subconscious Mind does exactly what the Conscious Mind tells it to do!

THE PROMPTER—PAIN REJECTION

Herein lies the problem. No one consciously wants to be sick. No one consciously wants to be poverty-stricken, unloved, unsuccessful. It would be impossible to elicit admission from anyone in the world that he consciously desired these negative things.

Yet, if he has them, just as surely as there is life, he has *ordered* them for himself.

He is the victim of "Prompters" set into the Subconscious Mind by the Conscious Mind. These have been buried by the Conscious Mind, much as a forgetful dog might bury a bone, remembering neither the place of burial nor even the fact of burial.

These Prompters in the Subconscious Mind are responsible for the great hordes of unhappy people who now troop to psychiatrists. They have spread more mischief for individual lives and for humanity as a whole than any other single thing. They have given the world insecurity, hostility, greed, corruption, and hate. They are broken keys in a divine instrument. They have thrown mankind out of tune with the Infinite. *They are the Lock that bars the door to self-realization.*

For example, Fred Smith is an unwanted baby. As an infant, his first searching for love from his mother meets with complete rejection. To cope with his hurt, Fred Smith develops an aggressive, arrogant attitude toward life. As he grows older, he forgets that he ever desired love from his mother at all. He takes pride in the fact that he needs nobody and nothing to make him complete, and he runs roughshod over people to attain his ends. Here is the making of a dictator or a murderer. Fred Smith hates life because his first reaching for life was rejected. He is simply rejecting that which first rejected him. He can't help himself. Consciously, he has long forgotten the cause, but the memory of the Subconscious Mind is perfect. The pain remembrance or Prompter buried there will not let him rest.

MAN AGAINST HIMSELF

The psychiatrist, as has been pointed out, has faced up to this problem by running down these Prompters in the Subconscious Mind and exposing them to the patient. For example, Miss B comes to the psychiatrist complaining that she has recurrent headaches. Investigation shows that these headaches always occur when she is cooking at her gas stove. It also develops that Miss B harbors a fear of fire. Running back through the subconscious time track, the psychiatrist discovers that when Miss B was two years old, her mother's gas stove exploded and in the resultant excitement Miss B's mother dropped Miss B on her head. Gas—gas explodes—pain in head; this is the simple subconscious memory that prompts Miss B's headaches whenever she must work around a gas stove.

Of course, the great majority of psychiatric treatments are not nearly so simple as this. The example is offered only to show how the existence of Prompters in the Subconscious Mind is widely recognized and that the damage they can do is unlimited.

Take the case of the man or woman who is poverty-stricken and desires money. No matter what he or she does there is always the unfailing outcome—little or no money at all. It would seem to this man or woman that the attainment of a comfortable amount of money is the most important thing in the world, but no matter the effort or time expended, only poverty results. Obviously, here is our Prompter at work. Strange as it may seem, the Prompter may be such a trivial thing as the subconscious burying of an infant-heard phrase: "There's never enough to go around." Think of that! The Subconscious Mind believes there is not enough, and lo, the manifestation of lack and limitation is all that this particular person can ever encounter.

The sick man wants to be well. That he cannot be well is evidence only of a Prompter. In this case the Subconscious Mind harbors such a phrase as "There's so much sickness in the world" or "I could have done better but I'm sick" or "You know, there are millions of dangerous microbes all around us." What chance has a person to be healthy with subconscious Prompters such as these?

The lonely person desires love and friends. Yet no matter the circumstance, he or she cannot seem to attract either a loved one or a social circle. There is a Prompter in this person that repels love, such as "Nobody ever did anything for me," "You can't trust anyone," or "People are just out to get what they can out of you." Or even worse, the Prompter may set up a sense of inferiority, such as "You're not good enough," "You don't amount to anything," or "Nobody loves you." Powerful Subconscious Mind! It manifests these beliefs into actuality.

Who can be successful with a subconscious Prompter that keeps convincing him that everyone is better than he? Who can achieve anything with a Prompter that convinces him that all achievement is worthless? Who can rise to heights with a Prompter that has him believing that he has no capability? The answer is *no one*. For the Subconscious Mind is the great creator, and it creates exactly what it is prompted to create.

SELF-MASTERY

Happily, you can remove each of these insidious Prompters yourself. What's more, you can, by understanding the laws and dynamics of life, remove the cause of them, so that they will plague you no more.

This reassuring fact we place before you; Nothing is impossible to the mind of man, for the Conscious Mind controls the Subconscious Mind and the Subconscious Mind is all-powerful.

Every condition, circumstance, and manifestation of your life can be changed to suit your conscious desires.

The commandments are only two: Know that fear is your enemy; and Understand the Lock.

For fear causes the Lock, and the Lock exists in the Subconscious Mind in the form of Prompters, placed there by the Conscious Mind.

Today, with this first chapter, we ask you to begin to undo the Lock. We ask you to eradicate from your mind all notion of yourself that has to do with where you live, where you were born, what you have done, and what your circumstances have been. We ask you to concentrate on only one thing and that is the spirit within you.

This real you, this conscious hidden intelligence that exists behind your eyes, is timeless, formless, and built from all the glory and magnificence that ever was. It is not a name or a job or a home; indeed it has nothing to do with circumstance or situation. The plain fact is that you exist. Dwell on that, nothing more.

I am.

Two more magnificent words were never put together. *I am.* This minute. This now. All the time that ever was.

ONLY ONE MIND AND YOU *MUST* USE IT

You are pure spirit, cast into human mold as a manifestation of divine intelligence, existing this little while on earth to help carry on the divine plan. Being pure spirit, you are a part of the only intelligence there is, and all the power and understanding of this intelligence are yours to draw upon.

There is only one intelligence, one mind in all creation, and everyone is a part of it. Thought transference, hypnotism, clairvoyance are only a few examples of the fact that we all are using one mind. Every book has been written by the same author, every building and bridge built by the same engineer, every picture painted by the same artist, every sonnet composed by the same poet, all music conceived by the same musician. You and your neighbor, us, everybody, one. That is the way it is.

The Universal Mind that flows through everyone knows no limitation or lack, and nothing is impossible to it. Its great dominant characteristic is creativeness. Since it is all knowledge and all substance and all power, indeed the only thing it does is create. *And it creates exactly what the mind of each individual person thinks into it.*

Now we are not discussing something that you can either use or not use as you see fit. We are discussing something that you use every day of your life, that you can't help using because it is a part of you, in fact, is *altogether* the real you.

This Universal Mind knows no big or little, rich or poor, great or insignificant. It gives of itself according to need, and it creates according to desire. It is creating for you right now exactly what you are thinking into it!

Construe this mind, if you will, as a great plastic medium containing all energy, all knowledge, and all substance. Conceive of it as a medium responsive only to thought and responsive in degree and time according to how such thought is sped with conviction.

We might then have a simple formula like this. Thought plus Conviction equals Manifestation.

There is manifested in your experience exactly that which you are convinced of!

However, even though our Conscious Minds desire success, if our subconscious Prompters believe it to be impossible, then our emotional thought is all aimed at failure, and failure will result.

The Lock that forbids achievement and happiness is the existence in the mind of subconscious Prompters that make automatons out of free persons.

EXPOSING THE SUBCONSCIOUS

Though hypnotism as a science is in its infancy, it illustrates perfectly the remarkable power of the Subconscious Mind and how it operates entirely by suggestion.

The hypnotist, through his methods of putting the Conscious Mind to sleep, simply removes the control which the Conscious Mind exerts over the Subconscious Mind. The patient, when under hypnotic sleep, acts on every suggestion of the hypnotist as if it were truth, for the hypnotist has now taken the place of the Conscious Mind. The hypnotist says, "You have no feeling in your right arm," and forthwith the patient has no feeling in his right arm. So deep, in fact, is this anesthetic that it far outdoes any drug known to science. The hypnotist may say to the patient, "When you wake up, I am going to count to ten, and as I count, you will gradually lose your hearing, so that when I get to ten you will be able to hear nothing at all. When I start counting backwards from ten, you will gradually regain your hearing, so that when I arrive at one, your hearing will be fully restored."

This is post-hypnotic suggestion. The patient is awakened, the hypnotist counts to ten, and the patient gradually loses his hearing. At ten, a gun is fired behind the patient, and not a single tremor indicates that he has heard. When the hypnotist counts backwards from ten, the patient's hearing is fully restored.

This is the mighty Subconscious Mind at work! This is but one small example of the miracles you can perform for yourself. For you, your Conscious Mind can take the place of the hypnotist, and your power is magnified a thousand times because you are working toward your own desires.

DISSOLVING YOUR NEGATIVE PROMPTERS

First, however, we must be concerned with removing all negative Prompters from the Subconscious Mind and installing in their stead a group of positive Prompters which will lead us in the path of attainment and happiness.

We need not remove these negative Prompters as an especial procedure. Since positive will override negative, all that is necessary is for us to install in the Subconscious a group of positive Prompters. The existence of these will dissipate all negative Prompters and allow the individual to expand to the full blossom of his power.

For example, if you are consistently sick, it is a long way toward recovery to search the Subconscious Mind for the Prompter that is causing your sickness. Rather, it is best to install a Prompter that says that it is natural to be well, that health and vigor are birthrights of mankind, that you exist in a spiritual medium that is perfect, and that your body as a manifestation of this perfect medium is perfect also. Once this positive Prompter is thoroughly installed in the Subconscious, the negative "Sick Prompter" will wither and disappear.

It is, of course, a great aid in this therapy to understand the origination of all negative circumstance in your life, the cause of all sin and punishment, *for heaven and hell are within you, and reward and punishment are simply cause and effect in your use of the great spiritual laws that govern all life.*

INTUITION

It has long been established that the principal compartments of the human mind consist of Memory, Reason, and Imagination. These three mental factors, however, when added together have failed to yield the mystical whole of the human personality, leading psychologists to believe that all the factors of the human mind were not being studied. For some time past, an additional factor has come under laboratory scrutiny—the factor of Intuition, the ability of a number of individuals to know the correct answer to a problem without being versed in the parts of the problem. It has been discovered that not all persons are so gifted, or rather that not all persons are intuitively "awakened," but where such an awakening exists, Reason and Memory have flouted all measurement.

Intuition, then, is a compartment of the human mind.

FAITH

Still a fifth compartment of the human mind is only now achieving widespread recognition, even though ancient philosophers long ago proclaimed it to be the most important of all. This is the compartment of Faith.

See how common these quotations are: "Faith can move mountains," "As ye believe, so shall it be done unto you," "Think big, do big." And yet, even though these written revelations are as old as recorded history, the world has blithely gone its way, disregarding them.

How many of them we have chalked up to coincidence! There was the neighbor who rubbed a rag across the wart on your finger, buried the rag and informed you that when the rag rotted the wart would disappear. You believed it, and the wart disappeared. A coincidence, your adult mind says, because your education tells you that there is no way a rotting rag could possibly affect the existence of a wart. With such a conclusion you are looking in the wrong direction, for it wasn't the rag but the *Faith* that caused the wart to disappear!

Consider the life of Jesus. There can be no doubt but that this enlightened man was preaching to the world of the magnitude of his discovery of Faith. Through revelation, intuition, enlightenment, attunement with the infinite, Jesus knew as perhaps no one before or after him of the unlimited power of Faith. Through it he worked his miracles of healing and spiritual understanding.

Such miracles as the Bible discloses are happening every day of our modern life. A patient suffering with cancer of the throat was informed of a new X-ray machine that would cure his condition. This man could neither read nor write, nor was he informed about any of the instruments or procedures of medical practice. When he first sat down in the doctor's office and received into his mouth a thermometer with which the doctor sought to take his temperature, he believed he was undergoing X-ray treatment. The doctor, alert to the practices of psychology, recognized this, and after leaving the thermometer in the patient's mouth for ten minutes, excused him and told him to return in two days. Three weeks of treatment with a thermometer cured this patient's cancerous condition! Obviously, it wasn't the thermometer that did it. It was Faith!

CREATOR

Here then is the human mind as we find it today. Principal conscious compartments consist of Memory, Reason, and Imagination. Conscious memory is the ability to recall the past, while subconscious memory is perfect and contains the Prompters which have been placed there as pain rejections of the Conscious Mind. Intuition is a characteristic of the Subconscious Mind, a phenomenon attributable to a contact made by the Conscious Mind with the Subconscious Mind. Faith, the mover of mountains, the worker of miracles, is the Conscious Mind acting on the Subconscious Mind. Memory, Reason, Imagination, Intuition, Faith: these equal the Human Mind.

For the purposes of what we have to learn here, we need concern ourselves only with Intuition and Faith, for by Faith we will overcome the Lock, and through Intuition we will contact the infinite.

Nothing is impossible to the human mind when the Lock is removed. Ships, planes, electricity, radar, rocket power, automobiles, engines, electronics, atomic power have all been the result of thought. Thought is the great creator, master and mother of the universe, God in man, the infinite in the immediate. And there is no end to individual power through the right use of thought.

Thought plus Faith — Creator.

But before we can truly use or understand this great creator, we must first understand the Lock that bars us from its proper use.

JOURNEY TOWARD GOD

Man is pure spirit, in essence a part of God, in actuality a manifestation of the infinite. As such, man is perfect but temporal. His earthly existence is a matter of a moment, his form is ever changing. In this earthly form, his spirit undergoes a sense of isolation and personal responsibility, which in his daily material life causes emotions of insecurity and isolation and frustration. These memories of insecurity, isolation, and frustration are unbearable to his Conscious Mind, his material mind, and he rejects them, hiding them within his subconscious memory where they act as Prompters of limitation, lack, illness, etc. These subconscious Prompters act as a bar to the door of the infinite, keeping man from full contact with the power of the great

Universal Mind in which he lives, moves, and has his being.

The complete removal of all negative Prompters in the mind, full contact with the infinite, complete recognition of the spiritual laws and the spiritual nature of mankind are the sum and substance of human existence and provide the path mankind treads on its journey toward God.

I AM WILL NOT BE DENIED

It is possible that you will be unready to accept with this first chapter the complete realization of your own divine origin and power. Perhaps the subconscious Prompters in your own mind are now urging you to the conclusion that you are an insignificant bit of matter, accidentally sprung to life in a chaotic universe, without cause, without reason, without destiny, without power. Yet inside you, a still small voice knows the truth, and no matter the strength of your rebellion away from your true self, the fact of your spiritual existence, the great I AM, will not be denied. Have no fear, then, that you will be lost. If, in this first chapter, there are statements made and conclusions drawn with which you cannot find yourself in complete agreement, it is only because you are now contacting those hidden truths that may not be learned without struggle. This, you have in store for you: These chapters are not merely expositions; they are demonstrations. You will be given things to do, experiments to conduct, proofs to achieve that will convince you beyond all shadow of doubt that there is a power far greater than you and which you can use to make your life happy and fulfilled. The understanding of this power within yourself will expand your life to new and exciting horizons, will embark you upon the greatest adventure it is possible to know.

THE RESULT OF SELF-KNOWINGNESS

Take for instance your body. According to measurement, it is short, tall, slender, heavy, handsome, dainty, rugged, strong, or weak. Within the scope of these measurements, you have established to yourself in some degree what kind of person you are. When you first came into self-consciousness in this life, your body was with you. You didn't order it. You didn't go to the great Tailor and say, "Make me a body with two arms and two legs and two eyes and two ears and a nose and a mouth, and make it better-looking than other bodies, and make it stronger than any other bodies, and make it so it won't wear out." If you had, you probably would have placed just such an order, but you didn't have the chance. Your body was ordered for you. You possessed it in an infant state and grew within it, even as it grew around you. The spirit clothed itself with a gown of flesh!

The result of all self-knowingness is form, and so your form, or body, is the result of your knowing yourself, being aware of yourself. Your body is an embodiment of life, is an expression of life, for through your body your spirit expresses Itself.

It matters not the form of your body, for it is perfect, even as the spirit within it is perfect. It is a perfect instrument for the expression of your spirit, and only the misuse of spiritual law can cast from it its perfection. All illness and disease is thus the result of the misuse of spiritual law and the lack of spiritual understanding. For God is perfect, spirit is perfect, and the body that expresses them must be perfect.

The answer to why you and your body came into existence is as simple as knowing yourself. You, as spirit, are eternal and never came into existence. Your body is simply a manifestation of your spirit, a changing form made from eternal substance, even as all form must change. It is difficult to analyze and probe this mystery with the Conscious Mind, but it is relatively simple to demonstrate to the Conscious Mind the existence of Infinite spiritual power.

THE ELUSIVE INFINITE

Man's words and conceptions, with which he demonstrates his earthly control, are hardly adequate in tackling the realms of the spirit.

Take the word infinite. Man has decided that infinite means never-ending. He understands a straight line. He claims to understand an infinitely long straight line. Yet if you were to take two crossed lines, infinitely long, and attempt to uncross them, you would find that, as you moved them away from each other, the point at which they were crossed moved farther and farther away from you. But since the lines never ended, they could never be uncrossed! You could, at the point you were grasping them, be holding them parallel to each other, and still they would not be uncrossed, even though they were straight lines!

Obviously the Conscious Mind, in its measurements and numbers, is scarcely capable of dealing with the infinite.

Again take man's conception of time, a matter of the earth's revolution on its axis and its path about the sun, a matter of seconds and minutes and hours and days and months and years and centuries. Time, you might say, is as fixed a conception as there could possibly be, an unvarying measurement.

Yet, in human experience, it has long been established that a second can be as long as a minute, an hour as long as a day. Einstein, in his *Theory of Relativity,* has expressed in the language of science the variability of time. Essentially, he has shown that the speed of light, 186,000 miles per second, is in man's conception infinitely fast. For at the speed of light, a mass would be infinitely big, and time would stand still. On the basis of this theory, it has been worked out that a space ship traveling 185,999.9 miles per second could circumnavigate the universe in a period of time that would be thirty years to the occupants of such a ship. Yet, to those on the earth, the space ship would be gone 10,000,000 years!

Yet, despite conceptual inadequacies, science has proven that every physical law of the universe has a corresponding spiritual law.

Science has shown us that matter and energy are one, that even the heaviest and sturdiest materials are simply a collection of free-moving molecules banging against each other, moving at tremendous speeds. Through the use of the spectroscope, elements have been discovered on far-flung planets that weigh as much as a hundred tons per cubic inch! Electronics may one day transmit masses around the world in a fraction of a second, even as pictures are now being transmitted! Certainly this is no age in which to hold the idea that anything in the way of bridging space and time and form is impossible to the mind or the spirit of man.

THE CHALLENGE OF THE INVISIBLE

There have been, in the records of history, many enlightened men; teachers, scientists, spiritual advisers, and poets; and each of them has had this thing to say in common: There is a great medium of mind and intelligence that is in and surrounds every human being. This intelligence is all-intelligence and knows and does everything. This intelligence, God, is an eternal creator, creating that which the mind of man thinks.

A doctor whose professed views on life were on a strictly material plane has said, "I have cut many a body open and I have never found a soul." To which it has been answered, "Undoubtedly true, but while you were there, did you ever find a thought?"

The invisible plane of human existence offers the greatest challenge and the greatest hope for all mankind!

A young woman, born and raised in the United States, not able to read or write and speaking only the English language, was sitting in the front room with her father not many years ago, when through the front door came a long-time friend of her father's who had just arrived from Greece. At the sight of him, the young woman rose from her seat and began speaking rapidly to him in his native tongue, a language she had never heard nor studied! The man from Greece broke down and wept, for the young woman had just informed him that his wife, back in Greece, had died!

18

Subsequent checking proved this young woman's revelation to be true. She had circumvented the barriers of space, time, and language to reveal this tragedy to this gentleman she had never seen before!

Another woman, whose contact with the universal intelligence was acute, was able to provoke physical occurrence through nothing but thought. In demonstration, under the surveillance of a group of highly trained scientific minds, she activated through nothing but thought, a light switch over which a soap bubble had been placed. The switch was turned on, the bubble remained unbroken!

THE TRUTH LIES IN LOOKING INWARD

So great is the new-found, newly recognized power of thought that groups are organizing throughout the world, aiming at the creation of peace through thought power. What else is this but prayer? What else is this but the transmission of desire into the creative mind of the universe? Done correctly and with power it must succeed!

The responsiveness of Universal Mind to thought has long been beautifully taught by Dr. Ernest Holmes and his Institute of Religious Science in Los Angeles. Dr. Holmes has authored a number of fine books on the healing power of positive beliefs, and maintains at his institute a spiritual treatment clinic that makes miracles an everyday occurrence. Yet Dr. Holmes smiles when they are called miracles. "They're only the use of the Law of Mind in Action," he says. "Change the idea of a thing, and you change the thing. It's that simple."

This great plastic creative medium, this Subconscious Mind, this mind of the universe in which there is all knowledge, all wisdom, and all power, is ours to use every day that we live. We are using it now; we can't help using it. We are using it in such degree and in such manner as we understand it; and more often than not we are using it in such a manner as to create unhappy circumstance and situation, delaying if not forbidding the realization of our own God-given divinity.

It is our purpose here to impart understanding of the great intelligence to which you belong, to point out the errors of thought and the false circumstances that have locked you away from self-realization.

This locked-in viewpoint, this limitation we impose upon ourselves must be dissipated. We have looked around us at the material world, made judgments about things and people and then imposed those judgments upon ourselves. By looking *outward* we have achieved what we believe to be knowledge about ourselves, and this is falsity of the very highest degree.

COMPETITION VERSUS CREATIVENESS

If you were to take an average person living in the United States of America, and ask him, "Who are you?" he would answer with either his name or his job or both. Similarly, he has an impression of his own success, his own wealth, his own ability, and his own desirability, which he has gained not from looking within but from *comparing* himself with those around him.

The essence of mankind is not competition; it is *creativeness*. In all this world there is not another you, nor has there ever been another you. Is it not ridiculous to attempt to mold yourself into a likeness of your fellows, to attempt to undo the work that God has done? For you, as an especial part of the universal intelligence, are manifested here on this earth in the form you now occupy to do work that only you can do! No matter how humble your job may seem, no matter how unprepossessing your position in life, take heart! The universe has sired no other person like you. Only *you* can be *you*.

Only *you* can draw upon the infinite for those divine powers that are yours.

There is a fine line of demarcation between competition and creativeness in the minds of everyone today. Yet they are black and white, complete opposites on the polar scale. Competition attempts to be *like*. Creativeness attempts to be *unlike*. Competition casts all humanity into the same mold. Creativeness makes of each man an individual counterpart of God.

Competition exists on the plane that makes you want to have a better home than Jack Smith, a better car than Jack Smith, a better job than Jack Smith. It leads you into the suffocating trap of not wanting the different but wanting the same, only better. It imposes upon you a scale of values that is not your own but belongs to a group.

Creativeness, on the other hand, is a world all your own. If you were to take brush and palette in hand right now and paint a picture in oils, the result—good, bad, or indifferent by the world's standards—would be all your own. *The finest artist living could not copy it exactly.* Does not this prove there is no other you? Conformity and competition are death knells to the spirit. Creativeness and non-conformity are an expansion into cosmic understanding.

ENLIGHTENMENT

Your security in life depends entirely on your recognition of your divine nature. Money, home, insurance policies, and position are like wraiths in the night. There are no banks in the hereafter, nor pockets in a coffin. All the things of the world change;

they are born, they blossom, they bear fruit, and they die. Only the great unity—your own association with the infinite, your own individual manifestation of the Universal Mind of God—only that is changeless. Your recognition and use of this great truth will provide you with such security as you have never dreamed, will cast into proper perspective every aspect of your life, will unloose in you such a flood of creative energy as to fill your life to brimming with success, accomplishment, and vigor.

There is a Key to this attainment. Could we but break down the barriers established by your Conscious Mind, remove your Prompters with but a word, the Key could be given to you now and your life would be changed this moment. But the Conscious Mind acting in accord with the insidious Prompters is strong. Only hundreds of pages of discourse and proof will weaken its prejudice. Only diligent daily application of the principles of this book will finally dissipate all doubt. For Faith is the great mover, the father of all creation.

With each chapter you will develop your powers of Faith and Intuition. There will come a time, an hour, perhaps a moment, when you will feel a flash inside you, when suddenly all the world will assume a shape and a mold that will seem divinely inspired for you alone.

POINTS TO REMEMBER

In the meantime, you must go step by step. There is no quick, easy road to anything worthwhile. Take from this first chapter the principal points covered and record them indelibly in your memory. They are:

1. There is a power, greater than you are, which you can use to make your life vibrant, successful, and happy.

2. This power is the Universal Creative Mind, the Subconscious Mind, and you are using it now; you can't help using it.

3. All of us live and move and have our beings in the great intelligence that makes up the universe and the world.

4. This Universal Mind is responsive to thought. It creates what is projected into it.

5. The reason our conscious desires do not always manifest themselves in reality is twofold: 1) We are not projecting our thoughts with conviction. 2) There are Prompters in the Subconscious Mind which cause our thinking to go astray.

6. The Prompters in the Subconscious Mind make up the Lock which bars us from

proper use of the great power of the infinite.

7. These Prompters are rejections of the Conscious Mind, buried in the Subconscious and long forgotten. They are primarily pain experiences, and thus are primarily negative, attracting and creating lack and limitation and disease and unhappiness.

8. This Lock, these Prompters, can be removed by understanding, study, and application of the great laws of spirit.

THE HIGH ADVENTURE

It is always necessary to understand something about a lock before you can use the key. It is equally important to understand a good deal about the key before you can use it to open the lock. In this first chapter, you have encountered the basic elements of the Lock that keeps you from enjoying but a small fraction of your God-like given power. Certain elements of the Key to the Lock have been discussed. In the following chapters, you will arrive at a complete understanding of the Lock and a complete understanding of the Key; so that you will, without further help, be able to embark upon the most productive and happy and vital years of your life. And you are not likely to ever again meet with such high adventure as you study and experiment with your own divine nature, as you discover for yourself the great source of power and wisdom that exists within you.

DON'T ARGUE WITH YOURSELF

Subsequent chapters will cover such subjects as Illusion, Mind, Form, Faith, Intuition, Love, Success, Health, Attraction and Immortality. The final chapter, *THE KEY* will reveal a great metaphysical secret.

Throughout the book we will undertake the study of Hypnotism, Thought Transference, and Clairvoyance, and we will show how they are all products of the vast power of the Universal Subconscious Mind.

Enlightenment, however, is not going to be as simple as just reading the chapters. You must devote at least ten minutes daily to the practice of what you have learned, for only with this cooperation and effort can the rewards of self-realization be achieved.

We ask you to spend ten minutes daily in meditation, projecting your thoughts into the creative Subconscious Mind, so that they can manifest into actuality. These meditation periods are designed to accomplish a purpose, to prove to you that you can achieve your desires through the proper use of mental law. Of course, if you spend ten minutes each day saying "yes" and the other twenty-three hours and fifty minutes saying "no," the "no" will result. Obviously, the only way the "yes" can be manifested is when you do more affirming than denying. *The Subconscious Mind always acts— and it acts on the most predominant thought.* Therefore, commit the meditation to memory or carry it with you. Throughout the day, when circumstances appear to be negative, when disillusionment, depression, or discouragement knock at the door of your consciousness, simply bring the meditation to your mind and say it over to yourself. *The simple saying of the words will immediately restore your peace and confidence.*

You must understand that as a human soul you can't quit using the law. You can't help using it a single minute of any day of your life. You're using it now. If you decide that you cannot achieve success, health, happiness, and peace of mind,—then failure, illness, unhappiness and confusion are yours. For the law still works, and you can't stop it from working!

The only question you have to answer is whether you desire good or evil, for the law must bring you one or the other, according to your desire.

MEDITATION—MANIFESTATION

"In the beginning, the word," and so it is with all creation, for the word is the thought. Speaking the word with conviction and maintaining that conviction with faith is the complete chain of manifestation from the thought to the thing.

The first meditation, which is given at the end of this chapter, is designed to put you in contact with the Universal Subconscious Mind, to provide you with a sense of peace, power and security, for only with this sense of the absolute can you go through the entire book to complete self-realization and unlimited power. Subsequent meditations will aim at achieving specific results in the realms of success, accomplishment, money, health, love and happiness.

During your meditation periods, you must be alone. You must be in a place of quiet and solitude, undisturbed by other voices or the movements of other people. You must set your mind at rest, forgetting for the moment all cares and problems and people. *You must let go—let go of everything you know except self.*

When you feel calm and peaceful, you will know that you are in contact with the Universal Mind. Then, and only then, speak the meditation aloud. But don't simply speak it. Understand it, feel it, project it. It will manifest for you in actuality.

RECOMMENDED READING

The Man Who Knew by Ralph Waldo Trine.

FIRST MEDITATION

I know that I am pure spirit, that I always have been, and that I always will be. There is inside me a place of confidence and quietness and security where all things are known and understood. This is the Universal Mind, God, of which I am a part and which responds to me as I ask of it. This universal mind knows the answer to all of my problems, and even now the answers are speeding their way to me. I needn't struggle for them; I needn't worry or strive for them. When the time comes, the answers will be there. I give my problems to the great mind of God; I let go of them, confident that the correct answers will return to me when they are needed. Through the great law of attraction, everything in life that I need for my work and fulfillment will come to me. It is not necessary that I strain about this, only believe. For in the strength of my belief, my faith will make it so. I see the hand of divine intelligence all about me, in the flower, the tree, the brook, the meadow. I know that the intelligence that created all these things is in me and around me and that I can call upon it for my slightest need. I know that my body is a manifestation of pure spirit and that spirit is perfect; therefore my body is perfect also. I enjoy life, for each day brings a constant demonstration of the power and wonder of the universe and myself. I am confident. I am serene. I am sure. No matter what obstacle or undesirable circumstance crosses my path, I refuse to accept it, for it is nothing but illusion. There can be no obstacle or undesirable circumstance to the mind of God, which is in me, and around me, and serves me now.

Chapter 2 - ILLUSION

Thy life is an image inexorably cast
By the pictures that form in thy mind
And that which thou see'st is that which thou hast
See'st thou evil, and evil is thine.

EVIL—THE GREAT ILLUSION

As the first step in our discussion of evil, let us sensibly get rid of both the devil and hell. *Make up your mind that the intelligence that exists behind the universe does not destroy itself!* The pain-ridden idea of hellfire as a place of punishment for sin is man's own morbid idea; evil is man's own morbid idea; disease and suffering are man's own morbid ideas. God does not know of the existence of these things. Since He created man free, He has left it up to man to conceive his own situations. *And man has thought into existence all evil!*

It is ego-absorption that colors everything in terms of good and evil. Never was this brought home to me more thoroughly than in the pre-dawn hours on the bridge of a destroyer on patrol in Nasugbu Bay, Philippine Islands during World War II. A forty-millimeter shell had just struck the chest of a Japanese attacking in a suicide boat. He seemed so close that I might have reached out and touched his hand. The shell exploded, and he disintegrated before my eyes.

The scene was seared into my mind. Throughout the battle it kept insinuating itself. This was the first violent death I had witnessed during the war. Surely this was an evil thing—that a man should die at the hands of other men.

Yet a great cheer had gone up when he had been killed. Had he managed to drive his explosive-laden boat into the side of our ship, we would have died instead. So we took his life and rejoiced. But was not that evil to him? Certainly his family, friends, and loved ones did not rejoice. Surely they were overtaken by the despair that everyone calls evil.

Good for us, evil for him; we rejoice, his family despairs. But *was* it good or evil? Was there even cause for rejoicing or weeping? Who judges? Whose judgment is adequate?

As we skirted the coast of Samar next night, I stood on the fantail of the ship and watched the wake spreading on the sea like a path of frost in the moonlight. Some of the night and the stillness seemed drawn into me. Then the word came.

VIEWPOINT

I felt the joy of discovery. It was only the viewpoint of the absorbed and limited ego that caused the appearance of evil. Evil was partial knowledge! To God, in whom was all knowledge, evil was non-existent!

And what I had witnessed in the death of the attacking Japanese had been simply the resolution of forces by which God was evolving truth through man. There was no victor, no vanquished, no evil. All was God moving toward manifestation of his perfection.

With new insight I recalled the words of Kahlil Gibran: "Only then shall you know that the erect and the fallen are but one man standing in twilight between the night of his pygmy-self and the day of his God-self."

Evil is the great illusion of all mankind. Religious thought of all ages has seldom offered more than a stumbling solution to this enigma, for nearly all religions offer a kindly and loving God who yet has created evil and is tempting man with it. Now, it is obvious that there is nothing kindly or loving about a God who visits disease and pain and poverty and suffering upon his children, any more than there is anything beneficent about a deity who creates evil so that he can burn in hell those he manages to tempt with it. The very plain fact is manifest. *If God is a God of love, He did not create evil!*

And so with the entire hideous conception of the devil and hell. If God created the devil and hell, He would have to know that He was going to send some of His children there, and it even follows that He would have a pretty good idea who they would be. So that would give us a God who created the temptation, who created persons unable to resist it, and who precondemned them to an eternal residence in the furnaces of Satan.

It is ridiculous, of course. Yet the extremely important point is this: as far as man's earthly life is concerned, if he believes in evil, he experiences evil; if he believes in disease, he experiences disease; if he believes in hell and the devil, he suffers all the tortures they offer each time he falls from what his own mind considers to be grace.

MAN ALONE HAS CREATED EVIL

All these things man creates into reality in his life on earth—evil, disease, poverty, hell and devil—but God has nothing to do with them!

Now we must understand what God is. God is obviously all wisdom and all knowledge. Since He knows everything, He never has any problems. There are never questions to answer, nor goals to be achieved; there is never knowledge to be gained, nor experience to be had. Everything to God is apparent. Each movement to God is automatically creation. Somehow mankind has insisted upon devising a God with a whole set of moral attributes, but since moral implies conflict with immoral, God couldn't possibly be either. He could not possibly be put in the position of wrestling, Himself, with good and evil and creating that which for the moment gained the upper hand. *It has to be understood that God only creates, and that He creates without the knowledge of good and evil.* It has to be understood that each human being is a living embodiment of God, that God is in him and around him, and that each human being creates through thought. Morally, the world-conscious human being knows right and wrong and good and evil, *therefore he creates them.* He creates them by his own thought. He. We. All of us. Not God.

For the act of creation in this life is accomplished by the Conscious Mind acting on the Subconscious Mind, and the Universal Subconscious Mind is the mind of God.

Mankind will never be able to accept an all-loving and just God who created evil. Mankind has never been able to reconcile such a God with the patent fact that disease and suffering fall like rain on the just and unjust. The thinking mind is emotionally torn to bits even dwelling on such an idea. But we needn't think of it further, for it can be proven that disease and suffering and evil of every kind are created by man and man alone.

THE SPIRITUAL LAW OF CAUSE AND EFFECT

The startling but very apparent fact is that we do not obtain to the good of life by being moral or righteous alone, but we obtain good by creating good by the power of our faith and thought.

"As ye sow, so shall ye reap" is one of the world's most veiled and misunderstood sayings. For centuries, religious belief has held that Jesus meant that the moral, ethical, and lawful misconduct of a man would be punished in the hereafter. Nothing could be farther from the truth. This saying speaks only of the spiritual law of cause and effect: a seed sown in the garden of the mind shall reap the blossom thereof.

For the Subconscious Mind is a garden, and like the garden of earth that knows only to cause things to grow, the garden of the Subconscious Mind knows only to create reality from the seed of thought. Whether this thought is moral or immoral, ethical or unethical has nothing whatever to do with the inexorable process involved. For the seed having been planted must grow, and grow it will, into physical fact, unless the seed itself is uprooted and another planted in its stead.

FREEDOM—THE ESSENCE OF MANKIND

Since we have likened mental processes to religious ones, and since we have said that God is the Subconscious Mind and that the Subconscious Mind, or God, does not recognize the difference between good and evil, there will be those among you who will be quick to assume that a God who does not know that suffering and pain and disease and war and disaster are attacking His flock is little better than a God who purposely looses these forces upon them.

Do not forget for an instant of a day in your life that you are *free!* That freedom is the most miraculous part of your existence. That freedom has allowed you to establish *exactly* what you are today and will allow you to establish *exactly* what you will be tomorrow. That freedom *must* allow you to obtain what to you is evil as well as good, otherwise it would not be complete freedom. The very essence of man's existence is a determination of what constitutes good and what constitutes evil and the subsequent choice of the good. For the good makes for progress, and the evil retards progress, and the purpose of all mankind is progression and creation! Only by creating both good and evil can mankind judge the good and the road of progress!

Even as you have nerves in your fingers so that when you touch a hot stove the pain keeps you from burning your hand off, so the pain, physically, circumstantially, and emotionally of all evil is designed to keep you on the path of progress. God did not create the evil; He simply endowed *you* with the prime function to create, and He allowed you to create what you will. He endowed you with the instinct of survival and progress so that when you create something contrary to your good, the lesson should keep you from creating it again.

But God made man only to create through thought. Beyond that, each man chooses his own road.

MORALITY AND SPIRITUAL LAW

It is a common misunderstanding that morality and ethics are at all times synonymous with good. Morality and ethics are *man's conceptions* of what is good, and, in the main, are right for any certain time and place, though they are constantly changing. But the irrefutable fact is that success and achievement and health and vigor are not directly the result of morality and righteousness. If they were, there would never be a maiden stricken by disease, there would never be a newborn babe with a crippled body, there would never be a poverty-stricken saint, nor a righteous failure. And the truth is that the world is full of all these.

So often you hear it said, "I can't understand why all this bad luck has overtaken me.

I've never done anything to deserve it." Or someone will remark with horror, "I work and work and yet everything I do seems to fail." Or again, "I try so hard to do the right thing and yet God always seems to be punishing me."

Get those thoughts out of your mind. Bad luck doesn't overtake you, you create it. Success isn't the result of hard work, it's the result of right thinking. God doesn't punish you, you punish yourself.

Put the seed of failure in the Subconscious Mind and it will develop failure for you. Put the seed of disease in the Subconscious Mind and it will develop disease for you. Put the seed of loneliness in the Subconscious Mind and it will develop loneliness for you. Put the seed of unhappiness in the Subconscious Mind and it will develop unhappiness for you. Evil, the tragic illusion!

THE IMPORTANCE OF YOUR NEIGHBOR

There is but one Universal Mind in which we all live and move and have our beings. There are billions of Conscious Minds thinking into the Universal Subconscious Mind, creating a physical reality with each thought that is sped with complete belief. This Universal Mind is reactive, creative, and it can create for your neighbor what you think into it for him.

Now consider that very carefully. The Universal Subconscious Mind tends to create for your neighbor what you think into it for him. *And it tends to create for you what your neighbor thinks into it for you!*

Is it any wonder that the second most important commandment of Jesus was, "Love thy neighbor as thyself," for even as your neighbor regards you, so shall it tend to be done to you.

Now, of course, you may be thinking of success, and your neighbor may be thinking of failure for you, and you may be successful, but only because the Subconscious Mind *always* acts. It always acts, and it acts on that thought behind which there is the most belief.

Perhaps you haven't fully absorbed the idea of there being only one mind, one Universal Subconscious Mind which we all use. May we point out to you the existence of thought transference, a phenomenon which can't be explained on any other premise than our all existing in the same ether or intelligence or mind? May we point out to you the existence of mental healing, done without any overt contact with the person being healed? May we point out to you "intuition" or "insight" which enables a person to have the answer to a problem even though he has never figured it out? Even the infamous Voodoo rites are not altogether superstition. Certainly the sticking of pins into a rag doll could never make any person sick, but the *faith* that accompanies such a pin sticking may cause a limb to wither, a fever to rise, a cure to effect itself, or a mountain to move.

SEE NO EVIL

Thought into the great creative Universal Subconscious Mind plus faith can equal only one thing and that is physical reality. It matters not whether the thought is good or evil, if the faith is there it will manifest, for that is the law. Thought plus faith creates!

Believe you will fail and you will. Believe you will succeed and you will. Believe you will be well and you will be. Believe you will be sick and you will be. Believe you are unloved and you are. Believe you are unattractive and you are. "Verily, I say unto you, if you have faith as a grain of mustard seed, you shall say unto this mountain move hither, and the mountain shall move."

Evil could not be anything other than the result of man's belief. Observe the triad of the orient, "See no evil, hear no evil, speak no evil," whence it follows like the night the day, there then can be no evil.

Stuttering mankind, grasping at the edges of truth since the ancient civilizations of the orient, has never been thoroughly convinced that his belief could make his life God-like in beauty and abundance and harmony and achievement.

MANKIND'S STRUGGLE TOWARD TRUTH

We must in this chapter dispel all notions of evil as existing as a separate entity in this life. We must see evil as it really is, simply illusion, simply pain response, a wrong track taken, an experiment toward truth, but always illusion, a wraith-like ephemeral thing that dissipates like the fog at morning when it is denied.

Evil as an existing reality, an entity separate and apart from man, has been taught since the beginning of recorded history. This fallacious assumption no doubt owes its origin to the fact that mankind has never been able to account for the *occurrence* of evil, which seems to follow no moral pattern, which falls on the just and unjust, the strong and the weak, the wise and the ignorant, the rich and the poor. Observing that a newborn child made its entrance into the world with a withered hand or an addled brain or a stunted leg, men mystically assumed that God must be punishing this child for the sins of his father. "The sins of the father shall be visited on the son"—how close to truth is this intuitive grasp of the law! It is not, however, the moral transgressions of the father that are visited upon the son; it is his errors of thinking! Not only of the father, but of the father's brothers and of every erring individual who projects his thoughts into the creative mind of the universe.

ONLY ONE CAUSE

Just like everything that exists, there is a reason for evil; and just like everything that exists, there is a reason for the deformity of the newborn babe.

Genetics may offer its cellular thesis that a defective chromosome in the egg or the sperm has blighted this young life, and indeed it will be difficult to dispute that such a physical occurrence did actually take place. But why? That is what we are concerned with here.

Everything on this earth is the result of thought. Now let us qualify that statement. This does not mean that everything has been created *by* thought. It simply means that everything has been created as a *result* of thought. The great universal plastic creative medium of the Subconscious Mind *acts* on all volitional thought that is placed there. The sum total of all life uses this mind. Every thought of every person who has ever lived has been indelibly recorded in this mind, which has been moved to action because of it. This Mind attempts to manifest all thought to the person thinking it, and it also attempts to manifest it to all the world.

Since everything in existence is the result of thought, all form maintains itself as long as the thought is held. As the thought changes, so does the form. Every newborn child is the result of thought, in form as well as substance, the event of conception being only a physical event in the chain of manifestation, as the carpenter nailing boards together is a physical event in the chain of manifestation of a house. The form must be the result of thought. And so with the newborn babe. *It therefore is inescapably true that deformity in a newborn child is also the result of thought.*

Now this may prove to be rather startling to you, as indeed no mother is likely to tolerate the premise that she has visited some deformity upon her child through a thought conception. But let us not forget that all thought is not *consciously* projected into the Creative Mind. A very great portion is projected by our buried pain remembrances, the insidious Prompters of the Subconscious Mind. It is also true that thought conceptions of other persons than ourselves, nay even every person who has ever lived, may show themselves in our experience.

31

ALL LIFE EXISTS WITHIN ONE MIND

In order to truly understand this, we must return once again to the Universal Subconscious Mind, the mind we all use and live in. This mind or intelligence is not in man alone, but in every living thing. Behold the process of evolution and you will see desire being projected into the Universal Mind and returning in physical reality. The fish experiences land and desires to walk and becomes a reptile. The reptile experiences air and desires to fly and becomes a bird. The reptile desires size and strength and becomes a horse. Bears, wolves, tigers, lions, snakes, everything that creeps and crawls and flies and swims and burrows and builds and desires—all are results of thought or desire projected into the Universal Creative Mind of God.

The fish has fins; the polar bear's fur is white; the chameleon changes colors to blend with the foliage—every reaching desire of conscious life is answered from a great inexhaustible source, without regard to suffering or good or evil, but simply in answer to conception and desire.

Should the temperature of this earth drop a hundred degrees, life would survive and adapt and evolve in different form. Should the earth and the planets fade away, life would survive and adapt. For desire is life, and life is change, and change is progress, and they all answer one immutable law.

Deformity in the newborn babe may seem a hideous injustice as we view it in terms of our own selves in a kind of self-identification. Yet the distant future may hold a day when mankind in physical form will not need arms or even legs, or may occupy a form that today would be regarded with horror by everyone. For today our thought conceptions of ourselves are what we see in actuality, and we are so firmly convinced of the reality of this evidence and the permanence of it that we cannot conceive of change in any other light than monstrousness or deformity.

The Subconscious Mind, or God, does not recognize suffering or pain or war or famine or disease. It recognizes only conception and desire, or thought and emotion, and it recognizes them only one way—by creating them into actuality.

THOUGHT AND FAITH—SOLE RESPONSIBILITIES

There are only two things you can do for yourself. One is conception, and the other is conviction. All the work of creation rests with another than you. For no man is responsible for anything in this life except his thought and his belief. All else is the working of the great creative Universal Mind, beside which the largest atomic plant in the universe is like a gnat on the face of the earth.

Jesus said, "Come unto me, all ye who are burdened and heavily laden, and I will give you rest. For my yoke is easy, and my burden is light."

Can you now gain an inkling of what this great man so thoroughly understood?

He said, speaking of his miracles of healing, "It is not I who doeth the works, but the Father who dwelleth within me."

He *knew* the responsibility of creation was not his. He *knew* that a power far greater than he would resolve into actuality any thought which he was convinced of. He did not stand at Lazarus' grave and restore Lazarus to life by a process of effort. He *knew* that Lazarus would rise. Beyond that, the responsibility was no longer his.

There can be little doubt but that the same power that responded to Jesus and restored Lazarus to life would, if approached with the same conviction, cause Lazarus to die.

This power manifests evil as well as good for it does not differentiate between the two. It simply creates according to image and conviction.

Thus with all evil. "God sendeth his rain on the just and unjust alike," for evil befalls the righteous and the unrighteous, *but it cannot visit him who sees and is convinced of nothing but good.*

TRUTH AND ERROR

The experience of evil and the selection of good is the path mankind *must* follow. Like everything else, this also has a reason.

Good is *truth.* Evil is *error.* The experience of error and the selection of truth are progress. When man knows all truth, man will be God, for he will have arrived at the same position as God, and there no longer will be problems or searchings, for everything will be known and apparent.

Perhaps we, in our lifetimes, are not to approach this infinity. It seems, at least, like a gargantuan undertaking, with our little knowledge and our little faith, to presume to banish evil from our experience within the comparatively few short years allotted to us here on earth. But this much is a certainty. If we know that evil proceeds from thought just as good proceeds from thought, we can establish eternal sentinel on our minds to guide our thoughts in the paths of good and progress. For even the ultimate is not impossible of attainment this very moment, could we but have the faith and have the image.

Since good is truth and evil is error, it is then apparent that evil is illusion. Evil is a wrong road, a mistake, a pain experience, simply a search on the road toward truth; and since it is not truth it is error; and since it is error it is illusion. Being illusion, evil dissipates with consummate ease. It is replaced by good with almost miraculous speed. Good can only be replaced by evil when the conception of good very weak and the conception of evil is very strong, for truth does not lightly yield to error, while error has few defenses against the illumination of truth.

For a man to know sufficient of truth to consciously exercise the power of the Subconscious Mind must necessarily deter him from exercising that power for the creation of evil. In other words, it hardly would be possible for Jesus, or any man as enlightened as Jesus, to use the same power with which he restored Lazarus to life for the attainment of Lazarus' death. For all humanity searches for truth, and the truth once revealed will not permit error. Since truth is good and error is evil, the knowing of good forbids the choice of evil.

WITHHOLDING SPIRITUAL KNOWLEDGE

There have been besides Jesus many enlightened men who have lived on this planet. There have been societies of these enlightened men whose perception of the truth has been so acute that physical manifestation from thought, thought transference, and intuition have been common in their daily lives. *Yet these men and societies have usually thought it dangerous to reveal this knowledge to humanity as a whole.*

Mankind, however, has come a long way in the last twenty centuries. It is no longer a case of revealing truth to the unready, as a loaded gun might be handed to a child. For all humanity now reaches out for an answer to the great why of human existence, and is searching for peace and knowledge. Though there is little doubt that the haphazard placing of mental power in the hands of the unready and ignorant could not help but have some negative effect on human progress, there is also no doubt but that mankind stands at the threshold of spiritual freedom this very day. It is not only needed and desired, it is veritably demanded by each person who lives that he gain access to the laws that govern his life so that he may use them for his own benefit and the benefit of humanity as a whole.

TRUTH CAN ALWAYS BE DESCRIBED

Many metaphysical treatises and some philosophical treatises deal with the outer world as though it were *all* illusion and the only reality a submergence in self, a sort of letting-go of consciousness to attain a sense of complete selflessness. This sense of the absolute, however, has never been fully described, and such failure has been laid to the inadequacy of the several hundred languages that are spoken by human beings.

Truth must always be possible of description! Since it exists, it must be known, and when it is known, it can be described. All truth exists in some form, somewhere. This does not mean that all physical circumstance is truth, for both good and evil manifest themselves.

But illusion—the only illusion that exists in this life or in the life of the spirit—is evil. Truth is reality, and reality can be described.

SIN AND PUNISHMENT—CAUSE AND EFFECT

Perhaps we are now better able to understand the ideas of sin and punishment. Sin is not a transgression against God or law in the sense of the violation of a moral code. Nor is punishment a vengeance enacted by society or God upon the transgressor.

Sin is simply error. And punishment is simply the inevitable result of error. If you are looking for a friend's house and you turn down the wrong street, you cannot expect to find your friend's house on that street. You have turned down the wrong street; consequently you will not find his house. Cause and effect. A law. That is all.

So it is with all evil, which is error. That which you think, good or evil, will inevitably develop in your experience. If it is evil, it is error, and if it is error, the effect upon you must be evil.

When you know that God is perfect, you will understand that God cannot err; and since evil is only error, God could not possibly be responsible for it.

So evil is error and is illusion and is created by man in his search for truth by his thought conceptions being projected into the Universal Creative Mind or Subconscious Mind.

From the experience of evil, man chooses truth. In other words, he progresses by a system of trial and error. Each error carries with it its own consequences, since we are dealing with a law of cause and effect. Therefore, the consequences of error are borne on this earth; they are not borne in a hereafter, each soul, returning into the Subconscious Mind from which it came, returns without moral stigma, without judgment of my kind, without praise or blame, without reward or punishment, for we all are branches on one great tree which neither chastises itself nor destroys itself, but is simply contemplative and creative.

Followers of certain religions which feature purgatory and damnation, will now raise the point, "Well, if the pure and the sinful are judged alike in the hereafter, what is the point of being good in our earthly lives?"

It seems highly objectionable to be restrained from the committing of evil simply because you wish to be rewarded with a harp in a nice cool place rather than a pitchfork where it is very warm, for this illusory promise of reward and punishment in the hereafter is a pale ghost alongside man's creative search for truth. You don't have to wait nearly so long as the doomsday to gain your punishment for evil. Steal your neighbor's purse and discover how soon your own is stolen from you. Kill your neighbor and discover how soon your own life is forfeit. That which you send out returns to you in this life, this *now,* this most important time that ever was, and it returns much sooner than you think.

DO NOT SUFFER REMORSE

Remember this: *Remorsefulness is a sin against yourself.*

As a human being, you will make mistakes in arriving at truth. Do not allow remorse to become a Prompter. Be joyful that error has disclosed truth.

The tragic picture of man dragging through life, chastising himself for every mistake, making discouragement and shame his bedfellows, and even frightening himself into immobility through a hideous vision of punishment in hell, is the source and cause of every Prompter of the Subconscious Mind.

To err is human. Evil is human. But evil is illusion, nothing more. It dissipates in front of good almost magically; and every error in your life is for the purpose of revealing truth to you and *not* to stultify your divinity in shame and remorse and fear.

There will be evil in the world until man completes his progress to a oneness with God. For there will be error until all truth is known. You will make mistakes. You cannot live and not make mistakes. But this you can do. You can suffer the consequence of each mistake only once and no more.

Let us face this very simple problem with the courage with which we are all naturally endowed. Let us not be afraid of making a mistake or of suffering the consequence if the mistake is made. If you have a desire, let it manifest; don't keep telling the Subconscious Mind "do"—"don't"—"do"—"don't"—until, weary of moving back and forth, it lays the weight of its indecision on your shoulders with a burden no one in the world could bear. Say either "do" or "don't," one or the other, for the Subconscious Mind is a vast army at your command, but it needs a clear-cut authoritative decision.

What results, then, must be either truth or error. If it is truth, your whole life will be immediately bettered. If it is error, you will suffer a temporary punishment, a setback, but from the knowledge of truth thus gained, you have progressed. For this temporary setback, like the error that caused it, is simply illusion and is actually progress toward the realization of truth.

Find a man who has suffered a score of defeats and you will find a great soul. He may know more of truth than the man who has won a half dozen victories. The man with the half dozen victories knows a half dozen truths. While the man with a score of defeats may know twenty truths!

DARE TO BE CONVINCED

You must *allow* the Subconscious Mind to create your desires into actuality. If you desire money, let it be an assurance, a conviction that the law must resolve. Then without doubt the money will be yours. *This, of course, does not mean that the attaining of the money is necessarily good.* It may be, on the other hand, that the consequence of your having the money fills you with vanity and lust for power that lead you into isolation and worry and the automatic attraction of the destroyers of your happiness.

Now this is by no means axiomatic. A great many people have attained wealth, prospered with it, done a great deal of good with it, and have been far better off through having it. Yet there have been just as many people to whom the attainment of money has meant the dissolution of family, the destruction of health, and the complete disappearance of enjoyment of life and peace of mind.

But if you want money, don't vacillate about it. Don't, on the one hand, complain that you do not have enough, and on the other, say that you don't care to have a lot. Seesaw, seesaw goes the Subconscious Mind and exactly nothing happens.

You must dare to be convinced on whatever it is that shapes up as a problem to you. Dare to make a decision, take a side, be convinced. Let that decision manifest itself in actuality, then shirk neither from the reward nor punishment.

For if you err, there is no one, nothing, that will hold you in account except the law of cause and effect, a strictly impersonal operating law; and once the consequence of the error has come upon you, you need have no fear that any others will be visited . . . *unless you create them yourself!*

For if you carry, from some error, shame and remorse and chastisement, these must act on the Subconscious Mind to create themselves in reality!

One bright day a young man starts out to open a business. At first things progress favorably, but in final consequence of wrong thinking his business goes bankrupt. Wrong conception, or error, carries only one consequence, and the day this young man's business goes bankrupt that consequence is brought home to him. But now is when he may make the greatest error of all. If he takes stock of what he has learned, discovers and recounts the errors in his thought, arrives at truth through examination of his error, then boldly strikes out once again, he is using the great powers of the universe as they must be used, and success will surely come to him. But if his error builds shame and remorse and self-pity, he will suffer added consequences as long as he carries these illusions with him, for they will continue to develop in his life as long as he thinks them into the Subconscious Mind.

MAN MAKES CIRCUMSTANCE

Now it must be thoroughly understood that we are not denying the existence of evil; we are simply denying the *reality* of evil, naming it illusion as it surely is. No great man or woman has ever lived who has not risen above circumstance, literally denying the reality of lack, limitation, illness, poverty, and inferiority. If you allow yourself to be a product of circumstance, then each encounter you make with evil will convince you of the reality of evil, and further evil will be created in your experience. Moreover, you will make despair and fear and unhappiness your constant companions.

Don't think for a single minute that circumstance makes the man. Man makes the circumstance!

Through the great law of attraction, all things come to him who believes in them; and every circumstance of your life inevitably has been attracted to you by your own beliefs. You are, literally, a product of your own thought. You are what you think; only that, nothing more.

You must right now convince yourself that evil is an effect, not a cause. Evil is the *result* of erroneous thought conception. Erroneous thought conception is the *cause* of evil. Evil is a circumstance; and you, as a divine part of the universal intelligence, need never be the result of circumstance. You *create* the circumstance. Only when you believe circumstance to be greater than you are, will you allow it to continue to develop evil in your experience.

MAN-MADE LAW VERSUS SPIRITUAL LAW

All moral and ethical laws are aimed at the general welfare of the human race as a whole. In other words, moral and ethical laws are designed as race preservatives. Since the first law of individuals or groups is self-preservation, there can be no doubt but that the evolution of all moral and ethical law consistent with the spiritual laws of the universe. This, of course, does not mean that moral and ethical laws shall not err, nor that they shall not, on occasion, promote evil, for all form (and man-made laws are no more than form) is but a temporal manifestation of thought and must change as thought changes. Consequently, we have the great evolution of human society from tribes of warring nomads to our gigantic cultures of today, where we dwell in relative peace with the main aim creation rather than destruction. It is interesting to note that the plan of ethical and moral laws is essentially the same as the construction of the laws of the spirit. They are both designed as true law—simply cause and effect.

Break a law of society and society will punish you for the transgression by imprisonment, by ostracism, by financial penalty, by retracting certain rights within the group. Whatever evil circumstance the individual creates in his breaking of the law, the law attempts to visit on him in return. Though the original basis of this law was laid on considerations of moral and ethical right and wrong, once the law is broken there is started a chain of events that moves without any consideration other than cause and effect and moves inexorably to its conclusion. Of course, because the laws of society are man-made, it sometimes happens that the lawbreaker escapes society's punishment for some time. Not so with the laws of the spirit. These laws work without the chance of error, and he who thinks evil, creates evil; and he who sends out evil will find evil returning home once again.

Moral law, therefore, is simply the effort of mankind to lay down rules of conduct which aim at eradicating error from society. Similarly, the laws of the spirit can be understood in such a manner and with such enlightenment as to eliminate error from the individual life.

THE PROMPTERS AT WORK

It is strange how often we recognize right from wrong and how often we follow in the path of the wrong, almost as if we *desired* evil. Scarcely a person lives who has not on some occasion performed some miserable act or deed in which he could not seem to help himself, as if some magnet lured him onward, as if in the performance of this wrong he found a secret martyred delight.

It has been convenient for society to propound that this only proves that the devil lives side by side with God and that evil is a thing in itself, a temptation tossed in the pathway of the righteous and the sinner alike.

Let us not be led astray by this type of abstruse thinking. God and the devil did not jointly author mankind. Obviously one or the other did, since the possibility of their taking up such a joint enterprise defies all rationality. If the devil made man, then God could not exist in man, neither could good, and all would be evil. Since evil is error, all life would be error, and as a consequence everything would be chaos, without design, without form. If God made man, then man is essentially good but being free is likely to fall into error in his search for truth. Isn't this mankind as we see it today? The devil is as illusory as evil. He does not exist in reality, neither do his fires.

What men have always thought to be the work of the devil, we can, in this age, say with certainty is little else than the remembrance by the Subconscious Mind of those pain experiences which have been rejected by the Conscious Mind.

FORGET YOU'VE MADE MISTAKES

Here we must point out the wonderful truth that Jesus Christ brought to the world— the revelation that the universe is owned and operated by a God of love.

It is difficult today to properly report the magnitude of this discovery, since mankind up to then had always lived in terror of a God of vengeance. But Jesus reported a God of love, whose very essence is one of tolerance and forgiveness. It is not simply a coincidence that the Christian world has progressed in two thousand years a score of times farther than all of mankind in the previous eons of existence; it is because Jesus taught that a man need suffer the consequence of error only once and no more, because the message that Jesus brought to a world fraught with morbidity and oppression and disease was simply that a man need never carry the burden of his mistakes with him.

How prominent was this point in Jesus' teaching! "Take up thy bed and walk, thy sins are forgiven thee." "Go and sin no more." It is a mistake to assume that Jesus was interceding between a revengeful God and a sinner, or that his speaking of sin had anything to do with morality or ethics. What he was saying was simply, "Forget that you have made mistakes and stop thinking about error. All is well. Good is everywhere."

Now we are not likely to have a world free of error for some time. There is little doubt that all of us will contribute some degree of error, regardless of how enlightened we strive to be. But the plain and comforting fact is ever present. We need never fear the consequence of error unless we insist on carrying it around in our minds as a burden that grows like a snowball, attracting other evil to it at an ever-increasing rate.

THE POWER OF THE WORD

Perhaps from the previous chapter you have been able to elicit sufficient understanding of the Prompters that exist in your Subconscious so as to make apparent the problem we are faced with now. The attraction of evil—limitation, lack, disease, poverty, etc.—can a thousandfold more be laid to the insidious Prompters than to any error honestly made in the search for truth.

Today you may be walking around with a Subconscious full of Prompters that would have you be sick, would have you be poor, would have you be lonely and unsuccessful. You must control these Prompters or they will control you. You must, by conscious meditation on the spiritual laws of the universe, install in the Subconscious a conditioned response for good which will automatically displace all negative Prompters. You must do this or there is not the slightest possibility of the full and good life. You cannot expect evil without creating evil.

After having performed meditation there no longer can be any doubt in your mind but that speaking the word means activating some power to create the conditions you desire. The word or the thought, since time immemorial, has been the first step in all creation, all achievement, all desire. The power of the word or thought is such that nothing will stand against it as long as it is spoken with conviction.

The Subconscious Mind is a brilliant deductive reasoner. In fact, there is valid reason to assume that deductively the Subconscious Mind reasons perfectly. Given a premise like, "I will make money," it can produce a series of brilliantly logical steps for the accomplishment of same. For example, under deep hypnosis, a patient was informed that he was in discussion with Plato; and from the subsequent discussion there evolved the most beautiful philosophical premises imaginable, as if they came directly from the mouth of the master himself. This discourse was far above the normal intelligence of the patient, and witnesses for some time believed that this young man had actually "contacted" the spirit of Plato.

Everyone is prone to attribute all things beyond his immediate understanding to the realm of ghosts and banshees and shades and shadows. But let there be no doubt. The Subconscious Mind has as its resources all the knowledge and wisdom there is, and all occultism is simply the use of the mind in which we all live and move and have our beings.

YOU ARE NEVER ALONE

In view of this intense discussion on evil and good and their creation in individual lives, you may be regarding the conflict between them as a battle necessitating your most valiant efforts. In other words, a great weight of tremendous effort may be settling on your shoulders as you think of the eternal sentinel you must stand at the bastions of your Conscious Mind to prevent the entrance of the forces of negative thinking. Similarly, since we are human and must err occasionally, you may be regarding future error with fear, thinking with indecision over courses of action.

Let us dispel this thought once and for all. Let us first dispel it by assuring you that you are never alone. Responsibility for your slightest action never rests entirely with you. Were it up to you, all by yourself, you couldn't walk across the street, speak to a friend, or even be in existence. Mark this fact well. *You didn't create yourself!* You cannot *by yourself* do the slightest bit of creating. The power into which you project your thoughts is the only creative force there is, and it builds and constructs all form and circumstance, but it does this according to how you think.

ACCEPT—DON'T WILL

Now it is absolutely impossible for you to *make* this power do anything. You cannot by sheer force of will bend this power to suit your needs. *You are not greater than God.* You cannot either stop or start this power in its creating, for it is greater than you are and it moves according to law. You cannot say, "I am going to make money" with all the determination and ferociousness you can muster and expect that you are creating in your experience anything other than belligerence and opposition. You've got to *accept,* not demand. *You can't will anything.* This does not mean a doctrine of resignation, far from it. It simply means that you recognize that it is not you who does the creating; it is a power greater than you are. This power creates what you believe and manifests to you what you are prepared to *accept.*

Be sure you understand this. All your will for money will avail you nothing, for that is the wrong use of spiritual law. Money will be created in your experience only if you *realize* and *know* that there is abundance all about you and you *accept* it. In other words, you don't demand money; you don't force money with the idea that there is not enough to go around and you don't have enough of it. You accept money; there is a great abundance of it about you, and you *know* that. Therein lies the true use of spiritual law as against the isolated exercising of the individual's will. For the force of your will against the Universal Mind must inevitably set up that same thing in your experience, so that you see opposition instead of cooperation.

When Jesus said, "It is your father's good pleasure to give you the Kingdom of Heaven," he meant exactly that. For all the power of creation is *given;* it is never yielded upon demand.

Expect and accept. Know and experience. Be positive and thankful. *For the great laws of attraction and creation are laws of attunement and never divulge their secrets to those who batter at the door with force.*

"Suffer little children to come unto me, for theirs is the Kingdom of Heaven." We must realize that Jesus was the greatest metaphysical teacher who has ever lived. Who has not seen a child completely accepting all good with an open heart and a knowingness? Only the "don'ts" we fear-condtioned adults impose on this God-like young mind ever set up conditioned "can'ts," "impossibles," lack and limitation. For the child accepts all good as a natural course of events, depends completely on all good being directed to it simply because of its desire. *Accept. Know and accept.* Those are the secrets of all prayer and meditation.

GUIDANCE THROUGH ATTUNEMENT

It is important for you to know that even with thought the entire responsibility need not rest with you. The power that creates is the power that knows; and it is possible, with perfect attunement, to achieve in each condition of your life a situation of *guidance.*

Now you cannot achieve attunement or guidance when you are consciously willing something to happen. The very idea of your will being imposed upon that of God's is indefensible from any kind of view. When you have completely accepted the power greater than you are, when you know it will create in your experience that which you believe, you will also find that it also will provide you with answers to your questions.

You must do this by letting go of your problem. Once the basic elements of the problem are clearly defined in your Conscious Mind, and once your general objective is clearly defined in your Conscious Mind, *let go.* Forget the problem altogether. One morning while you are going about your daily tasks, you will find the answer. It will strike your consciousness with such impact as to remove all doubt but that it is truth. The answer will be crystal clear, of such simplicity that you will be amazed that it never occurred to you before or that you ever held any doubt about it.

This is *guidance.* It is not achieved by any effort or will. It is achieved by confidence in the power greater than you are. It is achieved by complete acceptance of the power greater than you are.

If you are able to effect this complete attunement every minute of every day of your life, there can be little doubt but that pain and lack and limitation and disease will never more exist in your experience. But we must caution you against raising your expectancies higher than your faith. If you say to yourself in the morning, "I know I am working along the paths of success," and go the rest of the day complaining about every obstacle you meet, you may wind up the week expecting that success should be yours, but it won't be. Your faith must be with you at least fifty-one percent of the time before it will manifest in your experience. But a manifestation will come, one way or the other, according to the predominant thought.

BRIEF REVIEW

Here are the points to remember in chapter 2:

1. Evil is error and is illusion.

2. Good is truth and is reality,

3. Truth will dispel error, therefore good will dispel evil.

4. Evil is the result of man's thought, not God's.

5. Hell and the devil are illusions.

6. God does not destroy any human soul, for He does not destroy Himself.

7. God knows everything, therefore is incapable of error or evil.

8. The single function of the Subconscious Mind, or Universal Mind, is to manifest into form or circumstance the seed of thought.

9. Man has complete freedom of choice in the kind of thoughts he wishes to plant in the garden of the Subconscious Mind.

10. No human being can assume the responsibility for a single thing other than his own thinking, for the Universal Subconscious Mind does all creating.

11. Morality and ethics *do not always* follow the law of cause and effect; but the use of spiritual law *always* follows the law of cause and effect. This is because moral law is man-made, while spiritual law is the essence of God.

12. The proper use of spiritual law is *acceptance* and *faith.*

13. You cannot demand anything from the Universal Subconscious Mind by *willing* it to happen.

Guidance and inspiration in the paths of truth and achievement can be yours through faith and reliance in the power greater than you are.

STRIVE FOR BALANCE

You are now experimenting with the greatest force in nature. We caution you not to become so wrapped up in it that you forget your daily life. Do not search for contact with the Subconscious Mind to the exclusion of the exercise of the Conscious Mind, for as a human being your goal must be to achieve a perfect balance between the two. The ordinary people we meet each day scarcely use the Subconscious Mind at all, and their lives are directed and controlled entirely by circumstance. Men and women of genius are those in whom there is a perfect balance between the Subconscious Mind and the Conscious Mind. It is balance we strive for, balance between the great creative power of the Universal Subconscious Mind and the Conscious Mind.

Work at your meditation joyfully and confidently. Cast aside all doubt and morbidity and effort and strain. You don't have to make anything; it is already made. You only want to use it correctly. Accept! Believe! Know! Relax! The universe will provide you with all you desire.

AN EXPERIENCE WITH TELEPATHY

As an interesting experiment with the power you are dealing with, gather a few friends together and conduct a session telepathy. Join hands in a circle after one member of the circle has been blindfolded. In the center of the circle place a pack of playing cards. At a given signal, expose one of the cards to the sight of all members of the circle except the person who wears the blindfold. *Be careful to expose only one card.* Have all members of the circle concentrate on the exposed card and instruct the blindfolded person to report the card uppermost in his mind as soon as he has a clear picture of it. Let every member of the circle wear the blindfold in turn. Your results won't be perfect, but will prove to you beyond any doubt that there is a mind or ether or medium in which we all live and move and have our beings and through which we may contact each other through nothing but thought. This is the Universal Subconscious Mind!

THE MEDITATION

Our meditation following this chapter is aimed at dispelling illusion or evil. When you have settled yourself for your meditation, recall to mind all those circumstances in your life which you consider to be error or evil. Say to yourself that they are simply illusion and do not exist in reality. Then commence with your meditation. Within a month you will see some very startling changes.

In later chapters we shall become more and more specific with our meditations, until one by one we have laid each ghost and demon that springs from the buried Prompters in your Subconscious, until your life opens to unlimited horizons and great adventure, until you see the universe as it really is, designed specifically for you!

Know! Accept! Believe! Keep faith! There are more things in this world than you have ever dreamed.

RECOMMENDED READING

Creative Mind by Ernest Holmes. Published by Robert M. McBride and Co.

SECOND MEDITATION

I know that I am one with the Universal Mind. I know this mind is perfect and I may rely upon it for complete guidance in all of my daily affairs. This Universal Mind, this great Subconscious Mind, this mind of God knows no evil or limitation or lack. It simply creates in my experience that which I believe and accept. Therefore I deny all evil and all error. When my eyes and my senses are deluded with the apparent circumstance of evil, I turn away, lifting my thoughts to the perfection and abundance and love of all the universe. I know that God does not create evil; and I know that by using the power of God I am able to deny evil, which is only illusion, simply error, and will not stand before truth. For the great reality is good, which is always attempting to manifest itself. I know that error or evil is the result of my own thought, is the result of error on my part, is the result of isolating myself from the power of the Universal Mind. I know that the Universal Mind is constantly creating in my experience that which I think, and if evil is manifested, it has come from my own thought; and my own thought may as quickly deny it. I do not will anything to happen, for I am not bigger than God. I simply understand that the law of creation is bigger than I am and that I cannot help my thoughts and beliefs from becoming real in my experience. Therefore I hold my thoughts steadfastly on the good. I do not do this with effort, as if I were commanding something to act. I simply relax in contemplation of the good, secure in the knowledge that everything rests with a power much greater than I am. I trust this power. I have complete faith and confidence in this power. I rely upon this power for guidance in all my daily affairs. I refuse to accept evil, and evil is gone. I accept good, and the supply and love of the universe are mine.

Chapter 3 - MIND

Miracle of Ages, Master of All
O Mind that ever must be
Hark to the sound of thy Father's call
To the Throne and the Crown that waiteth for thee

THE MYSTERY OF MIND

How accustomed we are to regarding mind objectively! How conditioned we are to thinking of mind as brain, an isolated accumulation of gray protoplasm two inches behind our foreheads! We give our approval to scientific techniques which trace out brain convolutions and nerve networks and tell us of the storage compartments of memory, the cellular seat of reason, the pulpy mass that gives rise to imagination, the spinal network of conditioned responses. These, we say, are mind—these arrangements of matter which we generally investigate in dead persons or in partially inanimate ones. Yet how far from truth this is!

No one has ascertained the quality and quantity of "I" by investigating nerve tissue under a microscope! The impact and mystery of self-consciousness, the personal "I am," has never yielded its secret to the surgeon's knife or the biologist's probings. To objectively state that the body has a nerve center called brain does not bring man one step closer to an understanding of his own self-existence, a thing of such stuß as dreams are made, of which brain and nerve and tissue are but a result and never a cause.

In this chapter we shall turn from such half-truths into a world of personal consciousness, dealing with mind as divorced from the material, as pure thought and conception, as existing on the spiritual plane of cause and effect. In this manner we shall arrive at unity, the point where all things are one thing and thought is the only mover, the creator of everything.

THE INSTRUMENT OF SURVIVAL

We must first deal with the Conscious Mind and its so-called compartments of memory, reason, and imagination. This Conscious Mind of ours exists at the level of the five senses and is quite logically a product of hearing, seeing, smelling, feeling, and tasting. Its pursuit is to satisfy each of these five senses with sensations which provide pleasure instead of pain.

Each of us can remember the beginning of his Conscious Mind, perhaps at a few months of age, perhaps at only a few days of age, but the memory is there and available for recall and is invariably the recall of sensation, the pleasure or pain of one or more of the five senses.

The Conscious Mind, therefore, is a pleasure and pain distinguisher, and its compartments of memory, reason, and imagination are but names given to its total instinct to find pleasure and avoid pain.

All conscious organisms are endowed with the life urge to survive, and this life urge manifests itself in each as a conscious intelligence best adapted to cope with its surroundings. This survival instinct must necessarily be based on a pleasure-pain principle, for pleasure is an assurance of survival while pain is a warning of destruction. The system of warnings and assurances set up in each creature is that which we call Conscious Mind and has its focal seat in the brain and its network of nerves. On the survival plane, the conscious intelligence of the amoeba is suited to the surroundings of the amoeba, the conscious intelligence of the fish is suited to the surroundings of the fish, the conscious intelligence of the jungle cat is suited to the surroundings of the jungle cat. And when it is not, the conscious intelligence changes and so does the creature!

For the experience of pain brings forth the desire to avoid pain, and the desire to avoid pain brings forth an image to escape it, and this image is projected into the creative Universal Mind which manifests new form and new conscious intelligence to this life that seeks to cope with its surroundings.

Thus with all evolution; thus with all adaptation; thus with all of life in whatever form, for form is only temporary, a projection of conscious desire, inescapably the result of thought.

FUNCTIONS OF THE CONSCIOUS MIND

The Conscious Mind of man, then, remembers the circumstances which produce pain and pleasure, analyzes from experience which may produce pain and pleasure, imagines a flight into pleasure and escape from pain; and herein lie the compartments of memory, reason, and imagination.

Therefore, the Conscious Mind is a recording, analyzing, and selective instrument for sensation.

As an instrument of sensation, the Conscious Mind is finite, a thing of this world, a thing of the senses, a structural part of a working organism without use or purpose once that organism has ceased to be.

The Conscious Mind, then, must be as destructible as the body which houses it, and we concern ourselves with it here only because it is our means of contact with our true selves and we need to understand what its functions and limitations are.

Primarily, the Conscious Mind is a recorder, an analyzer, and a filer. It records sensation at the level of pain and pleasure; it analyzes this sensation according to circumstances which caused it: and it files such sensation away under one of two main compartments headed "Recall about Pain" and "Recall about Pleasure."

Now, of itself, the Conscious Mind has no memory. In other words, it does not contain a storehouse in which is laid up all experience and sensation. The faculty of memory as applied to the Conscious Mind is simply its ability to recall certain experiences and conclusions which have been recorded in the Subconscious Mind.

For the memory of the Subconscious Mind is perfect. Every thought of the Conscious Mind has been indelibly recorded in the Subconscious as well as every sensory perception of the individual. The great mass of this material is forever lost to the recall of the Conscious Mind, for it can only be so recalled when it has previously been filed away with instructions to the Subconscious Mind to release it for recall.

BENEATH THE LEVEL OF CONSCIOUSNESS

Thus it can be seen that subconscious memory contains a vast store of material—premises, conclusions, and perceptions—that exist without the knowledge of the Conscious Mind. This vast store of knowledge beneath the level of consciousness affords a great portion of the latent power in each individual person, for could you this moment but recall all this knowledge perfectly, your efficiency and wisdom as an individual would be increased a thousandfold.

These subconscious memories which exist beyond conscious recall are neither a plus nor minus factor in the circumstances surrounding any person. Since the Conscious Mind has never attached importance to them, has never arrived at conviction concerning them, they do not move the Subconscious Mind to creation, but simply exist, a huge smattering of experience and knowledge, lying dormant.

But there lies in the Subconscious Mind convictions which have been filed away by the Conscious Mind with the express order never to be available for recall—the Prompters!

Here in these pain rejections, these conclusions which the Conscious Mind could not bear to tolerate, these images of conviction which have been buried from sight, we find our illusory devil truly at work. For the nature of the Universal Intelligence is that it responds to conviction; and the Prompters move the Subconscious Mind to those very things which the individual fears.

The Conscious Mind, the pain-pleasure recorder and analyzer of individual existence, is but an infinitesimal part of a gigantic whole, the entire power and wisdom of which are within the reach of every intelligent person. In order for us to truly grasp the significance of the relationship between man and the Universal Subconscious Mind, we must start at the beginning, an arbitrary and assumed point, for there is no beginning to infinity, just as there is no conclusion.

THE ETERNAL SUBSTANCE

"In the beginning the word" does not imply that the beginning of the Universal Mind was a result of the word, but rather the beginning of our physical universe as we know it today. Indisputably, there must have been a beginning of the physical universe; undoubtedly there will be an end; but on the plane of Universal Mind we will find no such beginning and no such end. Our attempt to find a starting place for creation is simply an attempt to place ourselves in space and time at a point where our physical universe as we know it did not exist. But this on no account should be considered to be a beginning of all things; for the Universal Mind is infinite in time and space and substance.

It has only been very lately that our probings at the elemental substances of nature have yielded us the knowledge that mass and density are purely relative. *The astounding discovery of science that there is no such thing as a solid mass has revised the thinking of the entire world.* Even as you read this and consider that the chair upon which you are now sitting is simply a collection of particles which are moving about with the rapidity of express trains, your very credulity is threatened. When you consider further that there is a thousand times more free space between each of those particles than there is mass in the particles themselves, you are seized with the uncomfortable sensation that you are sitting on nothing. Now if you will hold this thought for a moment and consider that your own body is similarly made up of a collection of free-moving particles widely separated by space and moving about in frenzied agitation, then of a sudden you will see the affinity between the chair and yourself. You are both made of the same substance, which is simply a collection of the only substance there is; and the only differences between you and the chair are of form and consciousness.

THE ATOMIC THEORY

Not so long ago, science entertained a premise that certain elements were basic in nature and could not be broken down into other substances. This theory held that base metals such as lead, copper, zinc, and iron were eternal substances in the scheme of things for the reason that each of the atoms of which they were composed weighed so much on a scale of relativity. For some time this theory propounded that elements on the atomic weights scale were the substances from which all things were made. It was difficult for scientists to account for conscious life with this theory, but they seemed to have arrived at some sort of beginning and so they adopted it and proceeded from there. It seemed logical to assume that the smallest basic unit of mass and energy had been discovered in the atom, especially since all the atoms of a basic element had the same characteristics. Previously, the molecule had been suspect as the smallest unit of matter or energy, but with the discovery and statistical classification of the atom, a new era was ushered in.

It followed very shortly, however, that scientists discovered that even the atom was composed of other whirling particles, almost a small universe, in which the two principal components were called the electron and the proton. Speculation began as to whether protons and electrons might be freed of the confines of the atom, and one summer's day over Japan the final result of such speculation bore its fruit.

We shall not concern ourselves with the moral implication of science's greatest discovery being used on the battlefields of war, but rather with where we are going now that the elemental theory of atomic weights no longer gives us convenient classifications of bask substances in nature. For when the atom is split, the element disintegrates, and the question is what happens to it?

MASS AND ENERGY ARE ONE

Thus far we have only been able to say in general terms that mass is potential energy and energy is potential mass; that a certain weight of uranium, for example, is capable of unleashing a certain amount of power; and that a certain amount of power is capable of creating a certain amount of uranium. *And the only possible further conclusion, based on pure scientific research, is that there is only one substance from which everything physical is made and there is only one substance from which all energy is made and this energy, or substance, is infinite in time and space; it has no beginning and no end and thus is everywhere at all times, and all of it is anywhere at any time.*

This may prove to be a substantial dose to digest, but if you are going to throw off the shackles of limited thinking, you must strive to free yourself from conceptions of form, mass, space, and time as ultimate reality. You must say to yourself that you know that the physical world as you see it could not possibly answer the question of your own existence, so the answer must be elsewhere. You must reach into the furthermost recesses of your mind, for the answer is there and only there and never in the physical world around you.

We now know that matter and energy are one, that there is only one substance or energy or intelligence in all things. Since in its pure form, we can recognize this energy as nothing but invisible power, unintelligible to our five senses, there is not the slightest valid reason to assume that it is anything else than constant and never changing in its basic nature; that it always has been and always will be; in other words, that it is infinite.

UNITY

Now there can be no space or time in anything that is infinite. Infinity has no beginning and no end and there are no units within it. Infinity is one and only one. If you divide infinity into a series of units, you no longer have infinity but multiplicity instead. Since there are no units within infinity, nothing can be moved from one point to another, and since time is a measure of the movement of a unit through space, there is no time in infinity.

Now what we are saying is essentially this: Everything is *basically one thing,* has no beginning and no end, has no past and no future, but only one eternal now.

Einstein has said that, since a mass traveling at the speed of light would appear to be everywhere at the same time, the speed of light represents infinity. This premise is a small part of the master mathematician's Theory of Relativity, which he has stated came to him as an intuition or revelation. The entire theory was years in the proving by a group of highly-trained mathematicians working night and day, and even now there is room for doubt that it is exact, so difficult it is to cope with infinity with finite tools and measurements.

Yet few, if any, doubt the basic truth of the Theory of Relativity today. It is obvious that anything actually traveling infinitely fast would be everywhere at the same time which could only be one time or all time; and all of whatever was traveling at that speed would be at any particular point and all of it would be everywhere at all points.

INFINITY AND GOD

Infinity is a difficult word. Since words are attempts to convey thoughts, the word infinity has come to cover a multitude of so-called unknowables. Today, many people popularly use the word to cover anything that goes beyond their understanding, but it actually is as exact a conception as anything could possibly be, very probably the most exact conception mankind has ever been able to draw.

Infinity is the word that science has substituted for God. This is not to assign to science an irreverent attitude, for scientists as a group of men are the most reverent in creation. Scientists simply cannot work with an unknowable, and religion says that God cannot be known. Infinity, says science, is that oneness behind all creation that can be known. Thus the natural substitution of words.

But, of course, we are not talking about two different things at all. God is one; infinity is one. God is everywhere; infinity is everywhere. God is an everlasting now; infinity is an everlasting now. God knows everything; infinity contains everything. Religion, biology, botany, chemistry, electronics, physics, and all science, all philosophy, all the thinking efforts of man are but different roads which lead to one common destination: Infinity or God, whichever you will.

Infinity or God, eternal substance, eternal intelligence, that thing which is everything and yet is but one thing, that thing which is everywhere and yet is in but one place, that thing which is all time and yet is but one time, that thing which is all form and yet is but one form. *Infinite, eternal, only one, and never changing, that to which all things are known and in which every physical object has its being—this is God, and all of God is in us this moment, right now, and all the moments to come.*

THE GRAND CONCEPTION

If we have lost you now, it is only because your conception of the final reality of the physical world is so strong that for the moment it will not dissolve before your efforts to free your mind. If you are floundering, wondering whether this is dream or substance, fact or fiction, simply keep your resolve and your faith. You could scarcely learn to speak a new language in several months, and this language transcends all others. Be assured of this: all the mystery and complexity will disappear. As you continue to study and meditate, you will one day read again the portions of this book which seemed complex and will be amazed at how fundamental and simple they seem to you. For you are gathering from each chapter far more than you know, coming closer to an understanding of your true self, breaking down the finite bounds in your thinking, undergoing an expansion in power and conception that you may as yet be unaware of. Yet you can be sure that when the last chapter reveals the metaphysical secret which is so simple and yet so difficult to grasp there will be meaning and power in everything that you have read in these pages.

So let us stand for the moment on the conclusion that there is but one power behind the entire universe which is everywhere at all times and is the substance from which all things are made.

In the next chapter we shall cover in detail how form is called into being through and by this power, but for now it is enough to know that the same infinite intelligence pervades all life—all vegetable and animal life and even every inanimate object of our world.

This infinite intelligence, then, is the only mind there is; we are all using it; we can't help using it; for it is one and everywhere and is the stuff from which all things are made. It is as different from the human brain as night is from the day, for the human brain is a specific instrument for a specific organism for specific surroundings, while the intelligence behind all creation cannot, by itself, be specific in either time or place, form or circumstance. Being eternal and unified it does not recognize these things, except as projections of the consciousnesses that exist within it.

One mind only, which is everywhere and everything; this is the Subconscious Mind. And now, today, we are able to see it and to experiment with it.

HYPNOSIS EXPOSES THE SUBCONSCIOUS

First and most important of the tools with which we are able to reach the Subconscious is hypnotism, for through the techniques of this science we are able to temporarily put the Conscious Mind out of the way and deal directly with the God-Power, the infinite intelligence in every man, the Subconscious Mind. And the very startling discovery we make immediately is that this Subconscious Mind reacts entirely by suggestion. In other words, it has no volition of its own!

It does not by itself make choices, indulge in arguments, postulate theories, search for answers, wonder at possibilities. It only accepts and acts. Once it is given a suggestion, it immediately sets to work to make that suggestion truth, for it accepts that suggestion completely.

Now the unfortunate thing about hypnotism is that its evolution has been such that people tend to regard it as a type of trickery. Those of you who have seen hypnotists work may have been witness to a series of trivia, which, even though it has perhaps confounded you, has nevertheless left you with feelings of charlatanism or, even worse, an attitude of "so what?" You may have seen a man act as if he were a bear, shiver with cold even though the temperature was normal, break into a sweat in the same normal temperature. You may have seen a man put into a cataleptic state in which his limbs became rigid and he resisted great forces or held great weights; or you may have seen a person unable to resist post-hypnotic suggestion by reciting certain poetry on a word cue, picking up a certain object as a result of a gesture, or performing any one of a dozen other pointless acts. Without doubt, the stage hypnotist with his theatrics and flair for the bizarre has planted in the minds of his public a definite bar against regarding hypnotism as an experimental science.

What few people have suspected over the years is that the Subconscious Mind not only accepts suggestion as truth, but it has the capacity to make literal truth out of such suggestion!

For example, by the simple device of telling a patient under deep hypnosis that he has no feeling in his arm, we are able to effect this condition so completely that his arm may be amputated without anesthetic and he will undergo no pain whatever. Moreover, such a patient can be told that when he is awake all he will have to do to displace all feeling in any part of his body is simply say, "The feeling is going away." The day is not too far distant when each person will carry his own anesthetic with him in the form of this simple phrase. Consider how much suffering will be saved during accidents, disasters, and wars when an injured person can immediately allay his pain by simply saying, "The feeling is going away." *With isolated individuals such a situation has already become a reality in clinical tests!*

The cure and prevention of disease may reach undreamed-of perfection under the proper use of hypnosis. Cures as startling as those performed by Jesus himself are now being effected by those few who have perfected hynotism's techniques. A young lad who from birth had been afflicted by a hideous malformity of the skin, a thick crustaceous development called "Elephant Hide," and for whom medical science could do nothing, has now a normal skin through hypnosis. How? *By the simple expedient of telling him, when his Conscious Mind was out of the way, that his skin was clearing up!*

The Subconscious Mind is everything, contains everything, knows everything, and therefore can do anything. All it needs in the suggestion. All matter, all substance, all knowledge exist within it, and it rearranges them according to suggestion. And hypnotism is the first concrete way in which man has been able to reveal and study the workings of this mind.

LIMITATIONS OF HYPNOSIS

Now if hypnosis can accomplish the cure of disease and the anesthetizing of the body, it is reasonable to ask, why is it not more widely used? The answer is that it is coming to be, but no shrouded in superstition and ill-repute is this science, so fraught with misunderstanding and malpractice, that scientific minds have been reluctant to put it to wide usage. More than that, the scientific studies of the Subconscious Mind have revealed an instrument of such astounding power that scientists have hesitated to reveal anything of that about which they know so little. Nevertheless, hypnotism is coming into increasingly popular use in medicine.

Now where does the power of this Subconscious Mind cease? If you tell a sick man's Subconscious that he is well and he becomes well, if you tell an injured man's Subconscious that he feels no pain and he feels none, does this perhaps mean that you can tell an unsuccessful man that he is successful and he will become successful? It most certainly does. Given the proper suggestion, the Subconscious Mind will manifest success from failure, health from disease, prosperity from poverty, friendship and love from loneliness and isolation. For nothing is impossible to the Subconscious Mind and it operates entirely by suggestion.

From the foregoing it would appear at first glance that the only thing the world needs to cure its ills is to have one wise and kindly hypnotist put everyone into a trance and then inform them that they are healthy, prosperous, successful and loved, and presto, the millennium is here. Ridiculous as this may sound, if such a sufficiently enlightened and trustworthy person could be found and some method of effecting the hypnosis could be developed, the millennium indeed would be dawning. But the techniques of hypnotism are a far cry from this development today.

Thus far it has been fairly conclusively proven that with the present techniques of hypnosis only about one out of five people can be hypnotized. More than that, a hypnotic suggestion once planted in the Subconscious will eventually dissipate itself if it is not renewed, so that a hypnotized person who is told that he is recovering from a disease will show a definite improvement for a few weeks but if the hypnosis is not repeated and the suggestion replanted he will soon relapse to his former state. Why?

Simply because his mind contains a conditioned response, the Prompter, which is making him sick. A new conditioned response prompting him to be well has been planted, but this new seed must be watered and tended in order for it to grow. The old seed, the Prompter, is a flourishing weed, and its conditioned response, "You are sick, you are sick," must be overcome and disintegrated.

But regardless of insufficient techniques, hypnotism has revealed beyond all doubt that there is in man a mind with an infinite creative power and that this mind responds entirely to suggestion.

TECHNIQUES OF HYPNOSIS

Now, you may ask, why is it that a perfect stranger can tell your Subconscious when you are under hypnosis that you have no feeling in your arm and forthwith you have no feeling in your arm, while if you, yourself, in a normally conscious state say that you have no feeling in your arm, the feeling is just as lively as ever?

You are not able to accomplish this cessation of feeling because you think as well as speak. You are not simply telling your Subconscious that you have no feeling in your arm. You are forming the words in your mind or speaking them aloud, but this thought is accompanied by a dozen others, such as "This is silly, I know it won't work," "This, of course, is impossible," "I have normal feeling in my arm because I am aware of feeling now." In other words, you have so accustomed yourself to having feeling in your right arm that even when you say, "I have no feeling in my arm," a dozen others of your own thoughts are directed to your Subconscious to assure that you still actually have feeling there.

There is positively no other explanation for the fact that the hypnotist can accomplish what you can't. The very primary fact that he must put your Conscious Mind out of the way is all the proof we need. The Conscious Mind then, being asleep, cannot say "don't" or "it isn't possible." The Conscious Mind can do nothing. And the Subconscious Mind seizes on the suggestion of the hypnotist and attempts to turn it into truth.

The very techniques of hypnosis illustrate this point. The hypnotist begins by having the subject get into a comfortable position. Why? Because he knows that the Conscious Mind of the subject must go to sleep. He then begins to talk sleep to the subject. To facilitate this, he may ask the subject to concentrate his sight on some object, such as the tip of the hypnotist's finger or his eyes or any object in the room. The purpose of this is to incite a tiredness in the eye muscles of the subject and thus promote a sleepy feeling. Patiently the hypnotist talks to the subject about how his eyes are becoming tired. He may continue on this vein for five minutes, fully aware of how repetitious he is, for he knows that repetition is essential, that only through constant reiteration will he plant the seed in the Subconscious Mind. After a while, the hypnotist may begin to talk of how the eyelids of the subject are closing, how heavy they are getting, how it is impossible to hold them open any longer. When he sees that the subject's eyes are drooping and heavy lidded, he may say, "You cannot hold your eyes open any longer." If, at this juncture, the eyes close, the patient is well on his way.

The hypnotist now talks of how tired the patient is, how much he feels like sleeping, how delightful it is to sleep soundly. Once the subject is in a state of deep sleep, the hypnotist may simply leave him there for a while and then awaken him, confident that the next hypnotic effort will be accomplished with much greater simplicity and that the patient will go into an even deeper sleep. The deepest sleep possible on the part of the subject is what the hypnotist strives for. *Because he knows that in order to get directly at the Subconscious Mind he must have the subject's Conscious Mind thoroughly out of the way!*

Once deep hypnotic sleep has been induced in the patient, suggestions of health, prosperity, etc., can be given his Subconscious and they will tend to be manifested in the physical world. It is true that these new conditions may revert to their former states if hypnotic suggestion is not persisted in, but that is simply because negative habits of thinking, long ingrained in the subject's Conscious Mind, and the buried pain remembrances, the Prompters, will eventually displace the hypnotist's suggestions if they are not firmly implanted.

But the astounding fact is this: *Here at last we see pure God-Power, the infinite, the mighty Subconscious Mind at work; for it creates according to the pure word or thought and is the single power in all creation.*

THOUGHT TRANSFERENCE REVEALS ONE MIND

Now this Subconscious Mind belongs to no one man alone, for in it and through it all things live and have their beings. Since it is infinite, it is indivisible, and therefore irrevocably one, and thus all life is tied together by an invisible but powerful bond.

The principal experimental method and tool with which we may grasp this is thought transference. Second, and nearly as important, is intuition.

Thought transference is that phenomenon whereby one person may grasp another person's thought without any apparent means of communication. Experiments along these lines have been conducted for many years, more recently under the surveillance of trained scientific minds, and the occurrence of phenomena is indisputable. Original tests put subjects in different parts of the same building, one to transmit the picture of a simple drawing, the other to attempt to capture this picture and draw it with pencil on paper. Though results were far from perfect, they far exceeded any possibility of pure chance or coincidence, and even where the receiving subject was obviously in error, there was generally sufficient resemblance in his drawing to that of the picture held by the transmitting subject as to assure that a certain rapport had been actually established between the minds of these people. *Separating these subjects by miles, continents, and oceans has made no difference in the percentage of successes against failures.*

Thought transference exists. That the human mind does not grasp it perfectly is only testimony to the fact that the Conscious Mind has imperfect contact with the Universal Subconscious Mind. It is as simple for thought transference to take place across three thousand miles of ocean as it is for it to span several feet of space, for the Universal Subconscious Mind exists in only one place which is all places and there can be no distances or space within it.

INTUITION REVEALS AN ALL-KNOWING MIND

Intuition is that aspect of mental power which enables a person to "contact" certain aspects of the Subconscious Mind with ease. In most cases this phenomenon might be summed up as an intuitive grasp of universal law. Mathematical prodigies are cases in point. Ask such a one for the cube root of 21,952,000, and he answers immediately with 280. He does not stop to figure this, to factor, to add, to subtract, to multiply, to carry. The answer is apparent to him. It is apparent because he sees the law and the law automatically yields the answer. There is nothing mystical or occult about this. Since the Universal Subconscious Mind knows everything, it does not figure out anything; the answer is synonymous with the question. Intuitively, the mathematical prodigy is in contact with the Subconscious Mind, and he sees immediately, with the posing of the problem, exactly what the answer is.

Musical prodigies are similarly intuitive. Music follows the same universal law as mathematics, a fact that may be difficult to assimilate for some of you mathematicians who can't sing a note and some of you musicians to whom a problem in short division poses its own brand of terror. But the law is the same when it is apparent, and Joel Kupperman, not yet of school age, giving answers to complicated mathematical problems, and the child Beethoven composing a symphony are both using the exact same intuitive grasp of universal law.

Adela Rogers St. John, whose superb stories are read by millions, has a sure-fire method for creating her outstanding fiction. "My whole effort is to get myself out of the way and let Something take over," she says. "When Something takes over, the story gets written in jig time and is far superior to anything I alone could do. Naturally, I'd rather have Something do it. Happily, Something usually does."

Miss St. John is well aware of the limitless power for creation that flows through each of us.

Every great artist and engineer, physicist, chemist, and astronomer, all who seek after creation and answers, must perforce have some contact with the Universal Subconscious Mind. *This contact comes when they get themselves out of the way and let the only mind in all creation provide them with the answers.*

The characteristics of this great mind become apparent under deep hypnosis. It acts as if it can make anything, without doubt, without wonder, without fear, without hesitation. Though hypnotic experiments have not yet gone so far, there is little doubt but that the Subconscious Mind can do exactly what it undertakes to do, for it knows everything and everything exists within it and its only movement is to change the arrangement or apparency of its own substance. The success of thought transference is increased many times under hypnosis. The intuitive grasp of universal law is increased many times under hypnosis. The hypnotized person can, with vastly increased effectiveness, read the thoughts of other minds and answer problems where he has no known understanding.

METHODS OF REASONING

As science knows the reasoning methods of the mind of man, they generally come under two main classifications: inductive reasoning and deductive reasoning. Now inductive reasoning means to reason from the particular to the general. For example, given an individual cat that can see at night, inductive reasoning sets out to prove that all cats can see at night. Deductive reasoning, on the other hand, given the premise that all cats can see at night will arrive at the conclusion that a particular cat in a particular place at a particular time can see at night.

In other words, inductive reasoning observes a specific occurrence and attempts to arrive at a general law to cover all such occurrences. Deductive reasoning is already in possession of the general law and simply uses this law to determine what may happen in specific circumstances in which the law is involved.

It is apparent that inductive reasoning knows circumstance and seeks the law, while deductive reasoning knows the law and seeks the circumstance. The parallel can be seen immediately. *Man knows circumstance and seeks the law. The Universal Subconscious Mind knows the law and seeks the circumstance.*

The Subconscious Mind reasons only deductively. It cannot reason inductively because it already knows all law! It seeks only to determine circumstance from its complete knowledge of the law.

This characteristic of the Subconscious Mind, that it reasons only deductively, that it therefore has in its possession the full knowledge of all governing law, is an indisputable proof that it is the infinite substance, God in man, the ultimate or absolute of all creation. And it is obvious that the individual's complete use of this mind will provide him with all the power of creation.

THE SUBCONSCIOUS RESPONDS TO SUGGESTION ALONE

The great enlightening truth with which hypnosis has provided us is that this Universal Subconscious Mind responds entirely to suggestion. In other words, this Subconscious Mind attempts to create in form and circumstance that which the

Conscious Mind suggests to it. This Subconscious Mind does not direct man as an automaton, visit disaster and suffering upon him, govern his life. Indeed, it is the servant of man, and does exactly what man tells it to do!

To illustrate this towering conception, let us go back to the young man who was cured of "Elephant Hide" through hypnosis. What did the hypnotist say to him? "Your left arm is clearing up." That only! He did not enter into a series of whys and wherefores and ifs and buts. He simply said, "Your left arm is clearing up." Forthwith, the left arm cleared up.

It is ridiculous in its simplicity. The young man himself could not say, "My left arm is clearing up," and have any healing take place at all. Why? Because he was in complete rapport with himself, and when he said, "My left arm is clearing up," he was simultaneously thinking, "I've been this way all my life, and there's no hope"—"It isn't possible to cure this hideous skin by simply saying words"—"I see this ugly skin before me and it is there and I know it." So what did his Subconscious Mind receive? It simply received the young man's conviction that he had an ugly skin which continued to manifest in reality. For the Subconscious Mind always acts and it acts on those thoughts behind which there is the most conviction.

Perhaps you are thinking that it would be a wonderful shortcut to simply put yourself in the hands of a qualified hypnotist and have him solve all the problems of your life by planting the proper suggestions in your Subconscious Mind. It is true that any immediate problem of yours might well be solved in this manner, but it is certain that you would not relish the necessity of running to the hypnotist every time you were faced with a problem for the rest of your life. No psychiatrist or hypnotist can live for you, and it is unlikely that you would want him to even if he could. This is your life. You will live it to its fullest possibilities only when you are able to consciously exercise the great power that belongs to you. You cannot live by proxy, and live you must. The only answer is to arrive at understanding of the mighty forces of which you .ire a part this minute and of which you are a part forever-more.

Hypnotism you can and may practice either as subject or practitioner, but you will make a grave error if you regard it as anything else than an experiment. It is only one small facet of the study of the Universal Mind, and its principal use to us, at this moment, is to show us beyond all doubt that the Universal Subconscious Mind responds to suggestion alone.

MEDITATION AFFIRMS SUGGESTION

Thus our primary tool in attaining all our desires is the use of meditation. In meditation we are simply affirming certain suggestions to the Subconscious Mind.

We are simply repeating and affirming certain thoughts with faith and conviction so that they will be acted upon by the infinite intelligence. It is true that our percentage of successes will be low at first, for even as we affirm we deny. Even as you settle yourself for your daily meditation and affirm the good that is to come into your life, certain negative doubts, ingrained in your thinking over the years, will tend to project themselves into the Subconscious and thus negate all your affirmation. The Prompters themselves are difficult enough to overcome, and habits of negative thinking make the problem of successful meditation all the more difficult.

While the hypnotist might cure you of a specific illness in several sessions, you yourself, undertaking the same cure, may find that it takes you several months or even a year. But don't be misled into seeking solution through hypnotism unless your problem is so acute and time of such essence as to forbid any other procedure. For only by solving your own problem, only by attaining control and understanding of your own power will you be truly master of your own life. Even as chronic illness keeps you running to doctor after doctor, so will the solving of your problems by hypnotism keep you running to hypnotist after hypnotist.

Now this fact we must make very clear. If your appendix is ruptured or your leg broken, the person for you to see is a doctor. If an acute neurosis is leading you into intense melancholia or displacement of personality or any psychotic behavior that may be dangerous to yourself or society, the person for you to see is a psychiatrist. When a physical event or circumstance has reached its acute stage and the life or welfare of the individual is seriously threatened, the event or circumstance must be dealt with on the physical plane. Doctors and psychiatrists will play an important role in human welfare for many years to come. But the day will arrive when mankind understands that all physical circumstance originates on the plane of thought, and that day each person will stand individual sentinel against all disease and all emotional suffering and they will disappear from our world.

ULTIMATE REALITY

Our Conscious Minds, these instruments of ours which classify and analyze pain and pleasure and have their seats in our brains, tend to play a very disconcerting trick on us. Since the Conscious Mind functions altogether for the purpose of survival of the individual, it does all in its power to measure and weigh and classify everything with which it comes in contact. Through the sheer variety and exactness with which it performs these classifications, it tends to convince us of the final reality of the physical world about us.

For example, if we say in all truth that the chair on which you are now sitting is composed of sheer energy which is in a constant state of movement, the Conscious

63

Mind says, "No! I feel it, and it is hard. It has a certain shape and color, and it is real. I can leave it today, and it will be here when I return tomorrow. It cannot move by itself, for only I or someone who is capable of moving can move it. It is not alive; it is inanimate. It is a chair, and I know what a chair is."

This is a typical example of the reasoning of the Conscious Mind, but to consider it final reality is a bleak prospect indeed.

This is not to propose that you ignore the chair and attempt to walk through it, for you are likely to wind up with a nasty fall. This is only to state that the physical objects and circumstances of our world cannot be final reality. If they are, then this life is all there is and each human being is a poor thing buffeted around by a mad and ironic fate, and this consciousness of yours that is such an astounding thing is nothing but an accident. The great plan and design of the universe could not possibly permit such an appalling accident. You, your consciousness, must fit into this great design just as all other things fit; and the detail and purpose of all life is of such wonder and complexity that there could be nothing else behind it all than an intelligence of infinite scope and power.

You live in this intelligence. You have your very being there. This intelligence is the only mind there is; it responds to us as we recognize it, and it responds entirely by suggestion. What a towering wondrous world! We may call upon the power of all creation simply through thought and conviction. Nothing is impossible to man, for the intelligence in which he lives gives him anything he can visualize and have faith in.

So let us not allow our Conscious Minds to trick us into believing that the physical world is the ultimate reality. Let us go through our days following the dictates of the Conscious Mind in the physical world, for this pain-pleasure discerner of ours is a finely made machine for coping with the physical. But let us constantly reach outward for the infinite intelligence that is ours. Let us know that all form and circumstance must first originate on the plane of thought, that the first cause of all creation is simply thought and conviction. Let us know that we can contact the Universal Mind for the answers to all of our problems, that we create all of our own circumstances by giving birth to them in our minds, that nothing, nothing in all the universe, can stop our thoughts from becoming real in our experience, for that is the law of life and of living.

FIRST CAUSE IS MENTAL

You are immortal; not your body, not your Conscious Mind, but the real you, the part of you which exists forever in the Universal Subconscious Mind. You always have been; you always will be. You are inseparably one with everything that is, each human being in this world, all life, all form, all objects. One, just one, and everything answers thought and faith.

Later we shall undertake to show the origination of all form and circumstance in our physical world. We shall undertake to show the beginning of the universe and to explain the basic process and reason behind evolution. In the meantime, it is important for you to realize that the first cause of all circumstance in your life is thought. *All things and all circumstances must first be created on the mental plane.* When such creation is clear-cut and born of faith and conviction, nothing can stop this image from becoming real. Once this image has come into your mind and you have accepted it, you have done all that it is necessary for you to do. All the process of creation—time, place, and circumstance—must be left in the hands of the all-knowing Subconscious Mind. The physical circumstance you desire may come from a direction you expect or it may come in such a way and such a manner as you have never dreamed. Don't strain or urge or become impatient. Simply have faith and let go. Remember, whatever you observe closely causes you to entertain an element of doubt. You have nothing to do but create the mental image with complete faith, and with that simple act the process is completely done. Be assured that the image will become real in your physical world, for you are dealing with law and law alone.

REVIEW

Here, then, are the principal points covered in this chapter:

1. The Conscious Mind is an instrument for the recording of pain and pleasure. It measures experiences of pain and pleasure, files them for recall, analyzes the experiences that produced them, and imagines escape from pain and flight into pleasure; thus the compartments of the Conscious Mind: memory, reason, and imagination.

2. The Conscious Mind is a finely tuned instrument with the sole aim of physical survival of the organism.

3. The Conscious Mind is as destructible as the body of which it is a part.

4. The Conscious Mind has no memory of its own but simply a certain ability of recall.

5. The memory of the Subconscious Mind is perfect.

6. The Subconscious Mind is the infinite substance of which all things are made. It has no beginning and no end and everything exists within it.

7. The Subconscious Mind is everything and knows everything. It is everywhere at all times and all of it is anywhere at any particular time, for space and time cannot exist in infinity.

8. Inductive reasoning attempts to arrive at law through observing particular circumstance, and is the type of reasoning primarily done by the Conscious Mind of man.

9. Deductive reasoning attempts to arrive at particular circumstance through the knowledge of law and is the type of reasoning always done by the Subconscious Mind.

10. Hypnotism exposes the essence of the Subconscious Mind and allows us to see that it responds entirely by suggestion.

11. We cannot order our lives through hypnotism, but only through consciously exercising our control over the Subconscious Mind, which simply means consciously exercising control over our thoughts.

12. Meditation is the tool with which we seek to control Our thoughts and thus to control our world through the Subconscious Mind.

13. Thought transference is a proof that all of life exists within the one mind of all creation—the Universal Subconscious Mind.

14. Intuition is a proof that the Universal Subconscious Mind contains the knowledge of the law and will reveal it to the Conscious Mind of man when a proper rapport is established.

15. The Subconscious Mind has the power to heal the body, to create physical form and physical circumstance, but acute ill health must still be dealt with by the doctor, and acute mental distress must still be dealt with by the psychiatrist, for we have not come far enough in our faith and our conception to be able to remove all cause and effect from the plane of the purely physical.

16. The first cause of every object and circumstance is its creation on the plane of Mind.

THE MAGNIFICENT ASPIRATION

Gradually the barriers in your thinking dissolve before the weight of a greater conception. Gradually your mind turns from its concern with circumstance toward a beginning grasp of a greater and more towering reality than you have ever dreamed.

Think in terms of complete unity. You are one with every person who lives, ever has lived, and ever will live. You are one with every form of life that exists, every inanimate object of your world. For all things are made from one thing and thus all things are one thing, and objects and circumstances exist as the result of conception and desire being projected into the infinite creative substance of which we are all a part, in which we are all one.

Thought is the only mover. According to the degree of your conscious intelligence you will grasp the power that is yours. According to your conscious intelligence, you will project images into the Subconscious Mind which are great or small. Thus there will be returned to you only those circumstances of which you are capable of conceiving. But whatever you conceive will be returned to you; and if doubt and fear predominate your thinking, those very things that you fear will be visited upon you, for they are convictions that the Subconscious Mind must create into actuality.

We can't escape living in the Subconscious Mind, and we can't escape thinking. And we can't escape having our thoughts manifest themselves in our physical world. But we can control our thoughts. We can control our thoughts and thus we can control our destinies, and we can become as great and as powerful as we can conceive of being, for there is at our disposal the unlimited power of all creation.

The meditation that follows is aimed at creating harmony and effectiveness in your daily life. No matter what your work is, out of the home, in the home, manual, mental, employee, employer, you can create and attract circumstance and harmony so as to make each day full of achievement and satisfaction. Remember that meditation is the tool with which we work. It is our way of giving suggestion to the Subconscious Mind. You must not fail to engage in your meditation period daily. Only through the constant use of this great tool can you achieve control over your circumstance and your destiny.

You will succeed, for you cannot fail. You are dealing with life force, are a part of life force, and power through self-realization is the destiny of man.

RECOMMENDED READING

The Edinburgh Lectures on Mental Science by Thomas Troward.

THIRD MEDITATION

I know and recognize my oneness with all things. I know that all form and all circumstance are the creation of an infinite intelligence that is in and around me. I know that all things are the result of conception and desire, that my world is ordered according to my own thoughts and convictions. Therefore I concentrate on harmony. I see nothing but order and constructiveness all about me. I do not accept thoughts of destructiveness and disharmony. In my friends, my loved ones, my fellow workers, I see nothing but cooperation and assistance. I know that we all seek the same answers and the same goals. I know that each person must follow a different path toward his vision, and I understand the searchings and the copings of everyone I know and see. I have sympathy and tolerance for all things and all people. I know that inasmuch as I help others I help myself. In my brother's eye there is my own soul. In my friend's smile there is my own humor. In my neighbor's sorrow there is my own loss, I have compassion and understanding for all things, for this life in which I have my being strives for understanding of itself. I deny error; it is simply progress toward truth. I know that it is impossible to fail when faith is present. I do not order things to be made in my time or in my place, but trust the Universal Mind in its own great knowledge of the time and the place and the need and the way. Each moment of each day brings my life closer to realization. The objects of my work are being accomplished this very minute. Success and harmony, peace and confidence are mine.

Chapter 4 - FORM

The universe hums like a great harp string
Resounding a mighty chord
Answ'ring each thought by returning a thing
From the place where all things are stored

THE UNIVERSE IS LAW

As far as the eye can see, the mind project, and the spirit perceive, there is nothing but eternal and immutable law! Working with the tiniest unit of matter he can visualize, man observes that the atom has a nucleus and moving parts which circle this nucleus in never-ending motion. Working with the largest unit of matter which he can visualize, man observes that the Solar System has a nucleus and moving parts which circle this nucleus in never-ending motion. How strange that the smallest and largest units we know are identical in their construction! Indeed, it is as if there were many mirrors in the mind, reflecting one eternal law in infinite gradations of size. No doubt the atom contains many atoms of its own. No doubt the universe is but a part of many increasingly greater universes. How small and lost we seem as we perceive the vast reaches of infinity. *Yet all our perceptions exist in mind, and just as surely as we perceive them, we are the center of them.*

Our premise is that thoughts make things; and in order to substantiate such a transcendent truth, we must turn to the beginning of all form. What is the one basic substance that permeates all space and all time? If we take apart a substance and discover atoms, and we take apart the atom and unleash energy, we must eventually say that the basic thing behind all form and all creation is energy. What, then, is this energy? It obviously does not explode helter-skelter throughout all apace, but rather becomes apparent only in matter or in movement, and always such matter or movement attains an intelligent existence or moves in an intelligent direction. The design and flow of all energy is such as to leave no doubt that basic and eternal in the universe are everlasting and immutable laws of action which alone account for the accumulation of substance into form. Inherent in these laws are movement and activation which set up the atom and the solar system alike, without regard to size. Indeed, lacking a specific viewpoint or a scale of relativity, the solar system and the atom are identical, as they assuredly must be in the Universal Subconscious Mind.

A LIVING UNIVERSE

This Universal Subconscious Mind, this first cause, this infinite plan and energy, then, is the stuff from which all things are made. In its pure form, if indeed it is ever perceived as such, it is represented only by intelligent movement, or by a word which seems much more concisely to describe it: Law. Its first intelligible manifestation is in a center of force which on the smallest scale we know is represented by the atom; and on the largest scale we know is represented by the Solar System. Nothing extraneous to the law calls into being these centers of force; it is the nature of the law to manifest them, for the law is one of life and movement and energy which by its own nature congregates itself into units of similar frequency in a vibrating universe.

To consider this further, let us attempt to visualize all space as consisting only of vibration. We need not ask ourselves what it is that vibrates, nor postulate as to what causes the vibration, for the vibration is intelligence alone and the force it exerts is of intelligence alone. The vibrations in pure universal intelligence are established on many different frequencies and all vibrations of one frequency are inevitably attracted together to form a unit. This unit, this center of corresponding vibrations, we know as an atom, or as the Solar System, the first sign of visible form, the first evidence of tangible matter, called into existence by the very nature of infinite law acting within and upon itself.

The formed atom also sets up a vibration and seeks out other atoms of a corresponding vibration, and in this coalescence of units vibrating on the same frequency there is formed matter as we know it in our physical world.

Thus matter is formed from intelligence; and more important, intelligence is in matter, in fact, intelligence *is* matter. Since intelligence must be conscious, *it is an indisputable fact that we are surrounded by a living universe, that there is consciousness in all things.*

THE CONSCIOUSNESS OF THE ATOM

Now you must bear with this very necessary discussion of the beginning of things and the nature of substance, for we are out to show that thought calls form into existence, that form is no more than a part of the very intelligence that each of us lives in.

Thomas Edison was extremely preoccupied with what he termed "the obvious choice of the atom" in its infinite acceptances and rejections of the myriad combinations of chemistry. When two chemicals were put together in solution and some of the atoms of one combined with some of the atoms of the other, Mr. Edison was forced to ask himself why those particular atoms and not some of the others, and indeed, why any of the atoms at all? The only answer he could possibly conceive was that the atoms of each chemical exercised a conscious choice whether they would or wouldn't combine with the atoms of the other chemical. Now Mr. Edison certainly aired no views as to the *self*-consciousness of the atom, but only of the intelligence or *consciousness* of the atom; in other words, the ability of the atom to make a choice.

The atom, the building block of the universe, is a center of force, and the atom is conscious!

Working in accordance with law or universal intelligence, the atom seeks out other atoms which vibrate at a corresponding rate, and the coalescence of such atoms forms that which we designate as inanimate matter: water, earth, air, and minerals.

EXPANDING CONSCIOUSNESS

Now then, you may well say, this is all well and good as a plausible theory as to the formation of substance in a living universe, but how do you account for life?

Let us repeat: *The entire universe is alive.* There is nothing dead, nothing inanimate. When Jesus said, "God is not a God of the dead but a God of the living," he was revealing the basic truth of all creation. For all is living and all is intelligence and all is conscious; and the great motivating force of all life is its attempt to expand its consciousness. In other words, *it seeks to know itself!*

Though we can safely attribute consciousness and intelligence to the atom, there remains not the slightest possibility that the atom is self-conscious. In fact, all evidence points to the consciousness of the atom being of the lowest possible order. It chooses, but its choices are within the rigid scope of operating law. When a certain number of atoms begin vibrating together on a certain frequency and form, let us say, a rock, there is created in the rock a kind of consciousness which is on an infinitely lower scale than that of the atom, for the rock exhibits practically no ability to choose. Yet there can be no doubt but that there is actually a certain consciousness in the rock, for a group of conscious units must of necessity form a group consciousness. The rock exists, therefore it must be conscious. It consists of conscious intelligence and must then have some consciousness of its own, albeit so far below our level of consciousness as to be indiscernible to us.

From the rock and sand and earth and water and air to the formation of the pain-pleasure responsive amoeba, a thing that grows and feeds and reproduces itself, what gigantic step is this?

Expanding consciousness! Only that and nothing more.

First, we have energy moving according to law, congregating into centers of force by its own nature, setting up polarization (nuclei of positive polarity around which revolve electrons of negative polarity). These centers of force, or atoms, have lives of their own, are conscious. The nature of these little lives is to congregate with others vibrating on the same frequency, and thus matter is called into existence, which is basically not matter at all, but merely units of intelligent energy. Secondly, we have all form consisting of many individual lives, building up to a conscious whole, building up to a conscious entity which attempts to work out its own purpose. From these two conclusions we go on to a third: the form which results from the union of many individual lives or consciousnesses is the result of the consciousness of the whole. In other words, the form of the rock is the result of the consciousness of the rock. The form of the amoeba is a result of the consciousness of the amoeba, and the form of the human being is the result of the consciousness of the human being!

LIFE SEEKS TO KNOW ITSELF

Now once again you may say, this all sounds reasonable enough, but where does this consciousness come from?

The entire universe is caught up in a mighty work of expanding consciousness, because it is the nature of universal intelligence to seek to know itself!

God knows himself only as a thing!

Before you shout blasphemy or irreverence, tarry a while and dwell on this premise.

Visualize space. It goes on and on forever and ever. If, in your mind's eye, you retreat trillions of miles from the earth and draw a huge circle with the earth as the center and say this indeed is all of space, what, then, is on the other side of your circle? The only answer is more space. Space as we know it, or infinite intelligence as we know it, or universal law as we know it, or the Universal Subconscious Mind as we know it, cannot possibly have any limits or any boundaries. How is it possible for something which has no boundaries to ever know itself?

In order for it to know itself it must be able to say, "I am this." And in order for it to say, "I am this," it must become something with boundaries, something finite, a thing.

And that is exactly what the Universal Subconscious Mind is doing. *It is becoming things.* It is seeking an expanded self-consciousness. And that part of it which has achieved the greatest self-consciousness which we are able to observe is the human being.

What is evolution? *It is life expanding to a conscious oneness with God.* As time progresses and our consciousness expands, we are growing closer and closer to this attainment. Indeed, this is the clue to the mystery of life and evolution and the destiny of man.

Have no fear of your smallness in relation to the vastness of limitless space, for there are no limits to the mind and there are no limits to expanding consciousness. The destiny of mankind is that man's consciousness will expand to the point where he is one with all creation. On this great day it will be as simple for one man to be in thought contact with another five thousand miles away as it is now to speak to a friend in the same room. On this great day, the mind of man will span space and time and the limitations of form, and existence will be solely of the spirit in one eternal now. The past, the present, and the future will be one. All space will be one. All form will be one. Man's consciousness will be the consciousness of God.

SPIRIT INTO MATTER

All the great metaphysical and religious works speak of the evolution of consciousness as the descent of spirit into matter. The great allegory of Adam and Eve and the Garden of Eden is an illustration. The temptation of the serpent, the eating from the tree of knowledge, the final fall which culminated in awareness of self speak only of the beginning of self-consciousness. This awareness of self as a thing of free choice was the beginning of man's conscious choosing of modes of action and methods of thought. It was the beginning of error, the start of evil, the beginning of sin and punishment—all natural results of man's search for truth.

The great Universal Subconscious Mind acting upon itself according to the laws of its own nature sets up centers of force which are conscious and which attract other similar centers of force to form matter. This matter by the very nature of its overall consciousness (the sum total of the consciousness of all of its atoms) resolves itself into a particular form and seeks ever to know more about itself. As its consciousness grows, it becomes a living, expanding, feeding, and growing entity, that which we designate a living organism. As an organism its consciousness expands with ever-increasing rapidity, so that within a relatively short time the expanded consciousness or spirit can no longer tolerate the limitations of its form and abandons it. Thus is established the cycle of birth and death such as exists in all living organisms.

The process of evolution is now in high gear. The amoeba seeking to know itself unites with other amoebas and becomes a jellyfish; the jellyfish further develops its perception and consciousness and becomes a fish; the fish further develops its consciousness and becomes a mammal; the mammal further develops its consciousness and becomes a man. All along the path of evolution lie the many residual forms marking the way, for wherever consciousness reaches out to a higher level, there also consciousness remains behind. The very process of the conception and birth and growth of a human being, through the pollywog, the amoeba, the low scale vertebrate, the foetus and finally the human infant which grows into the magnificent consciousness of a man illustrates with remarkable detail the entire path of the evolution of consciousness.

COSMIC AWARENESS

Thus it can be seen that the purpose of life is the attainment of knowledge, the expansion of consciousness, a constant reaching upward and outward and inward toward a oneness with God.

Browning wrote:

> *Such men are even now upon the earth*
> *Serene amid the half formed creatures round*
> *Who should be saved by them and joined with them.*

In Palestine nearly two thousand years ago, a man looked at his neighbors and said, "Who hath seen me, hath seen the Father."

Adulterated and misconstrued, distorted and dogmatized, the magnificent consciousness of the man, Jesus, has been in the main but a confusing din on the ears of the deafened.

"I and my Father are one." One, one, one! One with all men, all life, all things, all substance! The attainment of the consciousness of the whole. The attainment of the consciousness of God.

Form is but the result of consciousness, and consciousness is but the result of thought, and thought is simply a contact and a borrowing from the Universal Intelligence that pervades all things.

> *Thought makes form! Thought makes things!*

EXPANDING SPIRIT CHANGES FORM

In this life, which ever seeks to know more about itself, which ever seeks an expanded consciousness, he who would i stop death would stay an infant forever. For as the spirit expands its consciousness it seeks new form through which to express itself. The body which you now occupy is but an instrument of your consciousness, an expression of your knowledge of yourself. By the very nature of your being, your consciousness must grow, and as it does, your spirit will gradually lay down your body and return again into the Universal Subconscious Mind whence it starts anew in its quest for a new expression.

This, of course, brings us to the subject of reincarnation. When you have truly understood that there is only one life, only one mind, you will understand that this life incarnates itself billions of times over in its search to completely know itself. When you have understood this, reincarnation will be as obvious as knowing yourself, for you will know that there can be no life without an incarnation of the one life, which is in you, which is altogether you. One, eternal and everlasting, that is the truth about yourself, and the terror that death holds for many is simply vain regret at losing the built up errors and illusions of the Conscious Mind, which is the silliest and most illusory fear of all mankind. We shall cover a great deal more of this in the chapter on immortality.

Law into units of force, units of force combining into matter, the consciousness of matter determining its form, consciousness seeking self-consciousness, self-consciousness seeking the consciousness of the whole, the consciousness of God—this is the diagram of all life.

For we are all one in reality, and our separateness is nothing but a necessary illusion in the plan by which the Universal Mind seeks to know itself by becoming a thing.

THE ETERNAL PRESENCE

Perception of the indwelling presence is often difficult to come by. The formative years of my own spiritual experience were certainly not spent in such knowledge. With chagrin I recall how sorely I must have tried the patience of Dr. Elton Trueblood, then Chaplain of Stanford University, when that gentle and erudite man tried to lead me out of the maze of my own circuitous questionings. Dr. Trueblood's excellent books are legion, and even at that date I had read a number of them. It was on the common ground of these texts and his own teaching in philosophy that we met afternoons in his study in the Stanford Chapel.

Shafts of sunlight poured through stained-glass windows as we settled in our chairs and explored territory we had covered many times. To my openly voiced doubt of the existence of God, Dr. Trueblood offered the immense variety of religious experience undergone by men of high repute through the centuries.

"But they could have been deluded," I insisted.

"By whom?"

"By themselves."

"Why would they delude themselves?"

"Because they were afraid of their own smallness, afraid of oblivion at death."

Dr. Trueblood smiled. "Strange that some of them were otherwise very brave men," he said.

"But certainly if God exists, somebody in all the centuries would have seen him."

"Many people have."

"Who?"

"I for one."

"You've seen God?"

"Yes."

"Then what does He look like?"

"Like everything."

"That means nothing."

"It means a great deal to me. I look at you and see God. Wherever my eye falls I see God. He is as real to me as you are, more real in fact, for He is the changeless in the changing, the immutable and ever-present spirit that inhabits all things."

In my mind those words still sound on the quiet air of the Stanford Chapel. Somehow I sensed the meaning in them even then, though I did not understand them. And as the years gradually enlarged my consciousness, there came a day when I too looked on all things and saw God. On that day my faith, weak and questing as it might have been, was tempered by the steel of knowledge.

UNITY VERSUS SEPARATENESS

Mental healing and creation of circumstance and form through thought may never be accomplished by him whose consciousness is one of separateness. But he who achieves the consciousness of the whole, the consciousness of God, may change form and circumstance and promote bodily healing through thought, for all things then will exist within him. This is the truth about Jesus, and he who shuts his eyes to the miracles of the man from Nazareth is blinding himself to the greatest truth which has ever been revealed to a searching and doubting world.

For a man may walk upon the water, raise the dead, heal the sick, feed five thousand with seven loaves of bread, change water into wine, appear and disappear at will. Such is the destiny of man that these things will one day be commonplace. Such is the destiny of man that one day there will be no necessity for form, for separateness, for differentiation in the mind of God. All will be one, complete unity, a self-conscious Universal Mind.

At this point, we beseech you not to isolate yourself in your room and attempt to move a chair by thought power, nor indeed to attempt to exert any of the powers of the mind that your consciousness has not as yet grasped. You must understand at once that it is not the impression of your will or your thought that will cause a chair to move without a physical force; it is only the final all-encompassing consciousness, a oneness with the intelligence in which you and the chair both exist. This consciousness has been achieved already by a very few individuals on a very few occasions. There is good reason to believe that these individuals and occasions are on the increase. Certainly on the lower echelons of demonstration, such as the healing of the human body through mind power, there have been a multiplicity of authenticated and accurately recorded phenomena such as to remove all doubt of the supreme power of the Universal Subconscious Mind.

THE SECRET DOCTRINE

There is in existence today a body of esoteric teaching which is aptly termed "The Secret Doctrine" and which for many centuries has been in the keeping of small groups of studious men who have learned its tenets and passed it down largely by word of mouth, though many allegorical texts exist in which it is described. This doctrine holds that the evolution of man will proceed through seven principal races and that we are now living under the great Fifth race, which began with the civilizations in Persia, Egypt, and the Orient. According to the Doctrine, the first race of man was largely spiritual, the second began to take on form, the third produced a race of giants that inhabited the continent of Lemuria, the fourth inhabited the continent of Atlantis, and the fifth sought refuge in Europe and Asia after the deluge (referred to exoterically in the Bible in the allegory of Noah's Ark) to produce the materialistic age of today from whence man will revert once again to spiritual unity through the sixth and seventh races.

Those who attempt to substantiate this Doctrine maintain that the continent of

Lemuria existed in the South Pacific Ocean and offer as evidence the gigantic statues which can be found on Easter Island. These statues are between twenty-seven and thirty feet high and show no evidence of having been built by scaffolding, but appear to have been molded by beings whose stature was approximately the same. As the old testament of the Bible says, "In those days there were giants in the earth," so the adherents of the Secret Doctrine maintain that colossal beings inhabited the continent of Lemuria which was swallowed into the sea during a great upheaval in which the earth reversed its poles, leaving nothing above the surface but Easter Island and an archipelago of volcanic rock extending from the Marquesas Islands to New Zealand.

These same adherents maintain that the continent of Atlantis was the home of the fourth race of mankind and that this continent existed in the Atlantic Ocean, its easternmost part where we find the Azores today and extending westward for several thousand miles. The men inhabiting this continent were supposedly eighteen feet tall and their civilization was such as to put our present one to shame, all of our present scientific advances having been made as well as the development of a culture far exceeding our own. As the Secret Doctrine has it, Atlantis was destroyed when the earth again reversed its poles. The water rose, Atlantis was swallowed into the sea, and its survivors (biblically Noah and his wife and their animals) found their home at the eastern end of the Mediterranean.

THE TENETS OF THE SECRET DOCTRINE

The proponents of the Secret Doctrine do not advance any reason for the periodic destruction of the various races of man's evolution, their evidence of the existence of the races is sketchy to say the least, and they fail to be clear about the author of this plan which they say has been irrevocably laid down for mankind to follow. But this much they are very firm about: that intelligence and law are the only realities, that mankind is evolving toward spiritual oneness, that it is within man's grasp to attain universal consciousness and thus control over all things.

The history and course of man's future, as expounded by the Secret Doctrine is difficult to accept, but we shall neither affirm nor deny it. Certainly, recorded history takes us scarcely to the doorway of mankind's past, and if the Secret Doctrine is not correct it is perhaps as allegorically correct as need be. It is safe to say that man's evolving spirit has inhabited other forms than we know today and that the process of evolution has gone on for perhaps millions of years. It may even be that the earth turns over every so often, for the precession of the equinoxes is known to every astronomer, which is simply another way of saying that the earth is slowly wobbling as it spins on its axis. Anyone who has observed a spinning top knows what happens when it begins to wobble in its spin.

The Secret Doctrine also holds that there are superior beings in the universe who are watching and guiding man's evolution on earth, that these beings send their messengers or teachers to our world in the form of Adepts (those whose evolution has progressed sufficiently to be able to gradually reveal the eternal truths to mankind). According to the proponents of the Doctrine, Jesus was one of the Adepts, as was Gautama Buddha, as was Plato. No information is given about what part of the universe is inhabited by those who send their Adepts upon the earth, but it is safe to assume that the inference is that these Superior Beings occupy the planets of our solar system, or else the stars.

LIFE ON OTHER WORLDS

Now it would be sheer blindness to maintain that higher evolved beings than man do not exist on other worlds in space. Indeed, since our premise is that all form is merely manifold differentiations of one supreme mind, since we believe that all is life, and consciousness is everywhere, it logically follows that life exists on other worlds. Has this life evolved to our level or beyond it?

We know already that some of the stars as well as a few of the planets are much older than our sphere. We know that some of the stars have climate conditions that may approximate those of the earth. As each year brings us closer to the day when space travel becomes a reality, it also brings us closer to the time when many riddles will be answered.

How the horizons of man will expand when he reduces the millions of miles of space to a comfortable journey, how his thinking will change when he looses himself from the pull of gravity, when the unimpeded acceleration of action in space sets up such blinding speed in his vehicles as to even affect the passage of time. Then, indeed, must man look at the physical worlds about him and know of his unity with the only intelligence and law there is.

THE RELATIVITY OF MATTER

Principal among the provocative phenomena man will encounter when he reaches new worlds is that of the relativity of matter. Today our spectroscope reveals the existence on far-flung planets of elements that may weigh as much as hundreds of tons per cubic inch! Consider that man knows matter only in its relative density to his own body. We judge all substance according to its varying degrees of hardness and softness, in other words, its density; and that substance which is least dense and which is still perceptible we call a gas. The air around us is such a gas. As we move about in it, we are aware of it, but we move unimpeded, so relatively scarce is its density in comparison to the density of our own bodies. A being whose bodily density was such that he weighed several hundred tons per cubic inch would move through our own bodies with even more ease than we move through the earth's atmosphere! He would not even be aware of us, for his physical perception would of necessity be on an entirely different plane of matter!

Such beings may conceivably exist on other worlds than ours. Others whose density is so slight as to be negligible in comparison to our own, may also conceivably exist on other worlds. Matter is purely relative to the senses that perceive it. In its essence it is pure intelligence, and it combines into such form as to be perceptible to whatever consciousness is attempting to perceive it.

The element which weighs hundreds of tons per cubic inch is made of the same basic stuff as our own atmosphere. Intelligence molds it into form, intelligence causes its form, intelligence is its form. Basically, it is neither more nor less than a conception held in the Universal Subconscious Mind.

THE RELATIVITY OF TIME

Spaceship travel offers another startling promise, that of extreme speed and an entirely new concept of time.

In free space, beyond all but a negligible attraction from interstellar bodies, a space ship would float, orbiting on some gigantic circle around whatever principal interstellar body it happened to be closest to. If a rocket were fired from the rear of this space ship, with such velocity as to create a reaction that accelerated the ship to a speed of one thousand miles per hour, the space ship would continue at this speed forever, unless some impeding obstacle or attraction or friction were put in its path. If another similar rocket were fired from the rear of the space ship, its speed would then reach two thousand miles per hour. If another were fired, speed would increase to three thousand miles per hour. If a thousand such rockets were fired, the speed of the ship would be one million miles per hour! Indeed, if sufficient numbers of such rockets were conceivably available, the speed of the ship could eventually be accelerated to 186,000 miles per second or 669,600,000 miles per hour! Since this is the speed of light and according to Einstein a limiting speed, we cannot go beyond it; nor, in fact, can we ever reach it exactly. His conclusion is that an object increases in size with its speed and though the effect is negligible at lower velocities it becomes startling as a mass approaches the speed of light. At this speed, Einstein maintains that a mass would become infinitely large. He also maintains that a minute becomes longer to those who travel at increased velocities; that at the speed of light, time actually stands still! Perhaps this is simply another way of saying that man cannot achieve the speed of light. Perhaps, even more than that, it is a method of scientifically describing the complete basic unity of all things in a world where time and space do not exist. One thing is certain, new concepts of space and time and distance and substance will be in sore need the day man becomes free of the pull of earth's gravity on his first adventure into space.

The promise is there. The promise is within the expanding consciousness of the mind of man, who will bridge all space and time, who will truly understand that he is the focal point of all creation the day he discovers that all things exist within him!

GROWING INTO UNDERSTANDING

We may, at this moment, seem far adrift for those of you who seek the solution to some specific problem in your life. But you must first understand what mind is. There are no words or formulas that must not first be understood. The Key itself is as concise as a diamond, but we must be sure your consciousness has been expanded to the point where you recognize that conception and thought are the alpha and omega of all existence. Patience is the virtue you can best exercise now—patience and practice of the meditations—and thoughtfulness with the conceptions you are now entertaining and evolving. Concern with space and time and the nature of matter and form are as essential to you in expanding your consciousness as was your original resolve to realize peace and power. Be assured. The road is well planned and charted!

REALITY VERSUS DELUSION

What remarkable phenomena are the myriad forms about us. Mountains, trees, brooks, seas, meadows, the infinite varieties of animal and vegetable life, the innumerable combinations of minerals, the astounding mechanistic forms made by the hands and ingenuity of man—their variety and number are awesome. Yet we pass them by, regarding them as natural and normal in the scheme of things, giving little or no heed to whence they have come and of what they are made. How sure we often are in our little moments in our little lives in our little material worlds. We attach our fleeting securities to the forms around us, vainly try to build up a sense of permanence in a constantly changing material world, forgetting the enigma of our births and the inevitability of our deaths as we put our main goals on the accumulation of wealth and goods. Yet all form is made of the same basic substance as ourselves, pure and eternal intelligence, the Universal Subconscious Mind; and that mind and all it contains lies within each of us.

To a being that weighed three hundred tons per cubic inch, the chair in your living room could not exist. He would brush it aside as if it were not there. If he stepped upon it, he would crush it but would never notice it. If the chair simply consists of atoms with more space between them than in the atoms, and if the atoms themselves contain more space than matter, if we regard matter as nothing other than pure intelligence, if certain matter, such as the chair, which is such a concrete thing to us, cannot be perceived by a being whose density is millions of times greater, then it is inescapably true that form may exist even though it is not perceived.

FORM IS CONCEPTION

This is an interesting and important point. Simply because the presence of the chair is not discernible to the being who weighs three hundred tons per square inch does not obliterate the existence of the chair. Such a being would perceive only such vibrations of light reflected from substances with a density comparable to his. He would hear only violent vibrations of sound. If one of his fellow beings told him that the chair existed, he would snort and say that if it did, he could see, hear, feel, or smell it. If one of his fellow beings pointed out to him that the place where the chair stood caused a slight variation in the quality of the light, he would insist that it was all just a crazy idea.

But he would know that an idea was involved!

That close to the truth he instinctively would come. The chair would exist for him, but only as a conception! To him the chair could be only an idea, a thought, which is all that the chair actually is in the first place, a conception in the Universal Subconscious Mind, made of the same substance as the Universal Subconscious Mind.

Now what we are attempting to illustrate is that form is no more than conception, that form is no more than an idea, that form always involves consciousness and that it is entirely representative of thought. *In its pure essence form is constructed of exactly the same material from which a thought is constructed!*

DUAL MIND

Thus has evolved the duality of our lives, and we live upon two planes at once: the plane of mind and thought; and the physical plane of things and circumstances. Our education and inhibition have been such as to teach us that thought has evolved in our attempt to deal with things, *while the truth is that things are no more than images that represent our thoughts!*

Such a parallel was drawn by Plato in his cave which represented the world. The men who lived within the cave, by their very nature, could look only on the wall of the cave, where they observed their shadows cast by the fire behind them. These shadows they believed represented the truth about themselves. When one of them turned about and noted that he was being gripped by an illusion, his fellows objected loud and long, labeled him deluded, and continued their observation of the flickering shadows.

All truth exists within man and never in the world about him. He who studies the world studies effects. He who studies his own mind studies the cause and source of things as they really are!

THE FOURTH DIMENSION

The world of science has long been working along the premise that we fail to grasp the full significance of form, that we do not see and observe a thing for what it really is. This extra quality of things science has labeled the fourth dimension, and many the tome and treatise have been written in an attempt to tell us in which direction the fourth dimension extends.

Since the first three dimensions are each perpendicular to the other, science has insisted that the fourth dimension exists perpendicular to the other three. With our present conception of space, such a fourth perpendicular is obviously impossible; yet science continues its patient attempt to place a fourth perpendicular in space, for it knows that three dimensions cannot possibly answer the cause and the existence of the things it is studying.

In a gigantic and complex volume entitled *Tertium Organum,* the Russian writer P. D. Ouspensky postulates that life is evolving to the recognition of possibly seven dimensions, that each dimension, when unknown, represents itself as movement. For example, he says that the amoeba lives in a one-dimensional world, that each thing that crosses the line on which his consciousness lives, represents to the amoeba only a point. On the next higher scale, the dog lives in a two-dimensional world, seeing and recognizing only width and height; where the dog observes the presence of the third dimension it is apparent to him as movement. To round out his conclusion, Ouspensky says that we three-dimensional human beings are perceiving the fourth, fifth, sixth, and seventh dimensions as movement also, and when man has evolved the full way along the path he travels there will be revealed to him an immobile universe possessing seven dimensions.

Thus Ouspensky is able to posit four dimensions more than the normal three, and he finds them all existing in what we know as time, for movement is synonymous with time.

Who dares dispute him? The world's greatest mathematical thinker has come to essentially the same conclusion, for he finds matter elongating itself according to its velocity, until, at the speed of light, it is everywhere at the same time, which is all time and anytime, for time will then stand still; which is simply Einstein's method of saying that time and space and matter are one when the velocity of movement has reached infinity.

A QUESTING GOD

What are these two outstanding thinkers driving at? Basically, they both see the same thing: that beneath the illusion of separateness there lies a great unity of all things, a unity in which space and time and individual form are all combined into one, an underlying infinite spirit or an intelligence, the Universal Subconscious Mind!

Here it is reasonable to ask: if this is so, what is the purpose of the illusion of separateness, what is the purpose of individual lives and individual things? And the only reasonable answer at which it is possible to arrive is that the Universal Subconscious Mind is seeking to know itself by becoming things, that, in effect, it cannot know itself as infinity.

The only possible conclusion is that there is only one purpose behind evolving life and that purpose is an expanding consciousness!

God seeks to know himself by becoming a thing!

Thus human evolution is destined to expand self-consciousness to infinity!

VIEWPOINT

The riddle of the universe is a riddle pure and simple. Like any other riddle, the true answer depends on a shift in viewpoint. If someone proposes a riddle to you, you put yourself in the place of each of: the persons involved in the riddle; you attempt to get each of their viewpoints. When you have gotten each viewpoint, you translate them into one central viewpoint. Then the answer becomes apparent.

It is viewpoint that gives us the illusion of separateness in life. It is this trick that consciousness plays on us that is forever provoking us into believing that we are negligible in the vast scheme of things. We sense that our consciousness is imprisoned within the fleshy limits of our bodies, and we presume that our personal "I's" are forever limited to the few feet of cubic space that our bodies occupy.

We see ourselves at the center of a tremendous universe. As far as we can see in all directions there is myriad form and infinite variety. The very grains of sand upon a beach refuse to be counted through sheer number. Yet something within us keeps insisting, "If I were not conscious and able to observe this, it would not be so." We analyze this statement somewhat sheepishly and admit that somebody else would be observing it even if we weren't, so it would still have to exist. What we fail to analyze is the personal, restricted, bodily-contained "I."

WHO IS "I"?

Bill Smith, Jim Jones, Mary Stuart, every conscious organism and thing that exists refers to itself in exactly the same way: "I."

When anyone says "I" he may think that he is referring to his name, where he was born, what he has done, every experience which he has ever had, but what he is actually doing, no more and no less, is simply saying, "here." He means: that thinking consciousness which is in a certain place is having certain thoughts and sensations which it wishes to express through speech or movement. "I am hungry"—that consciousness which is here wishes to be fed. "I wish to go for a walk"—that consciousness which is here desires to move somewhere else.

More than that, each "I" is far from being a stable entity, but rather represents hundreds, perhaps thousands, perhaps even millions or billions of "I's." Shakespeare said, "All the world's a stage and all the men and women merely players, . . . and each man in his time plays many parts." Millions of parts are the lot of each person, and every part represents another "I" on an expanding scale of consciousness. You are not the same "I" as you were ten years ago, nor are you the same "I" as you were one week ago. You will not even be the same "I" when you have finished this chapter. You are only a particular "I" at a particular moment, and the very next thought that traverses your mind makes you a different "I" on the succeeding moment. You are always a product of your thought, and represent at any time the sum total of your thought to that moment. Each new thought adds to or detracts from your consciousness. Your "I" is different from anyone else's in the world, for only you have had the exact train and sequence of thought which make you you. It is a practical truth that no two people have ever had nor ever will have the exact same train and sequence of thought until human consciousness has been expanded to the conscious of the Universal Mind.

THE ILLUSION OF ISOLATION

One of the biggest barriers in the explanation of the unity of life is that a person will say, "If true mind is universal and in all things, why am I me and not someone else or even everyone else?" And the only answer which it is possible to give is that you are someone else-and even everyone else basically. The differences you perceive between yourself and others is simply the difference between the thoughts they have had and the thoughts you have had, for each person is only what he thinks.

It is true that your consciousness tends to lock itself within a finite body. And because you tend to say, "My consciousness is here and nowhere else," it is difficult for you to perceive that you and your neighbor are one. How much simpler it would be if each thought affecting you and each thought you have had were identical in number and sequence with your neighbor's. Your consciousness then would have to be the same. Could there be any doubt in your mind that you then would both occupy the same body? No two completely identical things exist in the universe: no two grains of sand, no two snowflakes, no two trees. For the universe is engaged in making numbers of unlike things from a basic oneness. By its very nature, it cannot make two things which are completely identical. If two conceptions are completely alike, there is only one conception that will produce only one thing!

THE UNIQUENESS OF YOU

You are what you are only because of what you have thought. Because this thought is different from any person who has ever lived, you are a unique and separate thing in the universe. Most of your thinking is prompted by the sensations that come to you through your five senses, and since these belong to your finite body exclusively, you are constantly building up experience and thought that keep you locked away from oneness with the Universal Subconscious Mind. You tend to see all things about you as being external and different from you. You are, at this stage of evolution, acutely aware of self as a separate, isolated being. But be assured: the path upward leads to expanding that self-consciousness to include all things and all life.

THE KINGDOM OF GOD IS WITHIN

We must understand that all form and matter represent I only the same intelligence that is in us. We must recognize that all of this intelligence is ours to draw upon and to understand and use. We must know that thought makes form, that thought makes things, that thought makes us what we are. We must know that our separateness is only of evolving consciousness, that basically there is complete spiritual unity in all life. We must strive constantly to expand our consciousness by identifying ourselves with everything and everyone about us. We must search in our quiet hours for contact with the Universal Subconscious Mind, where all information and all thought have been indelibly impressed, which can guide us unerringly along paths of attainment and knowledge. We must understand the invincible power of thought, how it makes us what we are, how it creates form and brings circumstance, how it underlies and moves the universe. We must guard ourselves from being exposed to negative thinking; we must refuse to accept negative circumstance. We must, in our complete and positive expansion, in our soaring knowledge of the mighty work of the mind, teach our children to control their thinking, teach our neighbors to control their thinking, teach a suffering mankind that the way out of each of its dilemmas lies in the vehicle of its own thought, that the millennium is here, that the Kingdom of God is within everyone of us.

MIND IS GREATER THAN ALL

As you look about you at the panorama of your life, at the things that concern you, at the circumstances that involve you, expand your consciousness to include them as living parts of the fluidic medium in which you live. See through your own eyes a manifold living universe which is constantly expressing itself by becoming an infinite number of things. Sense your complete oneness with each of these things, know that the only real truth is intelligence and the only real form is thought. Somewhere, behind the barriers established by your habits of thought, there exists the consciousness of the whole, the intelligence that knows all things, the Universal Subconscious Mind. Nothing is impossible to this mind. All of its guidance and power are available to you. When you have fully realized that thought causes all, you will know that there can never be limits on you that you yourself do not impose.

As we work more and more with intelligence and consciousness, we will learn to disregard size in relation to our own bodies. By simply understanding that physical form and physical size have little or nothing to do with expanding consciousness, we may look on the vastness of space and the eternities of time with utter composure, in the knowledge that mind alone is the answer to all things and mind need never be limited by space and time.

Because a star lies a million light years away does not mean that you are small in the scheme of things. Does not your mind traverse this tremendous distance in an instant? See the power and scope of this mind of yours. So swiftly it dwarfs your body. With such great power inherent in his very being, is it not the worst of all evils for a man to place "no trespassing" signs on all avenues of thought and thus limit himself into poverty, disease, limitation and lack of every kind?

Nothing is impossible. All things are probable. Whatever the mind can conceive, the mind can do. Whatever the mind conceives the mind does. *There is only one way the path of evolution leads—upwards! There is no limit to the heights to be assailed, short of union with God.*

MAN IS THE CENTER OF THE UNIVERSE

Our home is a whirling ball amongst whirling balls in ringed space. Mercury, Venus, Earth, Mars, Jupiter, Saturn, Uranus, Neptune, and Pluto, eternal captives of the Sun, move in the immutable paths of infinite law. They are only specks in space. If the sun were a mile in diameter, Mercury would be fifteen feet across and thirty-six miles away; Venus would be thirty-eight feet across and sixty-seven miles away; Earth would be forty feet across and ninety-three miles away; Mars would be twenty feet across and one hundred forty miles away; Jupiter would be four hundred feet across and four hundred eighty-three miles away; and the last of the planets, Pluto, would be twenty feet across and three thousand seven hundred miles away! And this is but one of an infinite number of Solar Systems!

He who is a materialist and would account for life as an accident amid the immeasurableness of material form, is accounting for nothing, so small is man relative to the universe. Such a one may feel and touch his physical possessions each day, much as Midas counted his gold, but when his spirit lays down his physical form and departs he knows not where, it provides no entourage or vans or railroad cars for the transport of those things upon which the materialist has founded his truths. Matter and substance and form are but instruments of our thought, but pawns in a reaching game of expanding mind, much as chess players might play their game in their heads were it not so much easier to do it with a playing board and chess pieces.

Man is the center of the universe! Not in physical size assuredly, but in mind! For the Universal Subconscious Mind in everywhere at the same time, and all of it is at any place at any time, and all of it is in man, now!

THE MIGHTY TOOL

Form proceeds from mind, and mind controls all, and this knowledge properly applied can change your life. No longer need you batter at circumstance and things; no longer need you rail at the dealings of fate or frustrate your life against unwanted circumstance. Everything proceeds from mind, everything proceeds from thought; and miracles are wrought in quiet hours in still rooms when awakened souls harken their divinity.

You, as a person, know you exist because you think, and these thoughts of yours are far and away the most important thing you do; they are, in fact, the only thing you do. These thoughts of yours are the essence that makes form, that brings circumstance; they are your sole tool with which to expand your consciousness. Accordingly, there is no more paramount thing for you to do than carefully select those thoughts that you will think, those beliefs you will adopt, those attitudes you will take for your own, for by them you will be what you will be; by them you have arrived exactly where you are today. If you mean for your life to be progressive and full of achievement, vigor, love, and abundance, you will abandon each negative thought the moment it is presented to you. You will refuse to accept on the plane of mind any conception other than those that are in tune with good. You will think only positively! And the universe will shower you with more good than you ever dreamed.

REVIEW

1. Basic and eternal in the universe are everlasting laws of action.

2. A vibrating universe, acting upon itself, evolves centers of force such as are represented by the atom and by the Solar System.

3. These centers of force seek other centers of force with similar vibrations, and by their coalescence matter is formed.

4. Since intelligent law makes up the center of force, the atom, which is the building block of the universe, is conscious.

5. We have our beings in the midst of a living universe.

6. There is no such thing as inanimate matter, for all form is made from universal intelligence and is but a conception in the Universal Subconscious Mind.

7. That matter which we call living is simply that which has evolved sufficiently so that its consciousness is discernible to our senses.

8. That process which all life is caught up in is Universal Intelligence seeking to know itself by becoming a thing.

9. Evolution is the path of expanding consciousness.

10. Developed self-consciousness, such as is now possessed by man, is a necessary step toward the development of universal consciousness.

11. Man's destiny is to expand his consciousness to complete unity, to a oneness with God.

12. Form proceeds from intelligence, for form is intelligence. Therefore form proceeds from thought, and thought makes things!

13. All life is but an incarnation of the one life, therefore there are innumerable reincarnations until unity with the Universal Subconscious Mind is obtained.

14. The Secret Doctrine has been held inviolate by esoteric groups for many ages and teaches that mankind is evolving toward spiritual unity.

15. The Secret Doctrine lays down the past and future of man's evolution but this cannot be accepted as substantiated.

16. Matter is only relative, and is nothing more than a combination of centers of force or moving intelligence.

17. Space and time are also relative and represent concepts in the Universal Subconscious Mind.

18. Man lives upon two planes at once—the plane of mind and thought and the plane of things and circumstances-—but actually these two planes are only one.

19. Your "I" is a product of your thought and is never the same from one moment to the next, except insofar as it is confined within the fleshly limits of your body.

20. The real "I" is eternal, everlasting, only one, and contains all things.

21. The Kingdom of God is within us.

22. You are what you think, and thoughts are things; therefore select your thoughts with care.

PATIENCE

Still we have not come to grips with concrete problems in concrete lives. And two more chapters are to be read before we undertake to teach specifically how to apply the laws of mind to the realms of love, success, and health. We moderns are an impatient people, and always the first thing we want to know is what does it do? Then, the minute we find out, we want to get on with it as quickly as possible. We would like to be laymen one day and Doctors of Medicine the next, unnoticed one week and famous the following; and even when we recognize this sort of thing as a possible miracle, we forget that the workers of miracles must serve their apprenticeships also. It would be foolish to teach the powers of the mind without first getting it thoroughly understood what the mind is. It would be folly to undertake the vast and exciting subject that engrosses us without recognizing that if such answers were obvious they would long ago have been in widespread use by all mankind. Bear with us; the groundwork must be thoroughly laid.

THE INFALLIBLE LAW

You must understand that the teachings of this book are not to be regarded as patent medicines or wonder drugs, things that work most of the time, or some of the time, or not at all. The law this book teaches works all of the time and nothing or nobody on the face of the earth is big enough to stop it from working. We didn't make this law. We neither start it nor stop it. Our only purpose here is to impart to you a knowledge of its existence and methods of using it. The law works one hundred percent of the time. It never fails. If you apply it to achieve success and you meet with failure, it isn't the law that has failed—it is you! You have simply failed to do the one thing it is necessary for you to do to obtain the slightest good and that is to think only positively of that good. If an opposite develops, it has developed because you have been more convinced of it than you have of the good you want, and the law has still worked as it always must.

The cynic is his own worst enemy. It requires far less skill to run a wrecking company than it does to be an architect. The world has been built by builders, and those who destroy have no alternative other than to dwell in desolation. Throughout the world there are working groups who are envisioning the arrival of the Kingdom of God and Man, who see in the thinking mind of man the object of his own liberation. Thoughts are things, they say. Things are thoughts. Awaken, man, to your sovereignty over all. Cast aside your enemies: doubt, morbidity, fear, and guilt. Ask and it shall be given; seek and ye shall find; knock and it shall be opened to you. You cannot dream a dream too big, nor aspire too high. Nothing is impossible.

In our fourth meditation, we are recognizing that all form and circumstance are but manifestations of the Universal Mind, that everything and everyone is made from and has his being in universal intelligence.

Everything which you can conceive and accept is yours! Entertain no doubt. Refuse to accept worry or hurry or fear. That which knows and does everything is inside you and harkens to the slightest whisper.

RECOMMENDED READING

The Consciousness of the Atom by Alice A. Bailey, Published by the Lucis Publishing Company.

FOURTH MEDITATION

I know that all of life exists within me. Here in my heart and mind, in the recesses of my being, there is utter calm, a place of unruffled and placid waters, where the truth is apparent and the clamor of the world does not exist. I see about me the thoughts of all mankind, for these thoughts have become things. Whatever is good among these thought-things I accept; whatever is evil I ignore; for my concern is only with truth and understanding, which is forever the lovely and the good and the expanding. My mind moves easily to the furthermost reaches of space, in all directions, and just as easily moves back to me once again. I am the center of the universe. God, the Universal Subconscious Mind, has made Himself manifest through me. I know that my purpose in life is to reach ever upward and outward, to expand in knowledge and love and unity. I place my future in divine hands. I turn over each problem of my life to that great all-knowing mind to which all things are possible. I do not tell God how to bring these things about. I have complete confidence that every circumstance that comes my way is part of a perfect plan to convert the image of my faith into physical reality. Even now the universe seeks to answer my every need. As I believe in my heart, so shall it be done unto me; this is the law of life and of living. There is greatness in my friend and in my enemy, for we are all brothers seeking the same high mountain along many paths, God, who made all creatures, made no poor creature, for He made only of Himself. I am prosperous for God owns everything. I am vigorous for God is all vigor. I need only open my mind and my heart, keep my thoughts in the path of truth, and I am filled to overflowing with the power and abundance and love of the universe.

Chapter 5 - INTUITION

A mighty epoch of man draws near
What wondrous things there will be
Thy heart in place of thine ears shall hear
Instead of thine eyes thy mind shall see

INTUITION DEFINED

We are using the word intuition to cover a good deal more than the occurrence of "hunches." Under intuition we are classifying all the mysterious and apparently unexplainable phenomena which pass largely unnoticed in our world: clairvoyance, thought transference, materializing and demateral-izing objects, levitation, contact with the spirit world, in addition to an instinctive grasp of the laws of construction (such as in mathematics and music). Intuition describes our recognition and use of the great truth that mind is greater than matter and that the Universal Subconscious Mind contains the knowledge of all things and all times, is the substance from which everything is made, and is responsive to thought and desire.

THE STUDIES OF DR. RHINE

Dr. J. B. Rhine, through the work of his Parapsychology Laboratory at Duke University, has proved that the mind of man has the power to affect inert matter. Dr. Rhine had a machine throw dice. The frequency of each number appearing was strictly in accordance with the law of averages. However, when a subject sat nearby and concentrated on a certain number, this desired number appeared much more frequently than chance would allow. To test precognition, a machine shuffled a pack of playing cards, and subjects wrote down their predictions of the exact sequence of the cards from the top to the bottom of the deck. Again, the number of correct predictions ruled out pure chance. Dr. Rhine injected time into his test and had his subjects predict the sequence a week ahead of the shuffling of the cards. Once more, the correct "guesses" were far greater than the law of averages. Testing for telepathy, subjects were separated by an eighth of a mile, one looking at one of fifty-two cards of a playing deck, the other attempting to visualize the card and name it. As many as nineteen out of twenty-five cards were named correctly! Subjects have been separated by oceans and still the percentage of successes remains equally high. Clairvoyantly, the prediction of what card would come next from the deck has been successfully forecast twenty-six times in a row!

Now what Doctor Rhine has proved in his exhaustive scientific and statistical inquiry is this: the mind of man can affect inert matter; the mind of man can see into the future; *the mind of man can receive and transmit thoughts, regardless of the amount of intervening space between minds.* Dr. Rhine is now turning his research to spiritism. He feels that he has proved that the mind is independent of the bounds of space and time; thus, there must be survival of some kind on the other side of the grave.

These are the conclusions reached by a scientific study, using all the modern methods and statistical classifications that have evolved our gasoline engine and atomic energy, conducted at one of the finest universities in the world under the surveillance of an internationally known and respected scientist!

Dr. Rhine's measurements and investigations are proving the same truths that a man spoke on the plains of Galilee many hundreds of years ago: *The greatest power in all creation exists within the mind of man!*

PSYCHIC PHENOMENA

Had we not been blinded we should have seen it long ago. Many have shown us the way since Jesus, just as many lighted the road before him. And the truth has not always chosen the wise for its instrument.

A peasant girl from Lorraine liberated France. The voices of the Subconscious Mind revealed the future to Joan and cast her in one of the greatest roles ever played by a woman in the human drama. The young Bernadette knelt before a vision of her Subconscious Mind in the town of Lourdes and to this very day such faith imbues the sick and ailing who pilgrimage there that hundreds of cures are effected each year. The same applies to Fatima, Portugal, where three shepherd children beheld in the Universal Subconscious Mind a vision of Mary, the mother of Jesus.

Plato proved the existence of the great world beyond the flesh. The Universal Subconscious Mind possessed Leonardo Ha Vinci so completely that everything he touched was wrought by genius. Shakespeare clothed the eternal truths in the parable of human drama. Einstein and Edison applied mathematics and chemistry to arrive at God. Mahatma Ghandi visualized the great Unity in the brotherhood of man.

And this is far from all. Our world has daily demonstrations of the miraculous powers inherent in man's Subconscious. There are those who dispute, who scoff, who ridicule, those who would tear down the monument of man's Universal spirit to place in its stead the pygmy of physical man swallowed in unimaginable space and time. But the record will not be denied.

Saint Joseph of Cupertino could fly without wings. No less a personage than the Holy

Father himself, Pope Urban the Eighth, testified to Joseph's remarkable nights. Daniel Dunglas Home, the celebrated psychic, also was able to perform levitation. The great physicist, Sir William Crookes, testified to it, so did the Earl of Dunraven, Lord Lindsay, Captain C. Wynne, and many others. Through a lifetime of amazing psychic phenomena, under the strictest conditions imposed by all judging tribunals, under the minutest surveillance of the finest scientific minds of the day, no one ever was able to account for Home's miraculous demonstrations on any other basis than his having access to some tremendous power that was able to abrogate physical law.

Harold Sherman kept in contact with Sir Hubert Wilkins by mental telepathy when the famous explorer set out to the Arctic to rescue some stranded Russian flyers in 1937; this, when Sir Hubert could not obtain radio communication. Abraham Lincoln dreamt of his death in the exact manner in which it occurred, and he left a letter behind, written ten days before his death, to prove it. Robert Louis Stevenson, at death's door, testified when he recovered, that for a while he had got up and walked away from his body. For many years, Mrs. John Curran automatically wrote prose and poetry under the direction of Patience Worth, a personality adopted by her Subconscious Mind. Dante Gabriel Rossetti remembered a previous life when he wrote:

> *I have been here before,*
> *But when or how I cannot tell*
> *I know the grass beyond the door*
> *The sweet keen smell,*
> *The sighing sound, the lights around the shore.*

A skeptical world cannot look away any longer. If records were kept of all such phenomena, they would overflow the nation's libraries. The mechanistic and material age is passing. Man is evolving into the Age of the Mind, wherein his dominion over the universe will shortly be achieved. Mind over matter; mind over time; thus will come a future of many dimensioned proportions with man at the center and yet encompassing all.

GENIUS

Thought transference, clairvoyance, the affecting of matter and circumstance through mind power, contact with the spirit world, remembrance of previous lives are all results of the duality of the mind of man and the fact that the Universal Subconscious Mind responds to suggestion. All the powers which might fall under the heading of intuition are possessed by the Subconscious Mind alone, but they are available only when controlled by the Conscious Mind. The Subconscious Mind may see without eyes, hear without ears, leave the body to elicit information and return again. It may see into the future, see into the past, form circumstance and matter. Its existence is independent of the body, for it lives in all things and encompasses infinity. It is the soul of each man and the soul of the universe.

Inherent in the Subconscious Mind are the fixed laws of nature; and it is the perception of these laws, as embodied in our "geniuses," that we will undertake to discuss first.

One of the most remarkable mathematical prodigies was Zerah Colburn. Born in 1804, educated in nothing more than the grade school of a rural community in Vermont, he still was able to perceive immediately the correct answer to every , mathematical question propounded to him when he was not I yet eight years of age! He was able to raise numbers up to the sixteenth power, give the roots of numbers down to the same power, and perform all manner of number magic such as was not possible to a single mechanical contrivance of the day. And his answers were immediate. The remarkableness of his feats is all the more apparent when it is realized that the sixteenth power of eight is 281,474,976,710,656, a figure which it is extremely unlikely could even be read by our eight-year-olds of today.

Blind Tom, an idiot from birth, had a prodigious musical capacity. Even as a child, he could reproduce on the piano any piece of music he heard, no matter how long or how difficult. With equal facility he improvised an astounding array of musical composition. Beethoven was another such one, composing entire symphonies when still a child. Milton applied the fixed laws of the universe to the rhythm of his poetry.

PERCEPTION OF UNIVERSAL LAW

These laws of construction, or rhythm, or movement, are inherent in each of us, for they are part and parcel of the Universal Subconscious Mind. Time moves in accordance with these laws, and who is there who has not been able to wake himself from a sound sleep at an appointed hour simply because he consciously desired to before he went to sleep? Some never-sleeping presence within us keeps an eye on the clock or simply on the movement of the universe, and if we desire to be awake by six, so we are. Nature has thus fashioned the most reliable alarm clock of all, but our dependence upon mechanical contrivances dulls this faculty as it has dulled so many others.

Great artists perceive intuitively the laws of the combinations of colors. Great engineers perceive intuitively the sweep and scope of a building, bridge, or highway. Great writers perceive intuitively the innermost depths of the characters and stories they create and thus bring them into three-dimensional life from out of the printed page. Great scientists perceive intuitively the paths to new discoveries in physics, chemistry, and electronics. Did not Columbus himself sail toward the edge of a world which everyone said was flat? What else sustained him but his intuitive perception that the world was a sphere?

The universe moves and combines and builds according to certain fixed laws. These laws are part of the Subconscious Mind and are available to our perception if we will but clear away the doubt and skepticism and logical illogic that is forever cluttering up our Conscious Minds. The bud of perfection and the seed of genius dwell within each of us. It comes to everyone in some quiet hour and whispers of the truth. Who has not felt the excited certainty of an impending event, a new idea, a useful business, a new invention, a theme for a novel, a sunset that demanded to be painted, the precognition of a friend's devotion, a loved one's high regard? Who, in his quiet hours, has not looked at the stars and felt peace, as deep within his soul the magnificent order of the universe's laws was for a while apparent?

THE INDWELLING BUD OF PERFECTION

Can we, then, be geniuses, even as those the world has known? The answer is that we not only can, but we are! Great genius lies dormant in each of us, waiting to be awakened. We have only to take down the bars, unlock the door, invite our silent dweller forth. It is ourselves who have locked him within his prison, and he aspires to be set free. We build his cage and bars and lock each time we say, "I'm not good enough," "I don't know how," "It's too hard for me," "I'm poor," "I'm sick," "I'm tired," "I'm nobody." We make of this mighty mind a pygmy, cowering in his cell, forced to act and create all our negative fears and doubts into actuality and thus to reduce the temple of the universe to a sorry, fumbling, fear-ridden speck upon the earth.

Geniuses we all shall be when we know and recognize and practice the truth. Not geniuses begotten by a whim of fate, but geniuses because we have controlled our destinies, geniuses because we move in accord with the invincible power of an expanding universe.

THOUGHT TRANSFERENCE

Mental telepathy or thought transference is today perhaps the most widely known and discussed attribute of the Subconscious Mind. Scientific men, concerned only with the observation and statistical classification of phenomena, now tell us that if one man concentrates on an idea and another concentrates on attempting to determine what this idea is, it is very likely that the latter will grasp what the former is thinking about. There have been those who have attempted to prove that each human mind is like a radio transmitting and receiving station and that one man may "tune in" on another man's frequency.

The parallel is very weak. What manner of radio frequency curve could manage to support the billions of different frequencies assigned to the earth's population? And since it has been proved that the higher animals respond to thought, there are also these frequencies to consider. No method of measurement has ever been devised that showed more than the very weakest brain radiations, yet thought transference may span all measurable space.

No, thought transference means that we are thinking into or with *something* that is everywhere at the same time and is used by all manner of life. It means that the Universal Subconscious Mind is moved by a thought and this movement is perceptible to each living organism. Thus we are not actually *transferring* thoughts, but rather we are thinking them into and with the only mind there is; and they are then apparent to anyone who grasps the use of this mind, even vaguely apparent to those who do not grasp it. This mind is as big as infinity. Each person lives in it. Thus a thought impressed upon it is everywhere at the same time. We are not *transferring* thoughts. We are all one, with one mind, and our thoughts are community property, if only we can perceive.

CLAIRVOYANCE

Clairvoyance is an understanding or a vision of things to come. In no sense must this be considered as meaning that our lives are ordered or that our fates are predestined. Each of us is a product of his thought. The sum total of this thought determines our actions or opinions in any given circumstance. The next succeeding thought adds to or detracts from or alters what we are. In considering your own future you need only be concerned with the conviction you have concerning it. Whatever your conviction is, there is your future. Even the paths you will tread toward it may be determined by simply considering your convictions about each possible road. *The thing of tomorrow is the thought of today,* and he who sees the future needs but understand his thought.

But there is a great deal more to clairvoyance than this. A barrage of cases is reliably recorded in which dreams forecast certain events which came to pass. People from all walks of life have testified to visions in which they saw themselves involved in some action in a strange place, only to later find themselves actually doing this same thing in the very place in the exact manner they had envisioned. Professional clairvoyants whose mechanical instruments are the crystal ball or the deck of cards or the palm of the hand or the movement of the stars (though often times they are little more than shrewd psychologists), take from the Subconscious Mind an impression of their clients' thought and translate it into the future. There is no time in the Subconscious

Mind. Everything that has happened, everything that is happening, everything that will happen are all happening at one time in this mind and that time is eternally now. For this mind, being infinite, contains an infinite number of possibilities all of which are actual in an eternal now.

SUBSTANCE AND SHADOW

Materializing and dematerializing objects and circumstances verge on our conception of sorcery or we relegate it to the realm of witches' tales, yet once again we are dealing with that which has been reliably recorded and which must be, from the very nature of the Subconscious Mind, one of its inherent powers.

Jesus walked upon the water, fed five thousand with seven loaves of bread, turned water into wine. The Mate of the S.S. *Vestris* met a stranger on board his ship who told him to steer northwest, where this same stranger was subsequently rescued from a stranded ship. A hypnotized man may be told there is no chair in the room other than those occupied, and he will not see the chair. The thought, or idea of the chair, is gone from his mind. He may stumble over the chair, proving it is still there, but it is there only because it still exists in the Universal Subconscious Mind, planted there by the minds of those observing it, or every mind that ever has observed it. Is the chair not, in the first place, only a thought, conceived in the mind, made into physical reality by a man who thought he made a chair? Is it not true that if the thought connected with the creation of the chair had never existed, the chair would neither? The chair is naught but consciousness, resolved into form only by thought, made of the eternal substance of which all things are made, which is not substance at all, but merely intelligence.

God appeared to Moses; the blessed Virgin appeared to St. Bernadette; the ghost of Pickfair appeared to Mary Pickford; Jesus appeared to St. Paul; and the bridge which he builds appears to the engineer, in his mind, as a thought, *even as all the things of this world must first appear as thoughts!*

Similarly with levitation. Will Urban the Eighth be denied in his testimony that St. Joseph of Cupertino could fly? Will William Crookes be denied that D. D. Home could levitate himself from the ground? They were seen to do these things. Those who would dispute it can do so with no other argument than "It isn't possible," and the sorriness of that particular defense has been proved a million times.

THE SPIRIT WORLD

Contact with the spirit world also is one more manifestation of the power of the

Universal Subconscious Mind. We need not go so far as to say that those who have passed beyond the veil make themselves known to us only through certain "mediums." Rather, it is enough that we remember two primary attributes of the Subconscious Mind. 1) It responds to suggestion. 2) It possesses the power to manifest physical reality from thought. All the phenomena of the seance can be accounted for with these two facts in mind.

All the great mediums were and are possessed of another personality who assertedly dwells in the spirit world and makes contact with those departed souls who have something to say to friends and loved ones who have remained behind. In the trance, this spirit possesses the medium's body, usually assumes a drastically different personality from that of the medium, and proceeds to render acute and detailed information regarding present, past, and future events in the lives of people with whom the medium is barely acquainted or indeed has never met. Such information is often accompanied by disembodied hands and wraithlike faces hovering about the room, as well as objects moving and floating, seemingly under their own power, and accompanied by unaccountable rappings.

Now essentially what the medium does is to put himself or herself into a self-imposed hypnotic trance, during which the Subconscious Mind is exposed and is quickly responsive to any suggestion offered it. When it is suggested that it is the spirit of one who has been taken by death, it becomes so, and the information it is able to offer is proof that it actually believes this. Many investigators would have us believe that this is simply an illusion of the Subconscious Mind of the medium, that the departed spirit has not been "contacted" at all, that the medium has simply used the Subconscious Mind to elicit certain information that normally would be beyond his or her knowledge.

This is sheer nonsense. There is only one mind after all, and we are all living in it. Whenever this mind becomes Dick Roe, it is Dick Roe, and that is an end to it. What the complete details of existence are on the other side of death it will probably remain for one who actually returns from there to tell, but Dick Roe having been absorbed once more into Universal Mind still exists in Universal Mind. Whatever Dick Roe was in Universal Mind while alive, he must remain in Universal Mind when not alive, for the conception has already been placed there. Thus when the medium evolves from the Subconscious the personality and identity of Dick Roe, she is actually dealing with the spirit of Dick Roe, the conception which exists in Universal Mind of Dick Roe, for two absolutely exact conceptions are not two conceptions at all but only one, and the Dick Roe of Universal Mind responds to his call.

MINOR MIRACLES OF THE SUBCONSCIOUS

The phenomena of the seance have been exposed many times in dealing with those mediums who resort to trickery or legerdemain, but there remains a vast body of undisputed proof of moving and floating objects, ectoplasm gathering into hands and faces, spirit rapping, and the like, so as to leave little doubt but that the Subconscious Mind is often moved to perform these minor miracles at the medium's behest.

It is interesting to note that the "spirits" are always quite vague as to what kind of life exists in the afterworld. They say it is quiet there, that it is peaceful, that they are happy, but beyond that there seems to be a big breakdown in their communication. This would lead us to believe that the spirit conceived by the medium can effect no better description than the medium herself, or perhaps existence on the other side is so drastically different from that in the physical world that no words or conceptions can be communicated from the Subconscious to the Conscious. More likely, the whole practice of spiritism is the wrong approach to dealing with the Universal Mind and those who practice it are not armed with sufficient knowledge or concept of what they are doing to be able to effect any kind of perfect union.

This much we can say: Remarkable phenomena have been produced. The mighty power of the Universal Subconscious Mind is once again revealed. Once more we see the grandeur of man's destiny, how he is caught up in and is part of the entire power of the universe.

THE GRADUAL AWAKENING

What are all these phenomena? We shall gain no insight into them by calling them trickery or hallucination. Too many scientific inquiries have set out to do just that and gotten nowhere. This body of evidence exists, has existed for many centuries, tucked away in musty archives and pathetically labeled, "Can't be explained, so probably didn't happen." The startling thing is that man has been content with his fumbling examination of the physical world, deriving some strange satisfaction in perceiving order about him, always recognizing that the monument of irrelevant facts he accumulated was his own headstone, but seemingly extremely reluctant to pursue any type of inquiry that might expose his own divinity and power.

Only now, when scientific inquiry has had to reject its own notions of physics, of electronics, of time, space, and matter, *only when physics has had to evolve a new quantum theory which is much more philosophical than scientific,* have men reawakened to the possibilities inherent in the invisible world about them and turned once again to the examination of what lies within the mind of man.

The great British physicist, Sir James Jeans, has summed up the extent of scientific inquiry by saying, "It has become clear that the ultimate processes of nature neither occur, nor admit of representation in, space and time." Bertrand Russell says, "The distinction between mind and matter is illusory." Thus, like it or not, all investigation of man's nature and his control of his environment must take up for study those phenomena which have always been classified as the supernatural.

It seems strange that it has not been widely done before. Since natural events and things by their very nature give no clue to the truth of man's destiny, it would seem that long ago the physical would have been labeled the unnatural and men would have turned to the so-called supernatural for the truth about things. Whatever the purpose of the former by-road, it is upon this latter path that man has embarked today.

THINGS ARE THOUGHTS

We have said that thoughts are things, but the premise that we are forced to adopt now is that things are thoughts. In other words, every object and circumstance and form in this world is purely mental and represents nothing more than an idea or a thought.

This position will find many arguments directed against it, but they all will have the same basis. The disputer will maintain that if the clock in your kitchen is only a thought, then you only think you see it, which means that it will not be there in the silent hours of night when you are asleep; yet you wake in the morning and find that the hands of the clock have moved in accordance with time, which proves that the clock was there all night. Similarly, he will say that you may only think you see a red flower, but a camera can be rigged to photograph the flower when no one is around, and the photograph shows the flower to exist and still to be red, even though there was no one to perceive it.

Such a disputer makes a fine argument in proof of a point that we have no quarrel with whatever. We are not saying that the physical objects of our world would cease to exist if there were no one around to perceive them. Of course they would still exist, for they are not merely our conceptions any longer; they are conceptions in Universal Subconscious Mind. What we are saying is that these objects are only ideas given form by the Universal Subconscious Mind. As long as the idea persists in Universal Mind, so will the form persist. When the idea is altered in Universal Mind, so will the form be altered. When the idea disintegrates in Universal Mind, so will the form disintegrate.

And most important of all, we are saying that the original idea and all evolutions of the idea are placed in Subconscious Mind by Conscious Mind!

THINGS ARE CONCEPTIONS ROOTED IN UNIVERSAL MIND

A conscious thinking entity, or a group of conscious thinking entities, places an idea in Universal Mind, which by its very nature creates that idea into physical reality. Thus things are thoughts. They need no one around to perceive them in order to exist. They are rooted in Universal Mind, which holds them in form as long as the idea behind them persists. But this idea, this conception, this thought, was placed in Universal Mind by a thinking, conscious entity living in the physical world.

Thoughts become things. Things are thoughts held in form by the great creator, the Universal Subconscious Mind, *but a thing only becomes a thing as a result of a conscious thought!*

Thus man has ordered his world about him. Thus he lives .surrounded by an environment of thoughts become things, lie may change that environment by altering his thinking, but it most certainly will not change simply because there is no one around to observe it.

We all live in the same mind. There are a vast number of conceptions and ideas in this mind, placed there by every organism and life force which has preceded us. These ideas and conceptions once firmly implanted and crystallized are made known to us through our five senses as things which we perceive in the physical world around us. This world, in its essence, is purely mental, and all exists in mind.

What man concludes, God knows. What God knows, God creates. What God creates, man perceives. What man perceives he believes to be outside himself, existing in the world around him, but the truth is it exists within him, for it exists in Universal Mind and all of this mind is within man when his consciousness has expanded to encompass it.

Pascal said, "The narrow limits of our being conceal infinity from view," which is simply another way of saying that to understand how all of life lies within us, we must abandon our sense of separateness and isolation and expand our consciousness to include all things.

THE ILLUSION OF TIME

Now we needn't regard the law of thoughts becoming things as being attached to the supernatural. It would be a mistake to assume that what we are driving at in totality is simply a man sitting down and thinking, "I have a new car," with the result that, presto, the new car materializes out of thin air. Though without doubt this type of immediate result lies somewhere in the future of man's evolution, has indeed been accomplished occasionally by a very few persons who have evolved ahead of their times, it is nonetheless true that very few of us will reach it in our lifetimes. But exactly the same result can be achieved by each one of us, if we allow for the lag of time.

Wherever we see the logical procedure of physical events, we discount all that might be miraculous. If you sit down and quietly say to yourself, "I am going to get a new car," and keep assuring yourself of this over a period of weeks or months, you will first find yourself somehow getting the money to make the purchase, somehow visiting a number of new car showrooms, somehow finally arriving at the car you want, somehow buying it and driving it home. You may then return to the chair in which you sat when you first had the thought and be assured that you now actually have a new car. You thought you were going to get one; it is now outside in your garage. The only difference between its coming to you and to the man who might immediately materialize it by a miracle is the difference in time! *And time, we know, does not exist in the Universal Subconscious Mind.*

THOUGHT IS THE ONLY TRUE ACTION

Look around you. See your desk, your sofa, your bed, your refrigerator, your home, your radio, your television set. Each of these things is a thought. Somewhere, a man sat down and visualized each of them and said, "I am going to make this thing," and presto, here is the thing in your home, a thought a short time before, a thing now; and the only reason we do not see the miracle of it is because of the lapse of time when motors and machines moved and were guided to form the component parts, assemble the thing into a whole, and ship it to us. If we all live in Universal Mind, are we not simply daily creating into physical reality through this mind those very thoughts and ideas of which we think? We form every physical thing from a substance which is not substance at all but simply pure intelligence. We give this intelligence the form of our thought. We can neither start nor stop the process. We can only start and stop our thinking and our conceptions. As soon as we have crystallized the thought and adopted it, we are moved by the Subconscious Mind to perform those things which will give the thought physical reality.

Beyond the point of having had the idea, we are moved by a power greater than we are to give this idea reality. We needn't drive ourselves or worry ourselves or fret about the problems. These will all be solved by Subconscious Mind, and we will be moved in the directions we must be. Our only free action is our thought. We are what we think, we do what we think, we become what we think, and thus it always must be.

WHAT JESUS KNEW

What then of the miracles? What of Jesus turning the water into wine? Granting that Jesus conceived that the fluid in the bottles was wine instead of water, certainly he would in the normal course of events have been prompted to empty each bottle of water, proceed to the winemakers and procure the wine, and subsequently to pour this wine into each of the bottles. We know that he did none of these things. *He simply conceived that the bottles contained wine, and all of the acts necessary to perform this transition were performed immediately, and the water became wine.* What did Jesus know to be able to condense time and physical action in this manner?

For one thing, he knew that time (as has only now been proved by our scientists) is a dimension, and he undoubtedly was able to perceive each event along this dimension in response to each of his convictions. Secondly, he understood that the physical actions ordinarily necessary to resolve a thing from a thought are merely the movement of the Universal Subconscious Mind, or his Father, as he put it, and he knew this Mind needs no instruments other than itself to effect manifestation. Thirdly, he understood that this Mind by its nature is every-place at the same time and all of it is any-place at any time, so he knew that all of it was within him, and thus his consciousness was expanded to include the wine, the water, and the bottles. With such perception, along with his own magnificent conviction, he was able to transcend time and the movement of bodies in space, and to change the water into wine in an instant.

A miracle to us. The truth of things as they really were to him. He did nothing that any of us couldn't do, except compress time and circumvent the interaction of physical bodies moving through space.

Time is a variable, says modern science. The movement of bodies in space is purely mental, says modern science. *Jesus has replaced Newton on the shrine of physics!*

This then is where we are heading, into the unknown to make it the known. Those who cling to their little established worlds are holding onto mere dust. We are after the cause and source of all things. We are after true knowledge. Maeterlinck says, "The one sorrow of the mind is the sorrow of not knowing or not understanding, which contains the sorrow of powerlessness." Not knowing is powerlessness! *We* are after power; we want to know. Again Maeterlinck says, "He who knows the supreme causes becomes one with them and acts with them." Can there be any doubt that understanding the causes of universal power and moving in accord with universal power can give any less than universal power?

THE PROPERTIES OF LIGHT

Let us return to this ephemeral physical world of ours. One of its interesting phenomena is light. Light always takes the path of least effort. Least effort is ordinarily the shortest distance between two points, but where light encounters resistance, it simply reflects off in the mathematically most perfect angle so as to maintain its maximum energy. Light is inherent in the universe, and the universe doesn't fight and strain and snarl. *It does things the easy way.*

There are also some very interesting theories about light, which indicate that that which it reflects need not necessarily be true. Light consists of a stream of photons moving at 186,000 miles per second. These photons, of course, are invisible, but might best be described as approximating the shape of a silver dollar, though infinitesimally thin. One theory holds that these photons move perpendicular to the pull of gravity. Illustrating with a silver dollar, the dollar always must remain upright relative to the earth's surface. Thus, if the photons come at us from an angle from above or below, they appear smaller than they actually are. For example, a man standing twenty feet away and thirty feet above you appears much smaller than he actually is. It is this quality of his appearance, plus your own instinctive balance on the perpendicular to the pull of gravity, that allows you to determine how high he is above you. According to the theory, what has actually happened to give the man this appearance is that the photons streaming toward you look smaller, the man has not changed in size. For example, place a silver dollar at arm's length, face toward you, and perpendicular to the ground, then, keeping it perpendicular, move it upward until it is two feet over your head and still at arm's length. The dollar now will not only appear smaller, but will be an ellipse instead of a circle. Thus the photons of light streaming from the man who is at an angle above you cause him to look shorter; his breadth will be normal at his feet but will gradually taper towards his head. It is this aspect of an object in space that we perceive with "perspective," and it is the photons of light always moving perpendicularly to gravity that communicate this quality and relation of things to us. So says the theory.

WHAT DO WE SEE?

Now, the photons, moving at the speed ot light, have no measurable depths. In other words, looked at from the top or bottom, they are invisible. Here the theory takes an interesting twist. If, through some disruption of the pull of gravity or the imposition of some outside force, these photons could be made to lie on their sides so that they were parallel to the earth's surface, any object emitting them would be invisible to the eye. Scientists have worked along these lines for many years, with the thought in mind of disrupting the stability of the photons so as to make our machines of war invisible to the enemy. What man sets out to do, man does. Indeed, it will be difficult to remain attached to the final reality of the physical world the day man is able to cast any of his physical objects into invisibility simply by throwing a switch.

To this very day we do not know what it is we see in the world around us. We know it is something, but what we can determine about this something only convinces us that we know very little about it. Our postulate is that these things are thoughts made manifest, and when we are able to cast them into visibility or invisibility at will, who will dare maintain that they are things of themselves and completely apart from man?

Thus the shimmering ephemeral world about us is not a group of hard and substantial facts at all, but merely a world of shade and shadow, dimly perceived, flickering distortions on the walls of Plato's cave, vague indications of a mighty truth not seen.

HEIRSHIP OF GOD

Mental telepathy, clairvoyance, physical manifestation from thought, mental healing, any and all of the so-called supernatural phenomena of this world are possible to each man. He need not sweat and aspire and strain to achieve these things; he need only expand his consciousness to include everything around him. Through the unity of Self thus achieved he will perceive the laws of the universe as they are; and operating through and with them he will attain ascendancy over space and time and the limits of matter.

Jesus of Nazareth was clairvoyant; Jesus performed mental telepathy; Jesus healed through mind power; Jesus performed physical manifestation from thought. Jesus was a man and merely a man, but his intuitive perception of the laws of the universe was such that his wondrous works were regarded as miracles. Yet he invoked no new laws. He simply worked in accord with the highest laws, laws of such infinite magnitude and scope as to set our laws of the physical world to nothing by comparison.

Even as Zerah Colburn intuitively perceived the laws of numbers and mathematics, so did Jesus perceive the laws of the entire universe. Even as Blind Tom perceived the laws of music, so did the whole heavens open their secrets to Jesus. *The power that transcends reason is the power of intuition.* Instances of its amazing perspicuity could be multiplied a thousand times, but still, in comparison to the vast numbers of human beings, its instances are very rare. Yet this is not strange. Locked in the fleshly limits of our bodies as we are, puppets driven by the five senses, victims of the constant beat, beat of sensation which is always convincing us that the first reality is the world about us, it is a wonder that instances of highly developed intuition ever have come about at all. But still they come. Hardly a week goes by without another "unexplainable incident" finding its way into mankind's history. The power is breaking through, making itself known, confirming our heirship of God, our joint heirship with Jesus Christ!

ALL THINGS INDWELLING IN GOD

It is thus intuition upon which we must primarily depend in order to arrive at the wonderful gate. Only through conscious contact with the Universal Subconscious Mind will the truth be revealed. The discourses, arguments, and postulates of this book will help break down the barriers in the Conscious Mind, expose fraudulent convictions, cast off the limits shadow thinking and hopelessness, allow you to look upward into the heavens and perceive God as He is. You'll not need reason and argument to convince you then. You will see, intuitively perceive. The end of all searching will have arrived; the power of the universe will be yours.

Jesus of Nazareth was an educated man, taught secretly in the laws of mind by the most learned men of the day, gifted with such amazing powers of intuition that the lessons he learned were living tools in his hands. That which he knew he divulged only through parable and demonstration, for he knew the world was not ready for it. "Seeing they see not, hearing they hear not," he said to his disciples, "but to you it is given to know the Kingdom of Heaven." Every law he voiced, every work he did, regardless of how clothed in parable, regardless of how phrased to meet the mental grasp of those to whom he spoke, was yet an illustration of the universe's immutable laws—laws which each day our scientific studies are bringing to light and declaring to be fact two thousand years after this man from Nazareth spoke them on the plains and hills of Galilee. He intuitively grasped them. He needed not test tube nor laboratory nor cyclotron. He saw that the laws were within him, were part of him, were his very foundation and essence; and he placed in them his entire trust and confidence, made himself one with them, achieved the consciousness of the Universal Subconscious Mind, utilized the power far greater than he was, told a world astounded at his works, "It is the Father who dwelleth within me. He doeth the works."

It is the unity of all things indwelling in God which Jesus saw. It is the intuitive perception of that unity that we strive to communicate in these lessons. This unity was perceived before Jesus by Gautama Buddha, Confucius, Lao Tze, by the writers of the amazing Upanishads who said, "He who beholds all beings in the Self and the Self in all beings, he never turns away from it. When a man understands the Self has become all things, what sorrow, what trouble can there be to him who once beheld that unity."

FOLLOW THE HEART

This is a world in which the heart rules and never the head. The Conscious Mind of man has concerned itself with the frivolous ends of existence and has created a great Lock against the powers of the Subconscious Mind. The heart knows the truth of all things. It is the heart that is the seat of intuition, man's hope to arrive back home in the midst of and encompassing all the magnificent truth of his unlimited power. *Heed the voice of the heart.* Close your ears against the promptings of the Conscious Mind. The heart knows the way. In the innermost depths of your being it whispers the truth every minute of every day. Intuitively it perceives. Intuitively it communicates. Leave to your Conscious Mind the doing of that which is Caesar's; leave to your heart the doing of that which is God's.

Thus it is that as you proceed, you will find yourself being led more and more by your heart. The truth of a feeling that rises within you will ask for no argument or examination. It will come to you as a whole thing, and you will ask of no man whether it be fact or fiction, truth or fantasy, a good idea or poor. It will be a light that never was on land or sea, and you will follow it, for it will have penetrated to your soul. It will be a great deal more than that which up to this point in your life you may have termed a "hunch." It will be a great deal more than what you might formerly have thought to be a "lucky guess." It will take root deep within your being and become one with you, and you will take the paths of your life with unshakable vigor and faith to see that it is effected in the world about you. Thus success will come, thus health, thus love, thus peace, thus a grander purpose and sweep than ever existed on earth alone, for it will proceed from the heavens.

TRUTH VERSUS DELUSION

The duality of mind and the apparent duality of our world is a trying thing to cope with. If things are but thoughts and in true essence merely intelligence cast into form, what then of the ghosts of haunted houses, the disembodied faces and hands of the séance, the specters that we often attribute to the night; what of the fearful visions of our waking hours and the distorted images of our nightmares? What of the deluded and lost souls who people our lunatic asylums and fancy themselves to be Napoleon or Marie Antoinette? What of our psychotics and neurotics who dwell half in this world, now assuming one personality, now another? Where is the fine line drawn between thoughts becoming things and thoughts becoming delusions, even insanity?

Among the insane there will be found those who think they are birds, those who think they are persons from the past, great persons of our time, various kinds of animals. Among the insane will be found people suffering from all manner of fantastic delusion, which, in view of our saying that a man can become whatever he thinks, might prompt some persons to ask, why has this man, who thinks he is Napoleon, not become Napoleon, but only insane instead?

The answer to this well-taken question is that the very opposite of correct procedure has taken place in the mind of the insane man. Instead of his Conscious Mind controlling the Subconscious Mind, it has lost all control. The man is a victim of any passing fancy that may lodge for a moment within whatever conscious facilities he has left. Since there are billions of impressions available in Subconscious Mind for him to perceive, he simply grasps one according to its attractiveness and adopts it temporarily. He does not become the thing he fancies; his Conscious Mind flits too rapidly. He is buffeted about in the lap of intelligence by every movement of his Subconscious Mind. Control is gone. When control goes, there comes insanity.

Very often we are witness to the same thing in our very aged or infirm. The Conscious Mind becomes affected and begins to lose control, and before our eyes we see great changes in personality taking place. Such a person becomes helpless, his thoughts move at random, scattered and haphazardly, casting him now into irrationality, again into extreme lucidness.

THE CORNERSTONE OF PERSONALITY

We must remember that the Conscious Mind is the cornerstone of personality. It fills our lives with order and controls the Subconscious Mind in its great creativeness. When control by the Conscious Mind disappears, the individual disintegrates, becoming insane or infirm. That is why it is balance we strive for, balance between the Conscious Mind and the Subconscious Mind; therein lies the truth of genius. When the Conscious Mind vastly subordinates the Subconscious, we find an individual who lives beset by all manner of insurmountable problems, for he sees himself living in a world where all things are greater than he. When the Subconscious Mind subordinates the Conscious, we have an individual who is irrational, sometimes insane, even though on occasions he will exhibit some remarkable powers.

It must be remembered that the Universal Subconscious Mind responds to suggestion. The more ordered and authoritative the suggester (the Conscious Mind), the more ordered and clearcut are the manifestations of the Subconscious Mind.

TOWARD THE SUPERMAN

We need not set immediate goals for ourselves in the realms of mental telepathy, mental healing, and manifestation from thought. As William James so aptly stated, "All consciousness is motor," and immediately you become possessed of an idea or a desire, you will find that it sets you into action which inevitably results in its creation in the outer world. For the while, there is no point in attempting a shortcut through time and space by mind power. It is enough to free your thinking of its negative bonds, to allow yourself to take free part in the creation of your own wishes and desires, and thus to fill your life with achievement and good. But let us not forget that the possibility is there—the possibility of astounding shortcuts to all things, which will be ours the day we have rightfully claimed our places in the universe.

We are evolving toward the superman. We are evolving toward undreamt-of powers. The bud of this future lies within us now. We have only to loose it and it will begin working in our lives as a tangible vital presence for good.

In the words of Walt Whitman:

> From this hour I ordain myself loos'd of limits and imaginary lines
> Going where I list, my own master total and absolute
> Listening to others, considering well what they say
> Pausing, searching, receiving, contemplating
> Gently, but with an undeniable will divesting myself of the holds that would hold me.

OUR GOALS

It is our intuitive perception of the laws of the universe that reveals to us God as he is. We need only put all wishful thinking aside save the desire to know the truth. Expectation and desire will light the way. In the quietness of our meditations the inner eye will see and the inner ear will hear, and the truth shall be revealed to us, and the truth shall make us free.

We shall sense the future dwelling within us, know the thoughts and hopes of all mankind, know that the way we lived our yesterday has determined our today, know that the way we live our today will determine our tomorrow. True intuition will be ours—*the light that never was on land or sea!*

The soul of all life is your own soul. Wherever your eye falls it sees naught but a reflection of yourself. The mighty mind in which you live is all things to all life in all places, and it is the same to you. You are fashioned from the intelligence of God. You are one with the intelligence of God. You need only rub the mote from your eye, clear the wax from your ear, and there becomes apparent a universe which has cradled you in everlasting arms, a universe that responds to your every mood and need and desire.

We know where the path leads—ever upwards to a oneness with God. We know that the purpose of life is a constantly expanding consciousness, and we know it is within our power to expand our consciousness to encompass all of the life about us. We know that this is the secret of Jesus, that he saw the universe dwelling within him, that he intuitively perceived the laws that made up his being. *This is our destiny.* We may aid it or obstruct it as we wish, but we cannot stop it from eventually arriving. We may use it to fill our lives with good, or we may use it to fill our lives with error and evil; it matters not to the Subconscious Mind. For every soul who falls behind, another steps ahead. He who seeks will find; he who abandons the search as hopeless will find at once a hopeless life. It is a question of courage and effort; a question of desire. We either work in accord with the power within us or by opposing it destroy ourselves. It is for each man to decide.

We seek wisdom and knowledge. Our goals are power with pity; wealth with charity; health with temperance; love without lust. We accede to these goals through no moral pressure. They are true goals because they are truth. We are embarking on man's greatest age—an age wherein the first movements are apparent to banish disease and suffering and poverty from the face of the earth—an age wherein the brotherhood of man finally will arrive in all its magnificent peace and harmony.

REVIEW

Here for ready reference are the principal points covered in this lesson:

1. The studies of Dr. J. B. Rhine have proved conclusively the validity of extra-sensory perception.

2. All the truths that Jesus taught are now being proved by scientific investigation.

3. The overwhelming evidence of the super-physical power of the Universal Subconscious Mind has been recorded in all times by extremely reliable persons.

4. Genius perceives the fixed laws of nature in at least one aspect.

5. Jesus perceived the fixed laws of nature in entirety.

6. The bud of perfection, or genius, dwells within each of us.

7. The thought of today is the thing of tomorrow.

8. Things are thoughts, ideas implanted in Universal Mind.

9. We do not perceive the things around us in their true nature.

10. Our world is but a bare indication of the infinite possibilities of all things and all life.

11. The so-called "natural" world is the unnatural. The so-called "supernatural" world is the light of truth.

12. Space and time are illusions of man's locked-in viewpoint.

13. Things do not depend for their existence on being perceived, but on being implanted as ideas in Universal Mind.

14. Creation of any type is the manifestation of a miracle. We only regard it as natural because we see the processes of formation moving through space and time.

15. Expanded consciousness perceives time as a dimension and space as existing within.

16. Intuition will reveal the laws of the universe.

17. Intuition is not merely a "hunch" but an irresistible light which must be followed.

18. Jesus, as an example of expanded consciousness, compressed time and space to perform his miracles.

19. It is enough for us now to effect creation through the established chain of physical movement. This we can do by refusing to accept doubt and fear.

20. Follow the heart; it is the seat of intuition.

21. The Subconscious Mind must always be controlled, for it proceeds irrationally of itself and depends upon the planting of ideas.

22. Lack of conscious control of the Subconscious Mind is insanity.

23. Denial of the Subconscious Mind is the birth of fear and futility.

24. Genius attains balance between the Conscious and Subconscious Minds.

TRANSFIGURATION

Slowly we are moving through the maze of complexity that surrounds our existence. Slowly we are dissolving the illusions and half truths that inhibit our minds and our powers. Gradually the clutter is being cleared away so that we may perceive the great and edifying truth in all its simplicity. The age is at hand; the dawn is near. In the

113

words of Edward Carpenter, "When the individual is no longer under the domination of the body and its heredity, but rising out of this tomb becomes lord and master of the body's powers, and identified with the immortal Self of the world—such is Transfiguration. The whole of man's evolution is preparation for it."

This is our path and our goal, the purpose of this study. Long and persevering as it may seem, it is but a negligible flash in the history of man. To him who through it perceives that sublime feeling and power by which he is able to identify himself with the immortal Self, all the ages of nun will have directed him to that moment. There is no greater goal or undertaking within the realm of life and endeavor. What is a year in its attainment? or even a lifetime?

May we once again urge you to the assiduous practice of the meditations. Unless you put the meditations to work for you, this entire book becomes naught but philosophy. If you are studying only for mental exercise, it would be better that you turn to logarithmic tables or higher calculus. It is your immortal reaching soul that will find food here, and lest you provide it with the living tool of the practice of the meditations, the secret will pass you by, leaving you once again in the void of limitless space and darkness. Only in proof is there conviction.

Our meditation this time is aimed at intuitive perception of the unseen and unheard forces that surround us. Through reliance and immersion in Universal Mind we shall become aware of the directions our lives are to take; we shall perceive i lie purposes of our tasks and the manner in which they must be performed; we shall find guidance through each day to the appointed hours when we shall fulfill those destinies that only we can fulfill.

Put your faith and trust in the mind of God, and follow the dictates of your heart. Quoth Shakespeare, "To thine own self be true, and it shall follow like the night the day, thou then canst not be false to any man."

RECOMMENDED READING

Law of Psychic Phenomena by Thompson J. Hudson. Published by A. C. McClurg and Company.

FIFTH MEDITATION

I listen to the voice of the universe as it speaks within me. It is the voice of truth and it guides me unerringly along the paths of my life. Somewhere deep within me, in the perfect bud of my soul, there stands an immobile universe where all things and all law lie revealed. I reach within to this place of peace and quietness. I harken to the voice of my heart. I close my eyes and sense a living, breathing universe dwelling within me, and I dwelling in it. I am one with all people and all life and all things. I move in accordance with divine law. All the limitless power of creation is mine to draw upon, for it is in me and one with me and I am a part of it. The answer comes with the question; the path is lighted with the first step; the way is cleared with the looking; the goal is in sight with the desire. I know that I am fulfilling the fondest wish of God, for I place myself in His hands, taking each step of my life boldly and strongly, for it is God who prompts me, and God moves with sureness. I see tomorrow for I know today, and this day is father of tomorrow. The things of my life are the children of my thoughts, and my thoughts of today are even now hearing the children of tomorrow. All that is good I desire; all that is evil I refuse to accept. By attaining, I do not deprive. All that is and ever will be is available to every man; he need only ask and it shall he given, I bind myself to the power for good that surges heavenward all around me. The limits and inhibitions of my past are gone. Each day is a new birth of my soul. Each day is another step on ray journey to a oneness with God. I do not seek, I know. I do not strive, I am guided.

Chapter 6 - FAITH

If thou wouldst assume the Masters role
Wed unto Faith like a wife
Faith will sustain thee, nourish thy soul
And attain thee a mastery of life

FAITH—THE MIGHTY TOOL

All things are rooted in faith. Even those of us who have the most difficulty applying this law to our daily lives will find innumerable instances in which we use it with perfect aplomb.

We have complete faith that the food we eat will turn into blood and bone and muscle and tissue and fiber, yet we do not know why, or what causes it, and even the most erudite of us ran do no more than follow the chemical process with awe. We have faith that the air we breathe will combine with the .sugar content of the blood to oxidize and form energy for the cells of our bodies. We don't stop to wonder or doubt or analyze this each time we draw a breath; we simply breathe, confident that we are doing the natural thing to sustain vigor and well-being. We have faith that the sun will rise, that the earth will revolve uniformly, that the stars will maintain their places in the heavens. We have faith that we can walk across the street, talk to another person, understand him. We have faith in our own existence! Yet we admit we know the cause of none of these things. Our faith is blind! *How strange it is that we so often scoff at faith in the less tangible fields of human existence!* *Really!*

Faith led Moses to the Promised Land, Columbus to the West Indies, Pasteur to the microbe, Galileo to the stars, St. Paul on his ministry, Democritus to the atom, Magellan around the world. Sustained by the substance of things hoped for, the evidence of things unseen, these men departed from the beaten paths and followed their visions, and all the world has benefited from their faith.

Faith is the single most important tool of man's existence. In order to thoroughly understand this, let us return once again to the dual nature of mind.

RETURNING TO THE SUBCONSCIOUS

Our studies have shown us that the Subconscious Mind belongs to all persons and all things and all of it belongs to any one of them. We have further seen that this mind is the substance from which all things are made, is the intelligence that permeates all

116

creation, that its total and infinite effort is to become something in the physical world. What this mind becomes, we have seen, can only be the result of a thought or conception placed in Subconscious Mind by Conscious Mind. The Subconscious Mind takes each conception given it and attempts to make this conception manifest in the physical world.

We have observed that the Subconscious Mind cannot reason inductively; it cannot arrive at law by knowing a circumstance. It reasons only deductively. Whatever premise is given it becomes law and is created into physical actuality. The Subconscious Mind is dynamically motor. Whatever premise is impressed upon it, it must create. It cannot know a premise without following this knowledge with creation. This is its law and nature and most apparent function. Thus it can be seen that every circumstance and thing and form in the universe is the result of a conception in the Universal Subconscious Mind, or the Mind of God.

We have further seen that each being is a result of infinite Subconscious Mind becoming a number of finite things in order to better know itself. It cannot know itself as something infinite but only by becoming something finite, and thus it is constantly becoming a vast number of things. The intelligent faculty built up in each of these things is what we have termed Conscious Mind and is the Subconscious Mind's sole link with specific time and specific place. To illustrate, the Subconscious Mind is a vast intelligence without end, and each Conscious Mind is like a sense organ keeping this intelligence informed as to the happenings in any particular place at any particular time. Whatever conclusions the Conscious Mind forwards to the Subconscious Mind, the latter immediately returns in physical reality, for the law of its nature is to become whatever it knows.

Thus our thoughts are turned into things and we can neither start nor stop the process; we can only control our thinking.

THOUGHT PLUS FAITH CREATES

Now it is obvious that each of our thoughts is not turned into physical reality. Our Conscious Minds are capable of entertaining a hundred thoughts a second. If the Subconscious Mind were to create into physical reality each of the billions of thoughts entertained by humanity each second of every day, thus world be a very chaotic world indeed. It is apparent that i here is a great selectivity exercised in choosing which of the thoughts of the Conscious Mind are to be accepted by the Subconscious Mind, and it is equally apparent that such selectivity is not exercised by the Subconscious but by the Conscious Mind instead.

If we return to our discussion of hypnotism we are able to see that the Subconscious

117

Read again & again — the Truth!
that sets you Free!

Mind exercises no choice in the matter of which premises it will accept or not accept. When the Conscious Mind is asleep, as in the hypnotised person, the Subconscious seizes on every suggestion offered and immediately attempts to turn this suggestion into truth. Obviously, then, the Subconscious simply accepts any suggestion or any premise given it, and the only reason that all of our thoughts me not turned into physical reality is that they are not convictions of the Conscious Mind and therefore are not given in the Subconscious.

Wow! Why we must have faith. The Truth!

We are now able to see why it is that faith is such an important tool in the molding and determining of our lives. *Faith is simply that factor which gives the impetus of conviction to a thought and thus impresses the thought upon the Subconscious Mind as a premise or conclusion which must be manifested in the physical world.*

feelings

Thus anything you are convinced of must become real in your life, for thought plus faith creates!

Amen!

FAITH IS AFFIRMATION

As has been pointed out before, if some wise and omnipotent being were to live our lives for us, there would be no necessity for faith. This being could simply direct to the Subconscious all those premises for good which would make our lives full and happy, and they would shortly come to pass. But the whole purpose of our lives is for us to provide the Subconscious with conclusions, premises, and knowledge of what we encounter in our specific areas; and what we forward as convictions the Subconscious returns to us in physical reality. *P.23:7*

If the Subconscious Mind receives your conviction that you have money, you will have money. If it receives your conviction that you have health, you will have health. If it receives your conviction that you have love, you will have love. If it receives your conviction that you are successful, you will be successful. If it receives your conviction that you are wise, you will have wisdom. Whatever the premise, the Subconscious Mind will create it into physical reality. See how simple such a premise may be: "I have money," only that, and money is manifested. Why is it that we have such difficulty in doing this simple thing? *It is because we lack faith!* It is because the thing we want is expressed as hope, and in a million different ways throughout the day we affirm our faith in the very opposite! *One thing I do*

Let us remember what Jesus said to those he healed: "You are well." He did not argue or postulate or advance pros and cons on the matter. He simply gave the Subconscious Mind a premise upon which it had to act by its very nature. What does the hypnotist do? He simply says, "You have no feeling in your arm," and the feeling immediately departs. It is upon such simple affirmations as these that the

118

Subconscious Mind acts and always acts, and since we cannot think of anything without having certain convictions concerning it, the Subconscious Mind is always creating in our experience exactly what we believe in.

ALL DECISION IS ACCEPTANCE

For example, let us suppose that you set out to be a successful business man. At the start of your venture you correctly will have affirmed to yourself, "I will be a successful businessman." It is this affirmation that starts you on the road. Now let us suppose that you buy a quantity of merchandise and when you offer it for sale you find there are no takers. Your immediate premise is that you have made a mistake. This is followed very closely by the thought that you are about to lose a sizeable amount of money. Shortly you will be visualizing your business failure. Before long, you will have envisaged yourself as a bankrupt, without capabilities, without hope, beset on all sides by a cruel fate. What are you affirming now? You are affirming your business *failure* of course, and as long as these convictions predominate in your thinking there is no necessity for going to the office at all, for everything you do will be aimed at failure and failure will be inevitable.

You've got to think success to be successful. No one was ever successful by thinking failure. No one was ever a failure by thinking success. It is that simple. And the tool which we must use to prevent negative circumstance from entering our lives is that of faith.

To return to the above example, the crucial point at which faith must be exercised is the point at which it becomes apparent that there is no market for the quantity of merchandise which the businessman has purchased. At this juncture, he must refuse to accept this as a mistake, as a forerunner of evil, as an indication of a forthcoming failure. He must reaffirm to himself the fact that he is to be a successful businessman, and know that a power greater than he is directing him in the correct paths. He must understand that it is not up to him to determine the ways and means and exact sequence of events by which he is to attain his end. He must understand that the great Subconscious Mind, or God, will effect its own ways and means and time in which to accomplish it. He must take to his heart the words of a very wise and very successful man who said, "In every apparent failure, there is the seed of great opportunity, if we but have the heart and the faith to see it."

The moment our businessman has refused to accept failure, has seen in his apparent negative circumstance only a rung on the ladder to his ultimate goal, he will find the market for his goods created, perhaps in a far different manner than he originally had envisaged, and what could easily have been a disaster, he will have turned into a great victory, through faith and nothing more.

The key
Let God do it
His way

Wow!

never doubt His plan.

THE PSYCHOLOGY OF WINNING

J. Hampton Pool is the Head Football Coach of the Los Angeles Rams, one of the most successful teams in professional football. His quiet faith and dedication mark him as both man and coach, and well they should, for he learned them on the hard ground of painful experience.

At Stanford University, Hamp and I were team mates on a football team which was finishing a miserable season. We seemed to have good personnel, such outstanding players as Frankie Albert, Norman Standlee, Hugh Gallarneau, Pete Kemetovic, but with only one opponent remaining on our schedule, we hadn't won a single game.

Night after night Hamp and I sat around his Mayfield home grousing. How could we expect to win, we told each other, when we had no offense, no leadership, no coaching? We blamed the alumni who were about to fire the coach. We blamed the coach for allowing the alumni to intimidate him. We blamed injuries. We blamed the weather. We blamed everything and everybody but ourselves. And why should we blame ourselves? Certainly we tried hard. Sometimes we lost ten or fifteen pounds in a game, carried bruised muscles and gashed lips for days as souvenirs of our efforts. Oh, we were trying, all right. And so was everyone else. But the lickings continued monotonously.

At last we climbed aboard the train for New York and headed for our last game, this one with Dartmouth, the top team in the east. Certainly if we hadn't won a game all season there was nothing to hope for against Dartmouth. A pall of gloom settled over the entourage as we awaited this last defeat.

The train sped through the midwest on a bright winter's day, and Hamp and I sat in the club car and watched the white landscape. It was a pastoral scene, peaceful, strangely detached. Hamp turned to me.

"Stan," he asked, "have you played your best this season?"

I was quickly defensive.

"You know I have," I said. "You've seen me play myself into exhaustion."

"I didn't ask if you got tired," he said. "I asked if you played your best."

He was looking me straight in the eye. There was nothing to do but be honest.

"No," I said, "not even close to it. Have you?"

He shook his head.

"No matter how I've tried," he said, "I've fallen short." He looked out the window again. "Why?" he asked.

"Maybe we've tried too hard," I said.

"More likely not hard enough," he said ruefully.

"When the goal is impossible," I insisted, "just trying itself can be awfully difficult."

"You mean we can't win?" he asked.

"I mean we *think* we can't," I said.

He pursed his lips.

"Maybe you're right. Despite everything—the rallies, the fight talks, the good resolutions—I doubt we really believe we can win."

 "We have *faith* that we can't win," I said, "so we don't."

Hamp struck his fist into the palm of his hand.

"All right," he said, "let's accept right now that we not only can win this next game, but we will win it. How about it?"

I was pretty doubtful. Saying it and believing it were two different things.

"It's possible," I conceded.

"Then what's to stop us?" he cried.

"Eleven guys from Dartmouth," I answered. Then suddenly I grinned. "But, by golly, I believe we can do it!"

 At that moment the gloom evaporated from the club car and a load left my shoulders. I straightened. I began to feel good.

Something must have happened to Hamp too. He smiled and extended his hand.

"Shake on it," he said. "We'll do our best—better than our best if necessary—because we're going to win."

 As I took his hand I felt relaxed, serene and confident for the first time in months.

We had a good time in New York because the burden was gone from our practice

121

sessions. But most of all we had a good time playing Dartmouth. Men made tackles they had never made before, caught passes they had never caught before, blocked punts they had never blocked before. We won.

No one seemed able to understand it. How could a team that hadn't won a game all season manage to beat the leading team in the east? There were all sorts of speculation. There was even a little between Hamp and me.

We were in the locker room after the game.

"I'm not even tired," he said with surprise- "And I don't have a bruise or a scratch."

"It was almost easy," I said.

"Maybe it's always easy when you have faith," he said thoughtfully. "Maybe it's having faith that's the only hard thing."

ISOLATION BRINGS FEAR

We human beings are creatures of little faith. We isolate ourselves from God, from the roots of our being, and we are ready to see on all sides a hostile and preying world that we are constantly going about our daily tasks affirming our faith, disease, disaster, poverty, failure, and loneliness. Yet the reins of our destinies are in our very own hands. All things, and evil, have their beginnings in faith, and "as ye believe, so shall it be done unto you."

We shall have our beliefs anyway, why not make them beliefs in good, in the fine ends of man, in abundance, in health, in vigor, in integrity? Let us use the word faith to mean the overcoming of negative thought. Let us use the word delusion to mean belief in negative circumstance and negative thinking. "Be of good cheer," said Jesus, "I have overcome the world." He had overcome all things by faith only! This is the lesson he left us, the most magnificent teaching in the history of mankind. Let us refuse to accept delusion. Let us take up faith like a sword, and by using it, overcome all things.

The Subconscious Mind, then, turns into physical reality each of our beliefs. If we find lack, limitation, disease, and failure in our lives, we can be very sure that our own convictions have brought them. It seems strange most of us find it so much easier to attach our beliefs to negative things rather than positive, but there is no doubt but that this is mankind's tendency. Man isolates himself from God, from his sense of unity with the infinite intelligence; then, feeling himself a small and lonely animal in a vast universe, he supposes that the responsibility for all things in his life depends upon his own physical action. The moment any one of his physical actions is thwarted, he sees in this defeat the symbol of a bigger future defeat, and he feels about him a hostile world aimed only at thwarting his each desire. He sees in his smallness his own inadequacy and can forecast nothing for himself but those very fates that he fears. Thus he orders an existence the very opposite of that which he truly desires. Becoming convinced of failure, disease, poverty, loneliness, and suffering, he is likely to undergo all of them while their op-posites seem as unattainable as stars. Yet the truth is that these unattainable opposites might have come to him with the same ease as their bad counterparts had he only exercised his faith in the right direction!

POWER THROUGH UNION

No man can consistently exercise faith in all aspects of his life without the secure knowledge that God is with him every minute of every day. Unless you are willing to give up your problems and turn them over to God, you will find that you are making very poor solutions of them indeed, for you will feel your own inadequacy at every turn in the road and will shortly be projecting more failure than success into the Subconscious Mind.

Make your mind up right now that there isn't the slightest use trying to do anything by yourself. You just aren't big enough and that is the plain truth of the matter. The millions of facts and circumstances beyond your ken and scope make of you a microbe on the face of the earth the moment you isolate yourself from the Subconscious Mind and say, "I, all by myself, will do this thing."

The first very apparent thing you will discover is that you don't know enough. The second is that you find yourself facing gigantic forces over which you have no control and against which you have no weapon. Defeat in every undertaking is then certain, and the only end is to be reduced to a groveling, whining, complaining, fear-ridden speck.

But join forces with the Subconscious Mind and the entire universe speeds to answer your every need. Not without cause did Jesus refer to the Subconscious Mind as the "Father who dwelleth within me," for indeed this wise and omnipotent father knows of your every need before you voice it, and may effect an instantaneous manifestation in your life of whatever it is you are convinced of. The Subconscious Mind contains the knowledge of all ways and means and times, and you may rest your problem there with the surety that it will be answered with perfection. Do not keep examining the pot to see if the water is boiling. You don't have to double-check God. Don't make up your mind that your path should lead in a certain direction and then be disturbed because you find it is leading elsewhere. Know that your every step is unerringly guided on a perfect route to your destination. Whatever you consider to be a sideroad is not a sideroad at all but the best ot all possible paths, Hold fast and faithfully to your conviction.

Amen!

THE PERFECT PARTNER

He who takes up this life in full knowledge of his partnership with God will find splendor in everything he touches. He will see an ordered universe rushing to do his bidding; he will see the design of all things fitted to his every need. He will know that the Senior Partner is the one who carries out every decision, an infallible executive who never makes a mistake. He will begin to see himself as a beloved son, who needs only ask and it shall be given, who needs only knock and it shall be opened. He will make each of his decisions clear and without contradiction, and he will hold to them with complete confidence until they have arrived in his world in answer to his call. He will know of his Father's tireless energy and unbounded goodwill, but he will respectfully refuse to tax them by contradicting himself or by vacillating. He will not, for example, say "I am going to be successful," and then a few hours or days later say, "I am not going to be successful. He will not say, "do, don't, start, stop, give, withhold. He will have the courage and faith of his convictions and will reject all else until his desire becomes manifest in his life.

Key   *Fear Not*

Thus it is that he will achieve perfect faith, for he will know that all things rest with a power greater than he, that his image and conviction must become real in his life, for that is the law of the living. In his sense of oneness with God he will never be alone, *Amen.* and all the power of the universe will dwell within him. He will no longer have to fight for faith; faith will be as natural as breathing. *Amen P.116*

(Gen 11:6) Nothing they've imagined believed with conviction will be withheld."

CIRCUMSTANCE VERSUS FAITH

But in the meantime, short of having arrived at this conscious oneness with God, faith is the tool with which we may overcome the negative convictions of the Conscious Mind. The Prompters, buried pain remembrances which attract evil and limitation, may also be disposed of by faith. Are you beset by the lack of money? Then have faith that money will be yours. Are you ill? Then have faith that you will be well. Are you lonely? Then have faith that love and companionship even now are coming your way. Do you think you have failed at your heart's desire? Then have faith that you are following the path to its attainment. *Act as if it were impossible to fail!* Know with Jesus of Nazareth that "All things are possible to him who believes,"

So Key

Because our Conscious Minds keep insisting that the physical world around us is final reality, we must use faith to regain our spiritual values. Our Conscious Minds accept every negative circumstance of our lives and are forever assuring us that these circumstances control us instead of the opposite. We may awake to a beautiful morning, arise from bed full of faith and energy. This feeling may see us through breakfast and be with us on our way to work. Then a driver lurches his car in front of us in traffic, and we slam on the brakes with our hearts in our mouths. "You stupid fool," we say, maybe out loud, certainly to ourselves, and now we are irritated. The day is not so bright. We don't feel quite as good. We start thinking about the boss and the calling-down he gave us the other day. Suddenly it seems quite apparent that the boss is out to make our life miserable. We walk into the office with a chip on our shoulder. Shortly we may be in an argument. We don't like the job any more. It's underpaid. Nobody appreciates us. Fate seems to conspire to keep us from attaining success. And so it goes.

He who would use faith must use it to rise above negative circumstance, and he must never fall victim to that which goes on around him. Refuse to be trapped into believing that the cause of anything exists on the physical plane. Have complete confidence in the fact that first cause is mental and first cause once set in motion must inevitably manifest itself in the physical world. Do not deny negative circumstance. Simply have faith in what you believe and refuse to accept negative circumstance as final. This is the proper use of faith. For faith will overcome the deluded convictions of the Conscious Mind, build habits of positive thinking, which is the first step en the road to power.

POSITIVE THINKING

Faith is nothing other than a sustained effort to impart to the Universal Subconscious Mind that thought which you wish to be manifested in your experience. Faith means thinking the one thing and not thinking of its opposite. Faith means refusing to accept any negative circumstance or to entertain any negative thought. *Faith means complete reliance and trust in the power and goodness of God, and absolute trust that whatever you conceive with conviction will be returned to you in this world!*

There is no end to the power of positive thinking. He who banishes negative thoughts from his mind is caught up in the entire expanding power of the universe. Yet it is a difficult thing to do, so involved are we in our habits of negative thinking, so directed as automatons by our buried pain remembrances, the Prompters.

A man may have in his mind all the knowledge that exists in our libraries, but unless he becomes a positive thinker he will meet with nothing but failure in his life. He does not want failure. Who does? Who wants to be sick? Poor? Lonely? Unsuccessful? A man may even acknowledge that his own negative thinking is attracting negative circumstance to him, yet despite his efforts he seems caught up in a habit of thought that .will not release him. He may go for hours, even days, fighting off every mood of depression, turning his mind away from every negative idea, then

125

of a sudden, something, usually a small thing, the baby crying, the dripping faucet, a brusque word, will set him off, and he surrenders to morbidity and his accustomed habits of negation much as a chronic alcoholic might return to the bottle after a period of abstinence. He wallows in futility, actually seems to enjoy it. He takes a kind of masochistic satisfaction from being able to state to himself that the whole world is against him and nobody appreciates him and he never had a chance and fate conspires daily to do him a dirty trick. He finds an ache in his back; he rediscovers his indigestion, develops sick headaches from tension; his nerves will not let him sleep; he becomes jumpy and cranky with friends and associates alike. He is busy, yes indeed, very busy, attracting those very things which he says he does not want.

FEAR AND DELUSION—NEGATIVE FAITH

Oh, but if it were real easy, he would do it. If he knew that all he had to do was think positive thoughts for twenty-four hours and the next day he would have a fine job, lots of money, a happy home, prestige and achievement, he certainly would do it then, wouldn't he? But when it takes longer than that, he gives up the ghost, giving little or no heed to the fact that he is still working with the exact same factors, except now he is using his faith in the opposite direction, in the direction of evil, limitation, lack, and disease. *it's still faith*

A strange situation has evolved, a situation in which people today find it effortless to use faith to attract evil and in which they find it exceedingly hard work to use faith for good. Certainly this is a paradox. Certainly in the ages of man's evolution it is a temporary thing, but that doesn't dissolve its tragic importance to those who face the problem now. It seems easy for us to have faith in negative things because we have built up habits of negative thinking. These habits of negative thinking are as difficult to break as any habit which is as long-seated, usually thirty to fifty years, with most of us.

But if we know that positive thinking attracts good, and negative thinking attracts evil, then certainly we are all in accord that the primary immediate aim is to do away with negative thinking. In other words, break the habit. It is no more difficult to break than any habit and once broken need never bother you again, for you will then know its pitfalls and will not be tempted.

Your attitude will determine your altitude

THE BAD HABIT

It is often a very fantastic thing to observe a man accept temporarily the premise that positive thinking can change his life, then discard this transcendent truth as unworkable after the most perfunctory trial. He might, for instance, decide today to alter his thinking and approach to life. He might actually change his outlook and

126 *Faith can be faith in the negative by habit!*

attitudes very considerably for a period of a week or even a month. If at the end of that time, however, he has not been witness to a miracle, he all too often raises his hands in despair and shouts, "It doesn't work!" and falls immediately into his former habits of thinking.

A lifetime of negative thinking will not be undone in a week! Don't for a moment fall into the trap of thinking that unless results are immediate you are on the wrong track. It is a case of faith or fear, and fear is only the negative use of faith. No matter how you choose to think, you are calling into existence those very things you believe in. The choice then is simple: good or evil. There is in this life no alternative to faith other than fear and evil. No sane person, understanding this, will dally with his choice.

But how to undo the habit? That is the problem. A bad habit seldom yields to half-hearted measures, and negative thinking is certainly the most persistent and destructive habit ever assimilated into the mind and nature of mankind. To get at this fellow requires measures as sure and aseptic as the surgeon's knife, and thus it is we offer you the only tool possible.

BREAKING THE BAD HABIT

If a doctor discovers that your body is not receiving the proper nutrition, he puts you on a *diet*. His reasoning on this is simple. He discovers that certain elements and vitamins and minerals are lacking in the chemical composition of your body, therefore he would restore their proper balance by having you eat certain foods that contain them in abundance. In any event, he asks you to exercise a conscious choice in the foods you eat, selecting some and rejecting a great many more.

It is just such a procedure, confined entirely to the mind and spirit, which we shall ask you to adopt for the next thirty days. In other words, we are asking that you go on a thirty-day *mental diet*.

For thirty days, one month, you are not to accept a single negative thought nor dwell on a single negative premise. This does not mean that such thoughts or ideas will not occur to you. They most certainly will occur, as frequently or even more so than they have all your life. This simply means that you will refuse to *accept* any of them, discarding them immediately they occur, as fictional ideas, without basis in truth, delusions that are without foundation for they have no roots in your mind. In this manner, by consciously exercising a choice of that which you allow to become part of your mind, by deliberately planting only positive seeds in the garden of the Subconscious, you will not only set about an eventual harvesting of the greatest bumper crop of good ever to enter your life, but more important, you will be building up a habit of positive thinking that will become easier and easier, day by day. Eventually, you will no longer have to struggle with positive and negative, good and evil, truth and illusion. You will ally yourself with the forces for good in the universe and achieve an attunement and an effortlessness in life that once seemed impossible of imagining. *Re-born*

He's Your Father! *You're made the same!* *&*

THE MENTAL DIET *Focus the Goodness of God, Jesus Spirit* *Holy*

What are these thoughts that we are going to refuse to entertain? They are any thoughts that might in the smallest or greatest manner cast into a pessimistic or poor light yourself, your family, your friends, your social group, your state, your nation, or the entire human race. They are, in short, negative thoughts of any type, regardless of whether they seem personally aimed at you yourself, or even at an inanimate object.

Now don't be blind about this and say, "Oh, I never think negatively." And don't be fearful about it and say, "I couldn't manage to concentrate on that sort of thing for thirty days." Don't say you haven't got time. Don't say it won't work. We needn't even point out how and why each of these attitudes destroys the goal even before the experiment has begun.

Before you start the thirty-day mental diet, spend a day or two observing how your mind is working. Carry a notebook and pencil with you if you will, and keep a record of each negative thought you entertain for a period of two days. The result will astound you and convince you beyond all doubt of the absolute necessity of embarking on the mental diet.

You must master your thoughts!

This is going to be no easy time, discarding every negative thought for a period of thirty days, but it is something you absolutely *must* do. Until you become master of your thinking, you will never become master of your fate. If you fall from the path of your resolve and entertain negative thoughts, become depressed, apprehensive, pessimistic, there is nothing to do but start over. You must negotiate thirty days of positive thinking without any serious intrusion of negative thought. It is exceptionally important that you do this thing. Let nothing stand in your way.

During the period of your mental diet, you will be helped by understanding exactly what it is you are doing. You are training your mind to obey you rather than you obey it. You are training yourself to think more of less and less of more. In other words, you are developing the habit of concentration as well as the habit of positive thinking.

TOO MANY THOUGHTS

We humans think altogether too much on altogether too many things. In the space of

128

a single moment our minds may embrace a hodge-podge of unrelated ideas and half-formed conceptions such as could not be found on the printed page outside of the *Encyclopaedia Britannica*. We jump helter-skelter from one idea to the next, unguided, unguarded, seizing on whatever is presented to us across the moving screen of mind and declaring it to be real. We start the Subconscious Mind moving in one direction, halt it, start it off in another, recall it, send it off again, recall it, literally hundreds of times each day.

We have developed habits of absolutely undisciplined thinking, and very often where any discipline at all is present it is aimed at negative thinking. One moment we are happy and entertain happy thoughts. Then a shadow crosses the face of the sun, and we entertain unhappy thoughts. A friend pays us a compliment, and we feel important and vain. An acquaintance castigates us, and we entertain thoughts of resent ment and bitterness. Always we wait for impetus from outside to determine what thoughts we will accept and which we will reject, and thus we become victims of every wind that blows and every twig that falls, and the temper of our lives is determined by countless unending streams of circumstances over which we have no control.

Scarce indeed is the man who sets himself up to accept only certain thoughts and beliefs and, firm in his faith and foundation, outwaits the world to achieve his ends. The sea and the mountain, the storm and the stars shall not persevere against such a man, and he shall move the very ends of the earth.

DO WE THINK?

As human beings we have been tricked into believing that we think. In other words, we believe we make thoughts. It is a peculiar thing that we believe this, since no one has ever been able to say whence a thought comes and from what it is made, but nevertheless most treatises on the mind hold that man thinks up things and makes up thoughts. Yet if you carefully analyze the process of thought, you will find that it is not you who thinks at all, but it is rather you who observes thoughts as they flit across your consciousness. Stated differently, it is as if the real you occupied a still and guarded position in the very recesses of your being, from which you observe a purely mental world that consists entirely of thoughts. These thoughts parade across your consciousness in a never-ending stream, following one upon the other unceasingly, i Some you select and add to you, others you reject and send on their way. But the plain and irrevocable fact is that it is not you who sets the stream of thoughts in motion. *If you doubt this, try to stop it!*

You will find that all your efforts cannot stop your thinking for the essence of being is observation, contemplation, and choice; and though you may slow the stream of thoughts a very great deal, and examine each thought presented to you with much

129

more care, still they come, these thoughts from out of nowhere, exhibiting themselves before your consciousness, demanding of you that you establish a position and accept some while you reject others.

A writer who sits down and writes a novel does not "think up" his story and his characters. He simply puts himself in the position of someone who is going to write a story, then he observes the thoughts and ideas that cross his consciousness. On and on they come and he rejects them, until finally there comes an idea which appeals to him. This idea he takes unto himself and examines and then accepts. Now instead of just being in a position to write a story, he is in the position of writing a story about a man who is, let us say, alone on a desert island. He wonders how the man got there, and on the stream of thoughts come, and he accepts one, and now he is writing a story about a man who was marooned on a desert island by pirates. And so it goes with each of the facets and details of his story. In no case does he "think them up." His entire story, once assembled and written, is simply evidence of the thousands of choices he has made from the thoughts that have streamed through his mind. He has not thought up a thing; he has simply exercised choice. His story tells you what he has accepted; nothing will ever tell you the millions of ideas and thoughts which he has rejected.

WE CHOOSE THOUGHTS

Like the writer who authors a story, each of us authors his own life by his choice of what thoughts he will accept and which he will reject. Each of our lives is a story, unfolded by the silent contemplative author who dwells within us, who does nothing more than accept and reject, who is involved only in making choices. This indwelling Self says, "This is so," "This is not so," "I believe this," I feel fine in this circumstance," "I feel badly in this circumstance," "I am great," "I am nothing," "There is hope," "There is despair." And each of these choices is manifested in the physical world.

We are today living testimonies to the choices we have made from the thoughts that have streamed through our minds. We are literally products of the thoughts we have chosen to accept. We are what we believe we are, that only, nothing more or less.

So it is that the mental diet upon which we are about to embark is so important. We have assured the indwelling Self that it can be anything it accepts and has faith in, and we are now about to develop in it the habit of choosing only those thoughts and ideas that will constructively add good unto it. We are teaching ourselves to accept only good. We are teaching ourselves to reject all evil. We are deliberately compelling ourselves to accept all love, all kindness, all hope, all joy, all expansion, all abundance, all health, all vigor. We are deliberately compelling ourselves to reject all suffering, all sorrow, all depression, all morbidness, all inferiority, all aches and

130

The Key

pains. We are saying nothing is true but the great and the good and the beautiful, only these will we add unto ourselves. For thirty days we stand guard while the habit forms. Thereafter, though we may relax a little, we will not let go our sentinel, for we know that we are only what we accept from the thoughts that come to us, and more than ever the wisdom of Jesus is brought home, "As ye believe, so shall it be done unto you."

"As a man thinketh 231 in his heart, so is he".

St. Augustine wrote:

I, Lord, went wandering like a strayed sheep, seeking Thee with anxious reasoning without, whilst Thou wast within me. I went round the streets and squares of the city seeking thee; and I found thee not, because in vain I sought without for him who was within myself.

"Kingdom of God is within me", says Jesus, my Lord!

Heed the silent dweller in the recesses of your being. Know that to him all things are possible, according to what he accepts. You are what you choose to be, and your choice is made in the mind. Seek the high and forsake the low. A man adds all things unto himself simply by taking a position with impregnable faith.

The Key

RISING ABOVE CIRCUMSTANCE

The world is too much with us, and we think far too much. In the process of our thirty-day mental diet, we must learn to slow the stream of our thoughts and we must learn to deny the final reality of the physical world about us. The first of these aims may be accomplished by a simple breathing exercise and meditation; the latter is far more difficult.

Slow thoughts & Ignore your senses the flesh, physical

It is a fine thing to awake in the morning full of the exaltation of a vision that has come to us in the night, to arise from bed full of a vague remembrance of a brilliance and a peace that surpassed everything. We are uplifted, quickened with new faith and new resolve. For a few minutes we are nearly convinced that we have found the way, but how easily we let go of our faith, and how stupidly.

Cares of the world

There is a spot on the suit we had decided to wear, or our best dress has sprung a seam. The toaster isn't working properly and our toast is burned. We spill our milk or our coffee, or somebody else does. The car doesn't start or we miss our bus. We receive a fancied slight on the street. It is a bad day. Nothing ever seems to go right for us. The vision is long gone, and we seem to be little ants in a limitless universe, hemmed in on all sides by destructive and malicious forces and by designing and preying beings. We are angry and resentful.

Ignore them

NO!

Thus we are victimized. Thus we deny the magnificent indwelling Self. Thus we are prompting the Universal Subconscious Mind in those very directions we do not wish

131

Never

to go. Thus, because we have accepted the physical world about us as having a higher reality than that world that exists only in mind, we have become pawns in a game of physical fate over which we have no control.

It matters not whence the thought comes, whether it filters to your consciousness in the silence of your bedroom, or whether it comes to you in the clatter of a busy workaday world; if you accept it, then it becomes a part of you and will be added to you in the physical world. Thus you are continually accepting premises and convictions that are forced upon you by the circumstances and the people and the events you meet, even though they are often very contrary to what you really desire. It is this we mean when we say the world is too much with us. "Judge not by appearances," said Jesus. If you would win your way to the manifestation of those things that are your goals, you must not be swayed from your conviction and faith by any of the events or circumstances you meet in your daily life. Whatever is contrary to your belief you must reject as not having reality, as being only a temporary thing, a detour on the road you follow, not a setback at all but a necessary path to follow; for the whole plan rests in Universal Mind and though it may seem at the moment to be going against your desires, have no fear.

We will accept from the thought-things in the world around us only those which add to our faith and our conviction in the goals we have set or in ourselves. All other thought-things we reject as being only temporary and lacking final reality. Thus in the inner recesses of our beings we maintain a place of quiet assurance and contemplation, steadfast always in our knowledge that our faith will become manifest in our lives. It is then we who set the temper of our thoughts. It is then we who achieve mastery over our fates. Our positions are unassailable; we create from within and are never victims of circumstance.

THOUGHT CONTROL

Equally important in arriving at mental control and faith is our ability to slow down the helter-skelter streams of thoughts that flow across our consciousness. It is the flittering haphazard Conscious Mind, never unified in purpose, always prompting the Subconscious Mind in dozens of different directions, that produces chaos in our surrounding world. We must harness the Conscious Mind, control it, guide it in the paths we would follow.

Daily, just prior to your meditation period, you must practice the process of slowing your thought stream. Seek a place of quiet and solitude. Find a comfortable, restful seat- Relax every muscle. Start at the top of your head and move downward over your whole body. Relax the muscles around your eyes and forehead, your cheek and lip and jaw muscles, the muscles in your neck. Let your head loll. Move it slowly around in a circle on your relaxed neck. Relax the muscles in your shoulders, in your arms, in your hands. Let your hands hang loosely. Relax your stomach muscles, your abdomen, carefully relax all the muscles in your back, your thighs, your calves, feel the weight of your legs. Rest like this for several minutes and know that you are fully relaxed. Then concentrate on your breathing.

Gradually begin to slow the taking of each breath. Make each inhalation a little deeper. Breathe comfortably and peacefully, pausing at the end of each inhalation and exhalation, but do not pause so long that you begin gasping. Slowly your respiration will reduce itself until your breathing is scarcely noticeable. Slowly there will come over you a sense of peacefulness and drowsiness and security and comfort. Your mind will glide like a boat into a calm lagoon of unruffled and placid waters, and you will feel a sense of contentment. It is quiet there, so quiet that you can hear the voices of the soul. Think very slowly. Deliberately watch your thoughts as they cross your consciousness. Hold onto them and examine them, but let them go. Neither accept nor reject them. Notice how each thought follows one upon the other in an endless stream of traffic. Now ask yourself, "Who is it that observes this?" It will come upon you then that it is not you who thinks at all; *it is you who observes and decides, that only.*

WHO IS "I?"

Ask yourself who this observer is that you refer to as "I." It is not thought. It is not body. It simply is, has being, observes. In the contemplative sense in which you feel it now, it is neither past nor present nor future, but simply exists. *I am. I observe. I decide.*

Here is your true being. Here is your real Self, the unfettered, untrammeled, eternal spectator. To find this point of consciousness from which all things and thoughts and moods are a matter of observation is to find the spiritual center of gravity, is to know yourself in all your true freedom and joy. This "I," this observer, is the indwelling God, the real Self, the personal consciousness that is in all things and all life. To know it truly and at all times is to have the consciousness of Jesus the Christ.

Thus, in your daily practice of thought control, when you have slowed the thought stream after relaxation and breath control, turn always to the Self that dwells deep within you. Find the point of consciousness from whence all things are but observations. Then ask, "Who is this that observes?" Of this point of consciousness did Jesus speak when he said, "Seek ye first the Kingdom of Heaven, and all things shall be added unto you."

The arrival at this point of consciousness is the attainment of "the peace that passeth all understanding," and is the position from which all things are possible, without

Summary 30 day diet!

effort, without the exercising of will, but simply through contemplation and choice.

These things, then, we will do in our thirty-day mental diet. We will first reject all negative thoughts and ideas and circumstances, and refuse to add them to ourselves. We will entertain only positive thoughts of good and abundance and joy and love and kindness and success. We will daily engage in a period of thought control which we will achieve with the aid of breathing exercises, always aiming at arriving at that point of consciousness where all things and thoughts are a matter of observation. From there we will engage in our meditations each day.

This will prove to be one of the most rewarding times of your life, not only because of the manifestations you meet within the physical world, but also because of the lowering sense of peace and strength that will come to you as you grow to know the magnificence that is yours. You will sense the unity of all things, come to understand that nothing is done by man alone but all things are done by the Universal *God* Subconscious Mind, or the mind of God. You will further see that all of that mind is in you now and all the days to come, and you will understand that you have nothing to do but decide each of the issues of your life and put your faith and trust in the wisdom and omnipotence of this all-knowing mind.

Conviction!

LEAVE IT TO GOD

We are a civilization of people who suffer from a "I have to do it" complex. We believe that the responsibility for all things settles on our shoulders. Being materialists, we have great difficulty in analyzing anything except in a material sense, and our problems are largely confined to those of finding jobs, getting better jobs, and making more money. We sense our inadequacy as we set out to beat the world, and this makes us all the more frantic in our rushing around, hurrying back and forth, worrying about this, worrying about that. Though the slogan on America's silver coins says, "In God we trust," we deny this as we set out to collect as many of these coins as we can.

Henry David Thoreau wrote: *So true!*

Whatever we leave to God, God does; and blesses us;
The work we choose should be our own, God lets alone.

Perhaps the most difficult thing each of us has to learn is to "Let go and let God." As long as we keep our problems with us, dwelling on each aspect of them, lending reality to each negative quality we can perceive or construe, we are defeating our own ends. The mighty power of the Universal Subconscious Mind, recognizing our command that we are determined to do things by ourselves, filters into our lives in a

Wow!

134

So freeing!

tiny trickle, over the dam we have built against it. But once turn your problem over to the Universal Mind with the request, "Here, you handle it," and the dam is removed and the torrent flows and miracles are wrought before our very eyes, such miracles that we can only wonder with awe at how lucky we are or how beneficent are the circumstances that surround us.

DO NOT DWELL ON YOUR PROBLEMS *Cast your Cares!*

Never keep any problem in your mind for more than a few minutes at a time. Consider the issues and the possible paths or courses of action you might take. If you cannot decide what to do, turn the problem over to Subconscious Mind with the sure knowledge that the correct answer will be returned to you. You may return to your problem daily, thinking on its various aspects once again. It may be during one of these periods that the answer will come to you, though just as likely it will come upon you at any moment of the day, all unsuspecting. Whenever the moment comes, you will entertain not the slightest doubt but that the answer is truth. It will burst upon you like a light, and very likely you will chastise yourself for not having been aware of it before; it will suddenly seem so simple.

Rest

Once you have made your decision, forget about your problem altogether, secure in the knowledge that its execution rests in the most capable hands in the universe. Reaffirm your faith in your goal by meditation, but under no circumstances try to predict the manner in which the Subconscious Mind *[God]* will make it manifest. If you yourself have forecast certain steps that must be accomplished by a certain time, and you find that such steps are not taken and even opposite or conflicting ones are taken, don't turn craven and lose your faith. You have turned the execution of your problem or your work over to the wisest intelligence in all creation, and it is not your part to tell it what it should do or what it ought to have done in order to get where you both are going. If you really think you would be a better pilot, then there is nothing for you to do but take the helm. But if, like most of us, you have spent many years at that helm without chart or compass or navigational instruments, only to founder on the rocks and shoals of life, you will wisely leave the helm and the navigation up to one who knows, and not keep trying to tell Him where He ought to steer or saddle yourself with emotional upset and antagonistic thinking when He doesn't steer where you think He ought to.

FAITH IS TRUST

So Key

All of us are much too likely to predict the way things should happen, and when they fail to follow the pattern of our predictions we are sure our goals will be denied us; thus we defeat ourselves. A man decides to write a book. Assuming that his image

Not my way, Gods way! 135

and faith are clear, he actually sits down and after a period of time gets the book done. He sends it off to a publisher, and a while later receives the manuscript back with a rejection slip. He can now decide that the book is no good, do no more about it, and thus bring failure upon himself. Or he can entertain a respect for the publisher's decision, look the manuscript over carefully, and decide whether or not it needs rewriting. If it doesn't (and this is a rare case indeed), he should reaffirm his faith and send it off to another publisher, and keep sending it until the book is finally accepted, for accepted it will be if his faith remains true. More likely, however, he will rewrite it after each rejection, for what he has affirmed to the Subconscious Mind is that he will write a book *good enough* to be published, and his rejection slips are only part of the means by which he will turn the book into his best possible effort.

Wow! So key — not a bulldog — change to the key b

Faith is actually in the end little more than persistence, and a drop of water will wear a rock away if it keeps beating at it endlessly. Nothing stands against repeated effort. Bare feet wear cobblestones away. The soft morning dew repeated over years will dissolve iron. He who holds his image clear and true will arrive safely in harbor no matter the unsuspected seas or storms he weathers en route.

Faith is the end; more than persistence

But wherever we go, whatever we do, we must always know that the Subconscious Mind is our mighty and invisible partner. The Subconscious is our executive vice-president, our crew land staff, advisor and confessor. We have nothing to do but lean back in our chairs and observe and decide, and the mightiest force in the universe leaps to do our bidding. But we must delegate to our great partner full authority. He is the ways and means committee, and His nature is to work secretively. We cannot second-guess Him, countermand His various moves.

The Way, indeed!

He requires complete trust and confidence, and once He sets about a task we have given Him we must leave everything up to Him. Interference at any point He interprets as meaning a new goal, and He immediately sets about achieving this new one instead. We must learn to leave Him alone, to let go of our problems as soon as He has taken them. Once we have learned to do this we will find that His nature is to wind things up in jig time and in the most marvelous manner. Once we have completely given over to Him any one of our problems and been witness to the manner in which He solves it, we will never again doubt or disbelieve.

Yep — Amen!   *Summary*

FAITH VERSUS HOPE

One of the traps we so often fall into is the confusion of hope with faith. Hope has scarcely any relation to faith at all, and though many times more desirable than despair, nevertheless is a frail instrument indeed for moving the Subconscious Mind. Hope is a pessimist looking at things optimistically. Hope is a querulous wish for something better. Hope says evil is more real than good, with the timid reservation that everything might turn out all right anyway. It is no wonder that those who seek to better their lives through hope are very seldom witness to improvements.

It is an understandable thing that most of us set about the projects of our lives with hope instead of faith. Hope is a dimly perceived light, now flickering faintly in the darkness, now obscured by the gloom. Hope is wishing. Faith, on the other hand, is a radiance that bathes all things in illumination. Faith is knowing. Because we tend to attach primary importance to the material world, because we fail to perceive the design and purpose of our lives, because we refuse to let go of our problems, and labor under burdens of tremendous responsibility, it is extremely difficult for us to know and thus is extremely difficult for us to have faith.

Whatever we know to be a fact we have complete faith in, whether we understand how it works or not. You throw the lever on a switch with complete faith that the lights in the room will illuminate, yet the methods by which electricity is picked up in generators, transmitted over lines, distributed to your home and finally achieves the miracle of light by heating a tiny filament in a vacuum sealed by transparent glass are most probably little known to you. You know that the lights will go on when you throw the switch because you have tried it before and it works! Thus you have complete faith.

Similarly, on the intangible planes of human existence, we need not achieve the full knowledge of why and how everything works and is constructed; we need only try working with spiritual law, discover that it works, and thus come into complete faith through knowing.

But dealing with the spiritual and mental forces of the universe is far different than dealing with things of the physical world where our five senses are constantly giving sharp definition and substance to everything with which we come in contact. We are sure of the physical things we see, feel, hear, smell and taste. We have complete faith in the reality of their existence. Far less faith do we have in the reality of mind and the great forces of spiritual existence. "We hope for them. We timidly experiment with them. But because they do not follow the same pattern of demonstration as the physical world, we abandon them usually at the first failure.

FAITH IS MENTAL LAW

The truth is that the physical world has accustomed us to the wrong use of faith. In material things our faith habitually follows demonstration; while in spiritual or mental things faith must always precede demonstration. The constant analogy that we draw between things physical and things mental causes us to believe that mental law must parallel physical law, and we omit to notice the great difference. Physical law does *it was find*

Oh. MG! Amen.

not need our faith to be operative. Mental law follows our faith exactly, indeed, is faith; thus the difficulty in perceiving the great world of mind and spirit in which we dwell.

It sometimes sounds extremely childish to say to a person who is distraught with problems and griefs that he may overcome them all by simply having faith. The reason for this is that the person who is in such a position is acutely aware of physical circumstance and has denied the reality of the realm of mind and spirit. Knowing the physical so well, he has denied his true being and has lost faith.

Stay with God Day & Night.

It becomes almost Pollyanna-ish to insist that a person use faith under such circumstances, for faith is knowing, and at the moment he cannot know. Only by communion with the indwelling Self, the quiet assured place in the recesses of his being, will he come into the possession of true knowledge and thus complete faith. So it is that one man can never insist with success that another man have faith, nor can any man insist that he himself have faith when he is beset by doubt and fear. Faith only comes through knowledge, and the precepts that are contained in the pages of this book, plus your daily meditations and communions with the indwelling "I," will bring this knowledge home with full force and achieve for you a faith that will turn life into glorious adventure.

REVIEW

Here are the points covered in this chapter:

1. All things are rooted in faith, which is the single most important tool of man's existence.

2. The Subconscious Mind turns every conviction of the Conscious Mind into physical reality.

Beliefs - Intents

3. The Subconscious Mind knows specific time and place circumstance only through the convictions forwarded to it by the Conscious Mind.

4. Whatever the Subconscious Mind knows, the Subconscious Mind creates.

5. Thought plus faith creates.

& evil

6. Faith in negative things is delusion but nevertheless moves the Subconscious Mind to create them in physical actuality. *Wow! "As a man thinketh."*

7. Negative faith or delusion is caused by man isolating himself from the Universal *God* Subconscious Mind, and making fear and resentment and hate his companions

through his sense of separateness.

[handwritten: Conviction]

[handwritten: GOD]

8. Faith is attained through complete trust and confidence in the power of Universal Mind. *[handwritten: ½ through Knowledge & Success in it.]*

9. The unity of all things and all people indwelling in the immortal Self of the universe is the essence of faith.

10. Faith is a spiritual value and must be maintained in a spiritual manner; therefore it can never be dictated by the circumstances that surround you. *[handwritten: (physical) senses]*

11. He whose faith vacillates with the events of his life allows himself to become a victim of every wind that blows and every twig that falls, and is never his own master. *[handwritten: (James 4:8)]*

12. Faith is sustained effort. *[handwritten: Don't quit!]*

13. Faith is persistence. *[handwritten: even a persistent drop of water (it works) changes a rock!]*

14. Faith is knowing, while hope is little more than wishing.

15. Don't fall into the trap of hoping for things; it will avail you little.

16. Positive thinking is the cornerstone of faith. *[handwritten: Rejoice, as slow as (succeeds)]*

17. Refuse to add negative thoughts and circumstance unto yourself. Choose only the good and the great and the beautiful. The rest is delusion. *[handwritten: Meditate on lovely things 4:8]*

18. The mind may be trained in the habit of positive thinking through a training period called a thirty-day mental diet.

19. The inner Self does not make up thoughts; it only observes and chooses. Your life today is a result of the thoughts you have chosen to accept.

20. Turn your problems over to Universal Subconscious Mind; you will find the answers and be guided in the right paths. *[handwritten: God (Prov 3:5-7)]*

21. Don't, under any circumstances, tell the Subconscious Mind how to do things. Let go and let God.

22. When negative circumstance arises, know that it is but temporary, a necessary route to the goal you inevitably will achieve as long as your faith remains with you.

23. Daily seek the consciousness of the indwelling spectator, the place of calm and unruffled quiet, where all things are known and understood.

24. Seek to know. Subordinate all things to faith, for faith must precede all demonstration.

THE ROAD AHEAD

You now have arrived at the crossroads of understanding. There is much to do. There is, first, the thirty-day mental diet which you must perform faithfully and assiduously and which must be carried to successful completion no matter how many false starts you may make. There is, second, the breathing exercises and period of communion with the indwelling Self in which you seek contact with the eternal "I," your true being. And, of course, there are the meditations which you must perform directly after the breathing exercises and communion.

Once again may we caution you that failure to carry out the work will lose for you the greatest value that can be gained from your study—demonstration of good in your life. Only through such demonstration will the full knowledge come to you of your own self-mastery. Without this you are simply performing mental exercises. Knowledge without faith is like a ship without a sea; it may be beautiful to behold, but it does very little good. Do the work! Perform the meditations! Keep the faith I

RECOMMENDED READING

Power Through Constructive Thinking by Emmet Fox. Published by Harper and Brothers.

SIXTH MEDITATION

Here in solitude, in this time of peace, of meditation, I withdraw deep into the silent recesses of my being to a place of utter calm. Slowly the world retreats from around me, until finally I am alone. Walled away from all clamor and strife there is nothing but me. I am not body; I am not thought; I am not experience; I am not the past nor the present nor the future. I simply am. Across my consciousness comes a constant procession of thoughts and I observe them. I do not make up these thoughts. I know they come from the Universal Subconscious Mind, and I watch as they are presented to me. I glow the train of thoughts. I examine each of them, then let go, neither accepting nor rejecting. On and on the thoughts come, and I ask myself, "Who is it that observes this?" And I hear the answer, "Thou that art, always have been, and always will be—thou observes!," and I understand. Divorced from body, thought, and experience, I still exist as I always must. Here then is my true self, a thing independent of all but spirit, a contemplative "I," which only observes and chooses from the thoughts that cross consciousness. Whatever I choose is mine. Whatever I reject shall never touch me. I need only observe and accept, and all things will be added unto me by a power which leaps to acknowledge my faith and my decision. I sense such warmth and security as might overflow the world. I sense a fusion of my being with the great Universal Subconscious Mind, the mind of God. I sense the presence of the Father who knoweth no wrath, who does all things at his child's bidding. I sense my union with this Father by immutable and irrevocable bonds. I am one with all truth, all beauty, all justice, all love.

Chapter 7 - ATTRACTION

Like unto like doth the universe cry
What thou choose to accept thou wilt see
Skim the wide ocean, split the deep sky
Relentlessly bound on a meeting with thee

THE ENDLESS PRAYER

The human being is a center of life force, attracting some things, repelling others, according to his conceptions and beliefs. Universal Mind differentiates into centers of life force or atoms, which congregate with others vibrating on a similar frequency. And it is the nature of any unit built from Universal Mind to attract unto itself those thought-things that answer the mental vibrations it exudes.

We have seen that all the things of our world are nothing more or less than pure intelligence, cast into form by a concertion in the Universal Subconscious Mind. Intelligence responds to intelligence, and thought creates vibrations which inevitably attract the thing in the image. The one mind in which we all live contains an infinite number of possibilities all of which are capable of becoming manifest in space and time when the conception has been planted in Universal Subconscious Mind. Therefore whatever you choose and accept must develop in your experience, for it is attracted to you by in irresistible and immutable law, a law which isn't working me of the time, or occasionally, or most of the time, but every second of every minute of all the time there is.

Whether we like analogy or not, we are literally praying every minute of our lives, and every single one of our prayers ire answered. *There is no escaping this wheel of answered thought and belief.* It is the law of life. Whatever has developed in our experience has not been brought to us by luck or fate or coincidence, but is simply a physical manifestation of our thought and belief. Whether it has brought us good or evil, it is in effect an answered prayer.

Ralph Waldo Emerson wrote:

> *And though thy knees were never bent*
> *To heaven thy hourly prayers are sent*
> *And whether formed for good or ill*
> *Are registered and answered still.*

You are what you think; you attract what you think; your life is a product of your thought and belief; and nothing in the world can change this fact. *To alter your life the only single course open is to alter your thinking!*

THE PRIMAL FORCE

Since the shepherds of Asia Minor thousands of years ago discovered that the iron crooks of their wooden staffs were attracted to certain hard black stones (lodestones), the world of science increasingly has come to understand that behind all form and substance in the universe is a subtle but powerful attraction. This attraction manifests a high order of design and intelligence, and science has chosen to call it the Laws of Nature while religion has chosen to call it God. We, for the purposes of new definition, call it the Universal Subconscious Mind.

Studying the lines of force of a magnet, science has discovered that these lines never cross. They either repel or attract, one or the other. No matter how far a magnet is displaced from the lines of force in a free field, it will always return to its point of balance. So it is with the mind that sets up certain patterns of thought. Everything contrary to this thought is automatically repelled. Everything allied to this thought is automatically attracted. No matter how far such a mind is displaced from those things which it seeks, it will return to them as it must.

For example, such a mind as has built up habits of thinking aimed at poverty or lack must inevitably create such a physical situation, no matter how much prosperity it is thrust into. If the owner of such a mind suddenly finds himself with a hundred thousand dollars, he will shortly be dispossessed of it and return to a state of want, directed there by the thought habits of his mind and what they are attracting for him. *It is never money makes success; it is the thinking of the man.*

A conditioned habit of prosperity-thinking is usually ingrained on the mind of a person who is born to wealth and plenty. This habit of positive thinking in regard to money is as much a part of him as is the negation of money a part of the thinking of one who is born to poverty. As a consequence, those who are born to wealth seem to attract further wealth to themselves effortlessly. But it is not the money that accomplishes this; it is the pattern of thinking. Similarly, those born to poverty must exercise the greatest industry and perseverance before wealth smiles on them, for they must gradually condition their minds to think positively of money before money will be manifested. Each small success that comes their way contributes to building favorable thought patterns of confidence and faith, and so finally they achieve success and prosperity through being able to think right.

The subtle but irrevocable fact is this: *those things that a conscious organism believes are always returned by the Universal Subconscious Mind.*

ATTRACTION IS EVERYWHERE

The proton, vibrating in pure intelligence, attracts to it electrons of such frequency and number as to form an atom of a particular atomic weight: hydrogen, oxygen, iron, gold, uranium. The very earth itself exudes a magnetism that steadies the needles of compasses at sea and delicately counterbalances the centrifugal force of the earth's path around the sun. Dynamic attraction is everywhere present in the universe. Call it what you will—magnetism, polarity, electricity, thought power, moving intelligence—it is everywhere attraction. *Like unto like, the thing to the image, the circumstance to the vision, the answer to the prayer—on this law and this law alone are all things constructed from the atom to the solar system.*

A magnet may attract iron and have no effect on aluminum, and you yourself may attract disease and repel health, but there ends the comparison between physical and mental law. For the magnet by itself cannot change its properties of attraction and repulsion, while you, by changing your thought and belief, can set up an entirely new field of magnetism, and attract those very things that you were repelling before. Thus by refusing to accept ill health, and attaching your beliefs to the perfectness of spirit, you may banish disease from your experience.

STEPPING STONE TO THE STARS

Jesus spoke of the law of attraction and the habit patterns of the Conscious Mind when he said, "Unto him who hath shall be given, and unto him who hath not shall be taken away even that which he hath." He knew that the image and faith of the Conscious Mind was always materialized by the "Father." He knew that a person who saw abundance around him was by that very act calling into existence even more abundance; and he knew that a person who saw lack all about him was by that very act calling into existence an even greater lack. "As ye believe, so shall it be done unto you," he said, and in this simple sentence he stated the law of attraction more truly and concisely than it is ever likely to be stated again.

Every thought you entertain and accept becomes a part of you and inevitably will bring you the physical reality of your image. *All choice is made in the mind, and all acceptance is made by the spirit, and there are not billions of minds in this world at all, but only one, and it is in every one of us.*

It is sheer vanity to bemoan your fate for having been born into lack and limitation and disease, while some other person has been born into abundance and health and is, as a consequence, scarcely touched by evil. When you truly have come to understand that there is only one mind which is every place at the same time and is in all things, you will know that the differences between you and any person on earth are purely

144

illusory. Your "I" may have known lack and limitation, but when you cast these negations out and take on the knowledge of abundance and health, your "I" has changed and you are no longer the same person. True, you still occupy the same body, but even as your surroundings will swiftly change, so your body will become vigorous and unafraid, erect and purposeful, animated by the greatest power in the universe. You can be anything you want to be, do anything you want to do. Born high or born low makes not the slightest difference. Exposed to the veriest evil in the world, you may use it as a stepping stone to the stars, for the Kingdom of God is within, and all the power of the mighty Universal Subconscious Mind awaits your choice and your belief. No more is given to kings than to beggars. We are all born equal for we are all one, and he who disputes this point suffers from vanity, and vanity kills quicker than the hemlock of Socrates.

VANITY—THE KILLER

It is vanity, isolated ego, which is always our undoing. It's "I have to do this," "I have to do that," "I, I, I" when the truth is that "I" does nothing but choose and accept and all things are done by the Universal Subconscious Mind. Popular opinion to the contrary, vanity is more likely to be found among the failures and the diseased and the poverty-stricken than it is among the successful and healthy, for vanity is no more nor less than a sense of *personal* responsibility, an acute sense of ego as being separate and isolated from the Universal Subconscious Mind.

A person who falls prey to disease believes that he must take constant precautions against the invisible microbes which are constantly threatening him. He believes that the whole matter of his being free from ailments depends upon his taking the proper physical precautions at the proper times, and the ritual with which he calls forth the God of Health is contained in bottles and boxes of powders, liquids, and nostrums. It is true that very often these medicaments produce the desired result, for the very obvious reason that the person taking them believes they will. If he in the first place would simply have faith in the perfect spirit that has made his body manifest, he would let go of his sense of personal responsibility, invoke the power of the Subconscious for physical vigor, and never fall prey to disease at all.

THE EVIL OF ISOLATION

It is the same with failure. A man who sets out to achieve anything on the basis that it is all up to him will shortly be engulfed by myriad problems and decisions. *No man alone is big enough to do anything.* He didn't put himself upon this earth; he cannot save himself from departing. All the ingenuity of science cannot make so much as a single blade of grass. As long as a man carries with him a sense of having to do

145

anything all by himself, he will inevitably fail at what he attempts to do. But when he lets go of his vanity, sees his unity with all life and all things, rejects personal isolation, then he invites the great power into his life, and all things are arranged according to the good he desires.

Vanity is an acute sense of separateness. Vanity causes us to see all things and all people as obstacles in our path. Vanity would have us believe that all things are arranged in the physical world rather than on the plane of infinite mind. It draws us in. It closes us up. It causes us to lend reality to evil and negative circumstance. It gives birth to resentment, to belligerence, to hate, and even to violence. How silly and even stupid it is, and yet how difficult to abolish.

The two ends of life are equalizers. Into life we enter naked, and naked we depart. Yet the majority of us act as if the most important thing in all life is to get the best of our neighbors—better clothes, better cars, better jobs. We frustrate ourselves with our isolated egos and spill out our energies on the relentless blade of competition. We set out to deal with the world as if it were an enemy aimed at thwarting us, and the world turns out to be exactly what we conceive it to be, as it always must. The more opposition we see, the more frantic we become, hung on the endless wheel of our own thoughts and conceptions.

In Ecclesiastes we find the remarkable quotation, "Vanity of vanities—all is vanity." The writer of this most astute metaphysical observation knew that man's gravest error was concerned with isolating himself from God, or the Universal Subconscious Mind, in which all things have their being and in which all power is contained. So sad it is to see vanity in the high places or the low, for vanity preludes disaster, as "pride goeth before a fall."

ACKNOWLEDGING THE SENIOR PARTNER

The successful and vigorous person cannot be vain; if he becomes so, he is shortly reduced to failure and lethargy. A man sometimes repeatedly climbs the heights only to fall again to the bottom with a resounding crash. Each time he seems buoyed to the top by a "stroke of luck," and each time that he arrives at the top he chortles, "I did it all by myself, what a great man am I," and down he comes again. Humility regained and the Subconscious again allowed to enter his life, he once more begins the ascent, through another set of "fortunate circumstances." Some men have ridden this whirligig eight or nine times and still are no wiser for it; vanity is a sin so close to the human heart.

This you can rest assured of: The really great and outstanding people of our world have a constant partner, God or the Subconscious Mind, whichever you will; and this partner is consulted on all matters and is acknowledged to be the doer of all their deeds. They, like Jesus, attune themselves to all the power of creation when they acknowledge, "It is not I who doeth the works, but the Father who dwelleth within me."

LET GO AND LET GOD

Overcoming vanity and relaxing into mental attitudes of trust and confidence often have been expressed in the metaphysical saying, "Let go and let God." Yet it would seem from observation of many who quote this saying that they haven't absorbed it. On the one hand, they say, "I trust in God," and on the other, they act as if God were quite untrustworthy. They set out for certain goals, create the attainment of these goals on the plane of mind, and accept the image. But the very first time they observe that the path they are following doesn't coincide with the route *they* believe they should take, they are convinced that God has made a mistake or hasn't heard them in the first place. "I am not going to get there" is their first reaction, and naturally the Subconscious Mind then sees to it that they don't.

You can't predict the Subconscious Mind, and you can't outguess the Subconscious Mind; and if you try, you defeat those very things you have set out to do. It is strange that any of us ever try to tell God how to do things in the first place, since most of us will readily admit that we don't know everything. The Subconscious Mind always works with the perfect knowledge of all times and all places and all people and all things. It must answer billions of different conceptions. Only God knows the way a thing may be done; and man never will, not until his evolution has brought him complete unity with the Universal Subconscious Mind.

But whatever you conceive and accept with faith will be yours, regardless of the apparently circuitous paths and byroads you must follow to its attainment. The road you are guided to take is the only way, there is no other, and as long as you work with the Subconscious Mind your steps and routes are perfect.

TRUST THE ALL-KNOWING MIND

Each of us embarks on life's projects like a man who stands in front of a forest and desires to go through to a lake on the other side. Before the man starts, he hasn't the slightest idea which trees he will pass on the left and which trees he will pass on the right. He cannot foresee the culvert he will meet, or the mucky lowland, or the creek that must be forded. He sees in his mind only a straight line leading from his side of the forest to the lake, and along this line he starts as the shortest distance between two points.

A tree lies fallen across his path; he skirts it. He conies to the swamp; he walks around it. He comes to the culvert and again swings off his straight route to avoid an obstacle. Does he become discouraged each time he must vary from the straight line which he has projected as the shortest route to the lake? If he does he will say, "I can't get there," and the Subconscious Mind will turn him around and march him back to his starting point, and he will have failed. *But the Subconscious Mind won't have failed.* It will have answered his most recent conviction as it always must.

The man who says, "I can't," is a failure and unhappy, but he nevertheless arrives back at his starting place unharmed, guided to return there by the Subconscious Mind. It is the man who cuts himself off from God, the man whose vanity isolates him from the Subconscious Mind, who is in the real danger. He says, "God made a mistake and doesn't know how to do this, because I know that the shortest distance between two points is a straight line. Therefore I will climb over the fallen tree and proceed on my way." He does, and the tree is rotten and collapses on him, and the fall breaks his leg. Or if he safely passes the tree and proceeds through the swamp, he is caught in the quicksand. Or if he passes the tree and the swamp and walks through the culvert, he is bitten by a rattlesnake. Thus the man who predicts the way the Subconscious Mind must work is never following anything other than his own dictates, which will surely visit limitation and lack and even disaster upon him finally.

For our traveler by himself cannot know of the rotten tree and the quicksand and the rattlesnake, but God does; and he who conceives his goal with faith and never falters no matter the bends in the road will surely arrive at his destination; and always by the most perfect path.

THE INVINCIBLE GUIDE

From the twenty-third Psalm: "Lo, though I walk through the valley of the shadow of death, I fear no evil, for thou art with me." God is wherever you are, always guiding you. He forever guides you to each of your conceptions, for He answers in physical reality that which you conceive and accept in your mind. If you conceive and accept good you will be guided along the most perfect path to its attainment, no matter how winding and circuitous the route may seem to your limited knowledge.

Thus "Let go and let God" means to trust God, to trust in the perfect knowledge of the Subconscious Mind, to know whatever paths you travel toward your goals are the right ones, the only ones, the perfect ones, for you have been set upon them by the omnipotent mind of God, which makes no mistakes and will deliver you safely and prepared at your destination.

"Let go and let God" means to recognize that you do nothing but observe and accept, and whatever you accept is delivered to you by the Subconscious Mind. There is no personal responsibility for anything but thought, for accepted thoughts become manifest in the physical world.

AWAY WITH VANITY AND GUILT

Cast aside your vanity. You do nothing by yourself, and you are never alone. All things are done by the Universal Subconscious Mind, which is always right where you are. You are not isolated from the world; you are a part of it and at the same time the whole of it. The world is your friend if you are friendly with yourself. If you make it your enemy, you fight only yourself. Be humble in the fact of accomplishment, for you do nothing but conceive and accept it. God does everything. He writes all the books, paints all the pictures, builds all the bridges. His instruments are those who attune themselves to His presence and allow the power to flow through.

Cast aside your guilt. Who does not make mistakes? Do not feel guilty for mistakes in thought and subsequently in deed, for it is this path man must travel to become one with God. Guilt has no place in life. Mistakes are for learning. Guilt holds onto mistakes and makes them happen again. Guilt isolates you from the Subconscious Mind. Guilt brings about vanity, the vanity of being alone, without God. Vanity and guilt are the destroyers of attunement, errors of growing self-consciousness, creators of illusion and evil.

Feel your unity with all things and all life and you will see vanity slip away. Know only the eternal now of the Subconscious Mind, no past, no future, only a present that is always existing, and you will feel guilt dissolve. God is in you, has done what you have done, and God does not chastise himself, nor destroy himself.

Be born anew in the words of Emerson:

> *On this altar God has built*
> *I lay my vanity and guilt.*

Be done with it! Shame and remorse are poisonous weeds to plant in the Subconscious, and vanity isolates you from the power of the Subconscious Mind. Be alert for these harbingers of evil. Allow them to enter your life no more.

GOD KNOWS HOW

The law of attraction is the law of the manifestation of beliefs and desires, and the method by which this law may be controlled so as to produce only good is by refusing to accept evil. *When you have envisaged a goal and created its attainment on the plane of mind, nothing can stop you from realizing that goal but the creation of your failure on the plane of mind.* You may run into setbacks, into circumstances that appear to be preventing you from arriving at your destination, but these are not setbacks at all; they are steps forward. In fact, they are the only steps forward possible for you 10 make and still arrive at your goal. Since you don't know as much as the Subconscious Mind, you cannot predict the path by which it will take you to your destination.

In your limited knowledge of the things and circumstances and motives of the world, you may decide that in order to arrive at your destination it is necessary for you to take a certain step at a certain time at a certain place, when the truth is that such a step actually taken would result in disaster. When you are frustrated in taking this step, you visualize the defeat of your plans and come to believe that evil has been visited on you instead of good. Thus you lose your trust in God, in the Universal Subconscious Mind and the immutable laws of the universe. You start thinking defeat and evil, with the result that they inevitably will be visited upon you.

There is absolutely only one way to make the law work in your favor, and that is to trust it completely and not predict it.

IN EVERY OBSTACLE—OPPORTUNITY

The moment you start predicting the path you should take toward any goal, you will find your faith challenged at every fork in the road, at every by-path, at every apparent obstacle. But when you have learned to trust the law completely, you will begin to see every delay and every obstacle as opportunities whereby you may become fit and ready for what awaits you when you arrive at your destination.

For example, a young man decides to become an engineer. Were he to be given the job of building a bridge the next day, he would fail miserably. But as long as he holds his image and desire and faith clearly, the Subconscious Mind will deliver him fit and ready for his appointment with bridge-building. In the interim there may be five or six years of engineering education, perhaps several jobs in which he fully masters his science. And lo, the day arrives when the assignment is his and he is outfitted with the tools to conquer it, and every step of the way he has been in the hands of the omnipotent and omniscient Subconscious Mind.

There is no such thing as failure unless it is accepted. There is no such thing as defeat unless it is accepted. There is no such thing as evil unless it is accepted.

Let go of your feeling of personal responsibility and turn everything over to the Universal Subconscious Mind. Don't predict the way this Mind shall work. Accept your appointed tasks and circumstances with complete faith that they will provide the perfect path to the attainment of your desires. Evil and failure and defeat and disease cannot touch you if you will refuse to accept them. Only what you accept comes to you finally; all else is but temporary and merely a step to your goal. Such is the law of attraction, a law that never fails.

One more warning. Do not keep examining your goal to see if you have attained it. "A watched pot never boils" for the simple reason that you are watching it when it isn't boiling and this is the thought that you project into the Subconscious Mind. Rest assured of the eventual accomplishment of your goal and take pleasure and wisdom from each experience along the way. If life were only moments of victory, it would be very short indeed. Learn to enjoy the journey.

TRIUMPH OVER CIRCUMSTANCE

A middle-aged man in a midwestern city resigned a secure job and invested his life savings in a small manufacturing plant. Shortly afterward the aircraft parts for which his machinery had been designed became obsolete. There seemed no alternative other than to close his doors and face the loss of his investment. "Oh, but I was bitter," he said. "I felt the whole world was an injustice.

"Then one morning I read three words: 'Nothing is wasted.' I went down to the plant alone. It was quiet inside, and I wandered around. I picked up one of the gadgets we had been making, and it seemed different, as if I had never seen it before. It would make a terrific toy, I thought. Immediately I was certain of it. I rushed to the nearest phone and called my foreman. We worked all night on plans. Next morning we gave them to a sales agency. Within two weeks we were m production. Believe me, I'll never accept defeat again."

Today his toy manufacturing business is worth more than a million dollars!

A married woman with two school-aged children was near the verge of hysteria at the arrival of a third child. "To think, she wailed, "that I've gone through eight years of diapers, formulas, inoculations, laundry, meals, cleaning, and baby-sitters, always looking forward to the day when the kids would be in school and I'd have some time of my own. Now I've got to go through it all over again."

"Not unless you want to," she was told.

"Of course I don't want to," she said.

"Then try this. Make up your mind that the greatest thing that ever happened to you was the birth of your third child."

She was doubtful, but promised to give it a try.

Before a year was out her husband had made an astonishing success in his business, and they were able to afford help in the house. She herself was successfully operating a small mail-order business. She was playing golf once a week. She had just returned with her husband from a trip to Mexico City. She was brimming with enthusiasm and joy.

"What a tremendous lesson!" she said. "Now I know that everything depends on one's own attitude!"

An energetic business executive was disconsolate at being retired on his sixty-fifth birthday. He felt he had been "put on the shelf," that life had no further use for him. He used his leisure only to brood.

"I've been scrapped," he complained. "Life has passed me by."

"Not surprising," he was told. "Life usually passes by those who suffer from P.L.O.M."

"What's that?" he asked,

"Poor Little Old Me," was the answer.

He scowled, as if to take offense. Then he smiled. "Is there a cure for it?" he asked.

"Just quit feeling sorry for yourself."

His chin jutted out, and the cure was effected that moment. Today he and his wife have a busy stamp store and are so active in philatelist societies that he no longer has time to brood. And how pleased he is to prescribe the never-failing cure for a severe case of P.L.O.M.

A young clerk was struck by a trolley car and lost the use of his legs. His family and friends were horrified, certain he would eventually become a ward of the state. Only a short time later they were very surprised to find him operating a thriving advertising agency.

"However did you manage?" they asked him. "You can't even get out of bed."

"My mind can," he said. "That's all that's necessary."

THOUGHT ATMOSPHERE

It is an inescapable fact that each human being who lives is surrounded by a subtle but powerful thought atmosphere. We are accustomed to believe that thoughts are invisible, yet we mark the existence of thousands of them with our very eyes each day. The thought of each man stands written on his face, on his brow, in the expression of his eyes, in the set of his lips, the carriage of his head, his posture, his bearing, his demeanor, in the tone of his conversation, his character, his successes, his failures, his very life. Let a man walk into a room where you are, and you immediately are conscious of the thought atmosphere that surrounds him. Your very first reaction is that you either like him or you don't. It isn't the man that prompts you to this instinctive decision—*it is the kind of thoughts he thinks!* His mental atmosphere reaches out and contacts yours immediately. If it is similar, you are attracted to him. If it is opposed, you dislike him. Only a modification of thinking on the part of one or both of you can change this, for like gravitates to like in the Universal Subconscious Mind and throughout all nature.

Each of us seeks for good to enter his life. Even when we become negative thinkers and hopeless and defeated, it is still good we seek. The reality we have lent to evil has brought us to the final imbecility of thinking negatively and hoping for the positive. Patterns of negative thinking seem our only means of coping with a world which appears bent on denying all our goals and aims and desires. These are our Prompters, the crosses we bear as we go through life. *Karma* it is called by the Indian religions—that which would deny us the unlimited abundance and good of life. And it is sheer idiocy.

The Universal Subconscious Mind denies us nothing. Nature denies us nothing. We always get exactly what we have asked for. There is no lack, limitation, failure, or despair which we do not create for ourselves in our own minds. And it is just as simple, in fact downright simpler, to create abundance and success and health in our minds and thus experience them in the physical world.

NO LIMITATION

There are no limitations for God. There is no lack in the Universal Subconscious Mind. Whatever you dare ask for will be given; and you need only ask and have faith.

> *Hast not thy share? On winged feet*
> *Lo! It rushes thee to meet;*
> *And all that Nature made thy own*
> *Floating in air and pent in stone*
> *Will rive the hills and swim the sea*
> *And like thy shadow follow thee.* —Emerson

153

The great lesson we all have to learn is to think only positively of good. For in seeking good and thinking evil, we destroy our very lives on the sharp edge of the law of attraction and manifestation. Each negative thought that finds root in our acceptance brings upon us the very opposite of that which we seek. Frustration, illness, defeat, hopelessness, despair—are all the result of our desiring good and thinking negatively, for we have not the slightest chance of attaining good as long as we are creating evil with our thought.

Thus it is that we have embarked upon the thirty-day mental diet. Thus it is that you are advised today as Jesus advised so long ago: "Seek ye first the Kingdom of Heaven and all things will be added unto you."

THE CENTER OF CONSCIOUSNESS

The Kingdom of Heaven is the center of consciousness. The Kingdom of Heaven is that place of utter calm and serenity within the depths of your soul where your "I" becomes fused with the immortal "I" of all creation. It is the place where you no longer are the "doer" but instead become fused with the observer, the great contemplator, at the place where there is naught for you to do but choose and accept, where whatever is so chosen and so accepted becomes manifest in the physical world about you.

Communion with your center of consciousness, the practice of the meditations, the thirty-day mental diet will provide the tools with which you may banish negative thinking from your mind forever. Through these tools you will build strong habits of positive thinking that will be your bulwark against every negative circumstance that crosses your path. And negative circumstance *will* cross your path. That is, circumstances that *appear* to be negative will cross your path. They will appear to be negative for they will be detours from the path which you have projected for yourself, but they actually will be perfect steps toward your goal in the infinite wisdom of the Universal Subconscious Mind. It is only when you *accept* them as evil that they become evil; otherwise they are but temporary and dissolve immediately when they are refused the impetus of conviction.

Habits of positive thinking, firmly ingrained, strongly built, will sustain you no matter the height of the seas, the strength of the tempest, or the fury of the storm. "Peace! Be Still!" will be your order, and the seas will abate in the face of your faith.

> *Lowly faithful, banish fear*
> *Right onward drive unharmed*
> *The port, well worth the cruise is near,*
> *And every wave is charmed.* —Emerson

Know your center of consciousness. Retreat into it in your time of meditation until you *know!* Here is the place where all things in this world and the next are done, and once having arrived at it, there can be no terror or fear or disquiet for you ever again. Remember, the center of consciousness, the Kingdom of Heaven, is the place where you become the *observer,* where even thoughts are things to be *observed.* It is a place of complete calm and quiet, a place of absolute sureness, a place of communion with the Universal Subconscious Mind.

FIRST CAUSE

We have said a good deal about all first causes being mental and everything being first created on the plane of mind. We have said that each of us has no responsibility other than for his thoughts and his beliefs. And so the modern day Sadducees and Pharisees come to us and say, "Man is a builder and a doer with his hands, and it is falsehood to say that man can achieve by taking thought." Or perhaps you have confided to a friend that in your meditations you are treating yourself for some particular goal, and your friend has said, "What foolishness! If you are after what you say you are, then quit mooning around with that mumbo-jumbo and go out and get it." And many a man on the right track has been led off the path by such false counsel.

Nobody achieves anything by "going out and getting it." The very premise insinuates at the outset that he believes whatever he is after belongs to somebody else and he has to "take it away." When a man has created on the plane of mind the conviction that whatever he is after is already his, he will be guided in the proper paths and in the proper action that will achieve his goal. Action of itself produces nothing. There is true action and there is false action, and false action will not remove a molehill, while true action will dissolve a mountain. *True action is neither more nor less than true thought, for action follows thought.* If your thought is true, your action will be impeccably guided by the Subconscious Mind.

HOW TO USE YOUR WILL

We have previously raised cautions against willing things to happen, on the premise that will is usually directed at overcoming physical objects and circumstances which may very well be part of a perfect plan by which Universal Mind is guiding you to your destination. The danger of exercising will to attain specific things is that of isolating yourself from the power for good which you have invoked. On the one hand, you have called upon the power with faith and conviction; on the other, by the exercise of will you may easily deny it, or set it to working in another direction. Consequently all effort should be aimed at attunement with Universal Mind, at arriving at a point of consciousness where you have complete faith and trust that the infinite power of universal intelligence will deliver to you the image of your faith. Any subsequent attempt to direct your will at the circumstances that come your way is an imposition on the plan of Universal Intelligence. You are not bigger than God. Willing against the plan by which He is delivering your desires will abrogate that plan at once and set the power to moving in a different direction.

Do not direct your will toward the physical world. It avails you nothing, and in the end defeats you.

However, there is one very important place for you to exercise will, and that is in your choke of thoughts. When you retreat into your center of consciousness, to the place where you become but an observer, you may will the type of thoughts that cross your consciousness. Here is the basis of the law of attraction. *Whatever you will to think, you think.* Whatever type of thought you choose is automatically attracted to you.

It is therefore will which is the basis of the law of attraction, but will to think right only, and not will to change the objects and circumstances of your physical world through thought power or physical action.

Deliberately guard your thoughts. Deliberately choose to think only those thoughts which are in the image of your true desire. Refuse to accept any others. By this correct application of will on the mental plane, the outside world grows into the image of your desire.

From the Dhammapada: "All that we are is the result of what we have thought; it is founded on our thoughts, it is made up of our thoughts . . . Let the wise man guard his thoughts; there is no fear in him while he is watchful."

ATTRACTION IS MENTAL CHOICE

It is will to think right that attracts the proper thoughts. These thoughts move across your center of consciousness, are taken unto you and accepted. From that point the law of creation is invoked, and whatever you have accepted will be created for you in the physical world.

The law of attraction is neither more nor less than the law of attracting thoughts; and it is done by a process of choice. Whatever you choose to think is sent to you from the limitless reaches of universal intelligence. These thoughts, once having been accepted by you, will manifest in the physical world.

Willing to think the right thoughts is the basis of all accomplishment, all vigor, all success, all health, all happiness. *It is from here, this point of first choice, that everything in the universe starts.* It is first cause—consciousness making a choice. It is the primal question of all creation. What will you think? Once the choice is made, your life is but a reflection of your thoughts made manifest; you choose every circumstance and thing about you in that first choice when you decide what you will think.

Pascal says, "Thought constitutes the greatness in man." Schopenhauer says, "The world is my idea." The Vedanta philosophy of ancient India says that matter has no existence independent of mental perception. *Mind is the mighty mover!*

What will you think? The choice is yours and yours alone, the only true choice which you have in your life. Through it all things will be delivered to you, for good or evil, according to your choice. For the mighty power of the Universal Subconscious Mind will create in the physical world the image of your thought; such is its law and its nature and it can do nothing else. Hell or heaven are choices you make for yourself. The Universal Subconscious Mind knows neither; it only answers your thought.

THE PATH TO ILLUMINATION

Pascal says, "All dignity lies in thought. By it we must elevate ourselves, and not by space and time, which we cannot fill." He says further: "These are only two kinds of people who can be called reasonable; those who serve God with all their heart because they know Him, and those who seek him with all their heart because they do not know Him."

The first man is both reasonable and happy. The second is reasonable and unhappy. *But a man who neither knows God nor seeks him is foolish as well as unhappy.*

Thus the greatest adventure in life is to come to know the Universal Subconscious Mind for its infinite power, and to learn how to use this power to fill our lives with good and abundance. At the end of such a path lies a magnificent spiritual awakening, a transfiguration, a key to life's mysteries, an understanding of the meaning of "All things indwelling in God, and God dwelling in all things."

The Key itself is only three words, words which have no magic of themselves but contain such astounding significance that only a fully prepared mind may grasp it. You will do well to ponder on what this Key might be. Search the quotation above for possible meanings and dwell on them during your meditation periods, when you retreat into your center of consciousness. Illumination may come before the final chapter, is sure to be yours at the end.

MIND AND ACTION

Life is dynamic. All about you are the manifold evidences of nature's eternal process of becoming things'. Nothing remains static. Wherever you look your eye sees movement and flow and change. Birth and death are the rhythms by which Nature reaches ever upward, seeking, constantly seeking. Know! Learn! Build! These inexorable commands issue from every bud, egg, flower, bush, tree, in a crescendo of evolving life,

In view of this busy universe of ours, perhaps it seems strange that you are told that the path to power and accomplishment lies in getting your physical body quiet and working only with your mind. Perhaps, like so many others, you feel you should thrust yourself into the midst of the fray, take and grab and fight for what you want. When Jesus said, "Those who take up the sword die by the sword," he wasn't talking about soldiers only, for whoever enters aggressively into life with the aim of taking by force or cleverness will find himself dealt with the same way. Since life is bigger than he, the final victor is obvious.

Do not be concerned with action. Action is natural. Life and movement are synonymous. Concern yourself rather with guidance for your action. Know that all action springs from thought, that when your thought is true so will your action be. Action which is governed solely by stimuli received from the outer world is false action and can result in nothing other than the frustration of your desires. You dissipate your energies every time you attack an obstacle or a circumstance as a purely physical thing. No man is big enough to do anything by himself. The most frantic of your energies cannot change a wave of the sea, or the color of the grass, or the spread of a tree. *Man who made himself not, who knoweth himself not, who liveth among phantoms he knoweth not of, what imbecility possesses him that he should attempt to mold the world by force?* Wherever he looks he sees the work of the power greater than he is. He cannot fight this power. He can only attune himself to it, work in accord with it.

Thus it is true action we are concerned with, and not action for action's sake. True action springs from true thought, and true thought springs from a man's cloistering himself in meditation with the Universal Subconscious Mind. He who moves with God moves with power, and his action is rewarded. The great men of this world accomplish in an hour what other mortals accomplish in a year. Yet they are not more active. Their activity is guided, powerful, sure, because they are directed to their objectives by the unlimited resources and power of the Universal Subconscious Mind. To such men, lack and limitation and failure and disease are barely possible of understanding. They can scarcely conceive of them.

THE LEGEND OF THE "GO-GETTER"

This world of ours does not belong to the "go-getter." It never has and it never will. The frantic man who throbs out his life chasing power or prestige or fame is assured of one thing only—bad health. The worlds he fights he can never subdue; ulcers eat holes in his stomach, tired heart muscles give way, taut nerves come unstrung. Nobody can beat the universe, and that is what the "go-getter" sets out to do. He cannot be successful because he is too vain. Having no humility, he does not know that all things are done by a mighty lord, an unknown sage that inhabits all places and all times. Without this knowledge the "go-getter" is a molecule, vibrating and rebounding crazily in the limits he has imposed upon himself. He has no design to his life because he does not see the design of life itself.

Disdain the life of a "go-getter." Move with God, with dignity and surety. Give no thought to action, for thought produces action, as naturally as light comes from the sun. All things are decided in the mind, and all decisions are carried out by the invincible Universal Mind.

There is only one life, one mind, one "I," one Self manifesting an infinite number of things and beings. According to your awareness, you approach the power of this Self. Know that first cause is within, first decision is made by choosing which thoughts you will think. Whatever you think will manifest in your life. Think only positively; refuse to accept negative circumstance as having any final reality; keep your thoughts steadfast on the good; maintain your image with the fuel of your faith; and you will discover a universe of limitless supply and limitless reward, constant adventure, and everlasting love.

Know that every idea produces itself on the physical plane, in an effect exactly like the cause. Place no limits on your thinking. All things are possible. The moment they are considered probable, they become certainty.

Space itself is only that which accommodates movement. Matter itself is only that which illustrates movement. Space and matter and movement are nothing more than intelligence working with, through, and upon itself. Everything is made of this intelligence. It becomes all things; it can become anything.

THE REAL YOU

Don't confuse what you seem to be with what you really are. To the real you, the indwelling Self, the observer in the depths of /our soul, nothing is impossible. Give heed to this Dweller. Give Him homage and respect and humility. Your body is His temple. Would you surround it with evil and disease and want and lack and failure? Refuse to accept these limitations; they are illusions. The universe is all vigor and all health and all abundance. What you choose to accept and think you will see. *Wl you seem to be is but the barest fraction of what you really are.*

Refuse to think of yourself as a name, as a holder of a job, as a person who resides in a certain town in a certain country on a certain date, as a person who has had a certain history. That is what you seem to be. In the solitude of a silent room, in a shaded glen, on a hillside, in a meadow, or on a crag overlooking the ocean, turn your thoughts within to the real you. Slow your breathing until you feel complete peace and relaxation. Retreat into the depth of your being until your very thoughts are things to be observed. Ask yourself, "Who is this that observes?" *The real you is a mighty truth, a clarion call in the greatest age of man.*

Let the spiritual element rule your life. Give each of your problems to Universal Subconscious Mind and listen for the answer. When the answer comes, accept it with complete confidence and faith. Do not allow negations to steal into your mind like thieves in the night, for they will rob you of your greatest treasures. Close your mind to all evil, to all lack, to all limitation, to all disease. Into your consciousness come the most important of all things—your thoughts. They come not merely to visit with you; they come to take root and make themselves known as the physical things of your life. Bar the door to all negation. Post a permanent sentinel in letters bold and black. "None but the positive and the good shall enter here." And thus will your life be.

MUTUAL EXCHANGE IS THE LAW

See the movement and flow of life as a great exchange between all beings. All things must be paid for; mutual exchange is the law. You get because you give. You sell, but only so you can buy. There is no such thing as independence; it is a hallucination of the most foolish sort. We are all dependent upon one another, for we are all component parts of a great whole. You cannot live without your neighbor, and he cannot live without you. What you contribute to him, he will return in measure to you. Perhaps the measure is money; perhaps not. But whether the price is in dollars, or pesos, or francs, or bushels, or quarts, the price is there still. And what you receive you must pay for, and what you contribute you will be rewarded for. There are no bargains. The exchange is always equal, regardless of how it may look at the moment.

Retreat daily into communion with the Universal Subconscious Mind. Find your center of consciousness in the quietness of your meditations. Only in this way can you truly know yourself for what you really are and thus absolve any confusion with what you seem to be. The knowledge of what you truly are is at the center of your consciousness, the "I," the observer, the Self, unto whom all things are possible.

160

SLAY THE SPIRIT OF GRAVITY

We mustn't pursue these studies with long faces and melancholy. Life is laughter and excitement and joy. Life is singing and dancing and fellowship: The melancholy mien and the grave countenance are never worth whatever wisdom they might produce. They defeat the God in man because they cannot laugh. Nietzsche says, "Let us slay the spirit of gravity—not by wrath, but by laughter. He who laughs is full of hope, but he whose countenance is stony has given way to despair, and thus has defeated himself no matter what he has learned.

This is an adventure, a great excitement, that fills the heavens with its grandeur. "The good news I bring you," said Jesus, "is that the Kingdom of Heaven is within."

Can we possibly be morose or melancholy on learning that the entire power of the universe dwells within each of us? Can there possibly be anything saddening in learning that we can use this power to fill our lives with good and abundance? This is good news, big news, a news that calls for celebration, for singing, for dancing, for elation. The universe cradles us in everlasting arms. We are eternal, immortal, everlastingly one, and the nature of our true being will work for us here on earth even as it does in heaven.

AFTER THIS MANNER PRAY YE

Let us, for the moment, transpose the Lord's Prayer into the language of this study, so that we may thoroughly understand what Jesus knew when he said, "After this manner therefore pray ye."

I know the Universal Subconscious Mind dwells within me and is all-powerful

May the truth of this power be revealed to me, and may I work in accord with it, for it is perfect.

There is no limit to abundance, and the universe will provide me with all that I need.

I let go of vanity and am not tempted into thinking evil through seeing evil

I know the real truth and the real power is within me—one, eternal, and everlasting.

All things are made from universal intelligence. All things exist in universal intelligence. All form proceeds from thought, and thought is the first cause for all things. We are able to choose what we will think, and once having chosen, nothing can stop our decisions from becoming real in the physical world. Thus the law of attraction is the law of choosing thoughts. Whatever we choose to think we will think;

Summary

and whatever we think becomes real in our lives. Choose to think calmly that which you really desire; refuse to entertain any thoughts of what you fear; and you will find you are unerringly guided to your goals by a power greater than you are.

REVIEW

1. Every center of life force attracts those thought-things that answer its mental vibrations.

2. Because we think and desire, we are praying every minute of our lives.

3. To alter your life you must alter your thinking.

4. Every form and substance in the universe exudes a subtle attraction, powerful in proportion to awareness.

5. What man accepts, God creates.

6. Vanity is a sense of independent ego, and isolates a man from the Universal Subconscious Mind. *God*

7. Vanity breeds a sense of personal responsibility, and personal responsibility denies the power of the Universal Mind.

8. A human being has no personal responsibility other than for the thoughts he chooses to think.

9. He who lives by a doctrine of personal responsibility sees the entire universe as his foe.

10. He who lives by a doctrine of attunement sees the entire universe rushing to do his bidding.

11. Make your decisions in the mind, and trust the Universal Mind to carry them out. Refuse to accept apparent delay and detour as anything other than the perfect path'.

12. Don't predict the manner in which Universal Mind should carry you to your goals. It has the knowledge of all things and all times and thus automatically knows the perfect path. The human being has only a limited knowledge of a certain place and certain time and thus, by himself, cannot know the perfect path.

13. Don't batter and rail against unwanted circumstances, but "let go and let God." Denying the power that guides you will leave you adrift with insurmountable

give no power to unwanted

problems.

14. A man by himself is a microbe. A man attuned to his inner Self is a universe.

15. Mistakes are for learning and not to carry around with you as a burden. Refuse to accept guilt. God is in you, and God is not guilty.

16. Do not keep examining your goals when they are not yet attained. If you keep projecting lack of attainment into the Universal Subconscious Mind, you can expect nothing else in return.

17. When you have created something on the plane of mind you must know that it is done. Nothing can stop it from manifesting in the physical world. Keep your faith and conviction no matter the apparent obstacles. Look for opportunity in each obstacle.

18. The Kingdom of Heaven is the center of consciousness. Know it, and all things will be added unto you.

19. Action of itself produces nothing. Only true action creates, and true action springs from true thought.

20. The one place the human can exercise will is at the center of his consciousness, where he can will to think whatever he wishes.

21. Take more heed to your thought than to the world about you, for your thought brings the world about you.

22. In meditation ponder the meaning of "All things indwelling in God, and God dwelling in all things."

23. Be not busy or in a hurry. There is nothing to fight and nobody to beat. These are only things to learn and awareness to be obtained. God moves with sureness.

24. Don't confuse what you seem to be with what you really are. You are never what you seem to be, and always what you really are, which is within you, at the center of your consciousness.

25. Let the spiritual element rule every decision of your life.

26. Refuse to accept melancholy or sadness. The universe sings and dances.

27. Choose the thought. Once you accept it, the thing in its image will be yours.

SPIRITUAL TREATMENT

Be sure that you successfully complete the Thirty-Day Mental Diet. Only in this manner will you be able to completely demonstrate the power of positive thinking. Do not forget to seek your center of consciousness daily, just prior to your period of meditation. These procedures are living tools. Use them.

Each of the meditations in this book are spiritual treatments, aimed at bringing your life into harmony with good, into harmony with the power of the Universal Subconscious Mind. You may use these meditations to give spiritual treatments to your friends or loved ones, or to any one you wish to help. Simply substitute "he" or "she" or the person's name where "I" is used in the text, and you will shortly make demonstrations. Our Prompters are lulled when we give a treatment to someone else, and very often we are able to demonstrate for them before we are able to demonstrate for ourselves. Don't hesitate to tackle any of the problems of your friends or loved ones, but do not confide that you are treating for them. "The wise man doeth his alms in secret."

RECOMMENDED READING

Thought Power by Annie Besant. Published by Theosophical Publishing House.

SEVENTH MEDITATION

I do not confuse what I seem to be with what I really am. I am never what I seem to be, and always what I really am — host to the indwelling God. I quiet the movements of my body, slow my breathing, and glide deep into the recesses of my being, to the very center of my consciousness. Here in this place of infinite calm I become one with the immortal Self of the world, and I observe. My thoughts cross my consciousness in a never-ending stream. I do not create these thoughts. They come from the infinite reaches of the Universal Subconscious Mind and are directed to my consciousness, for I have attracted them. I may choose any thoughts I desire. I have but to decide, and the ideas and images I have chosen are directed to me. As I accept them so will they manifest in my world. I alone decide what I will think; thus I decide my entire life. I bar the door of my mind to negative thoughts or thoughts of evil. The door is always open to admit the positive, the good, the beautiful and the aspiring. I have complete confidence in the wisdom and the power of the Universal Subconscious Mind. I do not predict the manner in which each of my thoughts will manifest; I have complete faith that God moves in the most perfect manner. There is DO such thing as lack unless it is accepted; the universe has infinite supply. Vigor and health, abundance and success are mine, for I choose only such thoughts. Love abounds in a universe where I am one with the immortal Self, the Universal Subconscious Mind, God. My every decision is answered from a perfect and inexhaustible source of power.

Chapter 8 - LOVE

No gate too strait, no journey too far
When the path is lit by the gleam
Of the radiant rays of the guiding star
Of love, the law that's supreme

LOVE GOVERNS ALL

Much has been written and said of love. Poets have extolled it; musicians have sung about it; ballad and play and story are ever unfolding its many-sided drama. "Here is the truth about love," they say, and present romantic love, a half-truth only, and nearly all the world is deluded. The surging, welling, emotional searching that throbs within the breast of each human being can never be reduced only to a rapport between the sexes. Our literature and our education have inhibited us into believing that the end-all of love is the finding of a mate, and our divorce courts and psychiatrists' offices play host to multitudes of unhappy and disillusioned people who have discovered that this is not so. Into one of his strongest "physical drives, man has channeled his strongest emotional drive, and while there is riot the slightest valid reason that they shouldn't work in conjunction, it is apparent that often they do not. The home and marriage provide simultaneous release for man's sexual drive and the reproductive necessities of society, but neither of these very admirable institutions is in any way a school for love. *For no person cart love another unless he loves humanity first!*

Love is all. God is love. It is the nature of our basic unity, the underlying dim remembrance of complete spiritual oneness, that keeps us forever seeking union with others. From Universal Mind we have been differentiated into separateness, isolated within a fleshy prison, and throughout our incarnation in life we reach out to receive and to give and to commune —to return again to complete unity. Beauty, courage, loyalty, perseverance, creation are all born of love successfully given and received. Distortion, fear, iniquity, hate, resentment, violence, and failure are all born of love frustrated. Thus it is love that governs all—the supreme law of life.

Spake Jesus, "Thou shall love the Lord thy God with all thy heart and with all thy soul and with all thy mind. This is the first and greatest commandment. And the second is like unto it, Thou shall love thy neighbor as thyself."

THE CONSTANT SEARCH

We are evolved from pure and eternal spirit, from a place where space and time and number do not exist. From infinity we are thrust into finiteness, perceive space and time and number and separateness and other things and beings. Is it any wonder that the terrible longing grows within us, to have and hold, to take and be taken, to give and receive, to share, to reach for an earthly realization of that complete sense of belonging that can only be known in absolute unity? Love we seek above all things, for we have known absolute love and are lost without it; and all our hurts are received when our reachings for love are rejected; and all the Prompters of the Subconscious Mind are planted by the buried pain remembrances of our love rejections.

The Apostle Paul wrote:

Though I speak with the tongues of men and of angels, and have not Love, I am become as sounding brass, or a tinkling cymbal. And though I have the gift of prophecy, and understand all mysteries, and all knowledge; and though I have all faith, so that I could remove mountains, and have not Love, I am nothing. And though I could bestow all my goods to feed the poor, and though I give my body to be burned, and have not Love, it profiteth me nothing.

Love suffereth long, and is kind; Love envieth not; Love vaunteth not itself, is not puffed up, doth not behave itself unseemly, seeketh not her own, is not easily provoked, thinketh no evil; rejoiceth not in iniquity, but rejoiceth in truth; beareth all things, believeth all things, hopeth all things, endureth all things.

Love never faileth: but whether there be prophecies, they shall fail; whether there be tongues, they shall cease; whether there be knowledge, it shall vanish away. For we know in part, and we prophesy in part. But when that which is perfect shall come, then that which is in part shall be done away.

When I was a child, I spake as a child, I understood as a child, I thought as a child; but when I became a man, I put away childish things. For now we see through a glass, darkly; but then face to face: now I know in part; but then I know as also I am known. And now abideth Faith, Hope, Love, these three; but the greatest of these is Love.

In this life we are isolated from the Universal Subconscious Mind. In our separateness, we see through a glass, darkly. In our separateness, we long for the unity that rests at the crux of our Subconscious, and this is our motivating force, love. According to how we are able to give and receive it, all things in life come to us. The time will arrive when face to face we shall know as we are known, for the Universal Subconscious Mind is complete unity and thus is love itself, and we shall return to it.

SPIRITUAL UNITY

The negation of love is fear, and fear is the father to hate, and fear and hate through all their varying degrees are the seeds from which all evil grows. Is it any wonder, then, that love will overcome all, for with love there is no fear, and with love there is no hate; with love there is no opposition.

True love, then, is simply recognition of the spiritual unity of all life. Once you have realized completely that you and your neighbor are one, it is no longer possible for you to perform an unseemly act against your neighbor; it would be as if you performed it against yourself. Nor can you hate your enemy, for your enemy is also one with you, as like unto you as your very self. All life and all matter are but manifold manifestations of the one immortal Self, the Universal Subconscious Mind. It is not the nature of this Mind to chastise itself, to fight with itself, or to destroy itself. Anyone who regards life as a battle, who seeks to beat others or destroy them, is doing neither more nor less than beating himself or destroying himself. One! One! One! sings the Universe. We are all sprung from one intelligence. We all return to one intelligence. There is but one immortal underlying Self to all creation. Separated from it in our physical bodies, we desire to know this complete unity again, and it is to this emotional drive that we give the name of love.

The child in his crib desires all things, asks for all things, has complete confidence that all things shall be delivered unto him for the asking, so recently has he come from the unity wherein there never was denial. Only slowly does the child come to know that there are other beings than itself who must be considered. Day by day the child learns it cannot have this, it must do without that, it must conduct itself this way and that way. If the child perceives that these denials are directed to it with love, if it is aware of care and companionship and tenderness and concern, it rapidly becomes accustomed to consideration and mutual exchange. But if the child is aware of malice or anger with each denial, then rejection and fear take root. Once reality is given fear, hate is born; for people fear that which they think may hurt them, and once hurt, they hate the hurter.

Thus fear and hate are reactions to frustrated love. Fear is directed at that which we anticipate will reject our love, and hate is directed at that which has already rejected it. But always our motivations are aimed at finding fulfillment of the urge to unity that wells forever in our Subconscious.

HATE AND LOVE

So hate is akin to love and is the working of the exact same force. Hate is the negation of love, just as poverty is the negation of abundance. There is only one force at work in love and hate; in love it works positively, in hate it works negatively, and in fear it doesn't work at all, but chatters unfulfilled and undecided in one spot, now moving tentatively forward, now moving tentatively backward.

Few will dispute the power of love, but the vast majority of us have great difficulty bringing it into all aspects of our lives. Hundreds of buried pain remembrances, or Prompters, have set up coping mechanisms within our Subconscious so that we automatically are directed to greet certain circumstances or things or people with belligerence, aggression, cruelty, fear, timidity, or a thousand different other negations that backfire on us daily. Yet all of these Prompters can be dissolved by meditation at the center of consciousness, by finding the Kingdom of Heaven. At this magic center, where all things are known and understood, absolute love will banish fear and hate.   '

What of these two great cripplers? The greatest is fear for it proceeds phantom-like out of our darker thoughts, has no substance and thus is difficult to deal with. It hovers its distorted shadows in our dreams and in our waking consciousness. Its many demons lurk around each corner of our lives. It paralyzes, prostrates, immobilizes, bleeds off the stream of dynamic life like a monstrous parasite. It is fear that vanquishes our goals before we have even set out for them. It is fear that tarnishes the looking-glass of life. It is fear that squeezes our arteries, restricts our circulation, visits lethargy upon our energies, dulls the brightness of the day, casts a pall of murky foreboding over all the events of life. For fear is but the negative use of faith. *Fear is faith in negative things and negative circumstances.* Fear *believes* we are surrounded by a hostile universe and hostile beings all bent upon preying upon us and destroying us. All of which is sheer idiocy.

LOVE DISSOLVES THE PROMPTERS

How many buried pain remembrances does each of us have—a dozen? a hundred? a thousand? Psychiatry has shown us that they form an almost never-ending stream on the time track of subconscious memory, extending from this very day back to the dim perceptions of prenatal experience when egg and sperm were but recently united in the womb. A great deal of good has been done by psychiatric treatment, but the tedious search for and exposure of each of these innumerable sore spots with the end in mind of building a psychologically sound person is a gigantic and unwieldy process indeed. It is like a farmer who year after year harvests crops which have been afflicted with the blight. From the great mound of wheat he accumulates, he patiently examines each stalk for evidences of disease, discards those that are affected and stores those in the barn that are whole. Much more time does he consume with his examination than he does in planting and harvesting his entire crop, and what a pitiful supply of whole wheat he has to show for his labors. How much more sensible for him to take care with his planting, to exercise caution against the disease of his crops by keeping them adequately sprayed and watered and cultivated. He will work far less and harvest far more.

Thus it is with the Prompters of the Subconscious. They must be dealt with en masse, at the roots of their beings, and all negative thinking and fear and hate must be cast out of the mind by choice at the center of consciousness.

We are jealous of our love. We are fearful that we may lose our love objects, and our love objects are our very sustenance in life. They have so much power over our happiness that sometimes our love for them runs negatively and turns to hate for the space of an hour, a day, a week. We become fearful and apprehensive that we may lose the things we love, or they may turn against us, and resentment grows within us, and we strike out in our blindness.

Oscar Wilde wrote:

> *For each man kills the thing he loves*
> *Though each man does not die.*

And so the gallows and the barred cell are constant hosts to a procession of lost men and women whose love has run to hate, so close akin are the two when they are without the firm and solid foundation of unity with the Universal Subconscious Mind.

He who loves God and understands that God is love, loves all things. His love does not rest on the shifting sands of the world, nor does it wax hot and cold as the -winds that blow; but he knows his complete oneness with the Father whose very essence is love. He seeks not, for he has all. Wherever his eye looks, he sees but a reflection of himself. All things return his love, and his prayers move the very foundations of the world.

> *He prayeth best who loveth best all things both great and small.*
> —Samuel Taylor Coleridge

ABSOLUTE LOVE LIES WITHIN

Love is the supreme law, for through it we throw off the bonds of separateness and perceive the great spiritual unity in which we have our being. Through love we attain a rebirth of consciousness, unity with the Universal Mind, such as Jesus spoke of when he said, "I say unto you that unless a man be born again he shall not enter into the Kingdom of Heaven."

We need not drive for love. Love is in us, complete and absolute. It cries out for expression from the very depth of our being, but we lock it in. We consider it smart and adult to build a fence around love and submit to loneliness and pride and vanity. How dear to us our vain little errors are, and how smug! We hurt only ourselves. He who deprives himself of the expression of love, deprives himself of all things. He hurts no one but himself, for love moves through all the universe, expresses itself through every bud and bush and flower and rain drop, and needs no man for its fulfillment. Loves makes the world go. It will make you go too. Just let it!

CREATION SPRINGS FROM LOVE

Life is creation, and all creation is a labor of love. Nothing springs full-bodied from the vast creativeness of the Universal Subconscious Mind unless there is first a desire to contribute to humanity. The essence of creativeness is love of life, for such love guides a man to do something better or bigger or more enlightening than has ever been done before. Such love catches a man in the great unity and the great purpose, and he instinctively perceives the direction in which life moves, becomes one with its efforts, contributes, and creates.

Life seeks for knowledge, and creation is the measure of what has been learned; thus creation is the purpose of life, and creation springs from love. Each of us has a talent, sometimes several, given especially to us, for through us God has become something unique in the universe. Love develops our talents, sets us free to do the special work that we can do. No matter what else we do in life, we are never completely happy unless our talents are developed, unless our destinies are fulfilled, unless we enlarge the vision and knowledge of God for which all humanity strives. By allowing love to work in our lives as a power for good, we become free to develop our special gifts in accord with an expanding and seeking universe; we become free to *contribute*. This contribution, when it is individualized and expressed in such manner as is unique with each of us, advances all humanity along the road of knowledge and thus moves in accord with the very nature of life itself.

The most pitiful spectacle of our time is presented by those people who do not realize that failure and unhappiness are their own fault. He whose cries of outrage and resentment are heard along life's pathways has yet his greatest lesson to learn. It is not fate or luck or an angry God that has dealt him his unsavory condition—it is himself! The perfect seed of success and happiness lies within each of us, and there is a channel in each of us through which it may become perfectly expressed. This channel is as manifold as there are numbers of people, but in every case it is opened only by love, and nothing may close it but the lack of love.

LOVE OR DIE

Love is the motivating law of life. On all sides of us we see the inexorable command of the universe: *"Love or die."* Through love we serve, and by serving we multiply abundance and good and knowledge and beauty and comfort; but through lack of love we grow selfish and bitter and complain ing, and we sow the seeds of hate and destruction, and we wither and die and detract from life. By working with love we add all things unto ourselves, add all things unto humanity.

"God is love," said Jesus. "He dwelleth within me, and I in Him. He doeth the works." Thus the great teaching he left us is that all humanity dwells in love and love dwells in all humanity, and all things good, great and small, are wrought by love.

It avails a man little to recognize the law of thoughts becoming things, if he has not love. Despite all his will to think only positively and to accept only the good, he will find his thinking warped into patterns of selfishness and bitterness and resentment every time he is faced with a crisis in his life. If love has not made itself fully known to him, he sees a hostile world about him and regards other people as hostile creatures bent on beating him or destroying him or taking from him. As long as this type of belief lies at the crux of his subconscious, he is creating an environment exactly the opposite of that which he wishes to have. "Love never faileth," said Paul, but faith and knowledge and prophecy wither and vanish with time.

OPEN YOUR HEART

It seems so difficult for us to open our hearts to love. We are so mindful of our petty little hurts and rejections, so super-sensitive to the opinions and circumstances about us, so steeped in our own self-centeredness, so pulled in on our own little problems and victories and failures. We isolate ourselves from the great unity; like hermits we retire into our caves; like hurt animals we lie in lonely retreat and lick our fancied wounds; and always we build our walls—walls to protect us from further hurt. Far from protecting us, our walls visit upon us the greatest hurt of all, for by them we slowly kill ourselves, not only physically, but mentally and spiritually as well.

Open your heart. Allow love to enter. What matters a hurt when it is but a step toward fulfillment? Life is for living, and some experience of pain and sorrow is essential even to distinguish pleasure and joy.

Wrote Walter Chalmers Smith:

> There is no gain except by loss
> There is no life except by death
> There is no vision but by faith.

Love heals the body, comforts the lonely hour, illumines the darkest path, redeems from sin and evil, brings prosperity, overcomes fear, builds character, and reveals the meaning of life.

LOVE OR SUFFER

As individuals in this great God-seeking drama we know as life, we have but two main choices: *Love or suffer!*

Every moment of every day we are engaged in the spiritual force of creating. We hope, plan, consider, desire, act, speak, fear, use our will, love, hate, are joyful, embittered—always we are creating. There is only one force in the entire universe; it creates all things according to what we conceive, accept, and allow. The right use of this power creates a blessing; the wrong use creates a harm, even a disaster. This power pervades the universe, is in all things, is all things. It serves us or masters us according to our perception. *But the choice is always up to us.*

This power is accessible to all men, and all of it is accessible to any man. It works for evil through hate and resentment and bitterness and coldness. It works for good only through love. Love recognizes that all things are accomplished through the many manifestations of God. Love sees that all things are . the One Thing that lies back of all creation. Love knows that your neighbor is yourself, that your enemy is yourself, that there is only one power behind all space and time and form. Love understands that God is sought by everyone, each working in his own way toward his own vision, and each sustaining the other through his discoveries. Love knows that each man advances all men. Love knows that the only activity worthy of man's heirship of God is creation. Love fuses all beings and all life into a great common purpose: to share and contribute and advance along the common path toward God. God is love; love is life; we are love. He who denies love denies himself and destroys his part in the human drama.

All the evil Prompters of the Subconscious Mind are buried memories of love rejections and love frustrations. They form dams that prohibit the free flow of love through our consciousness; they engender bitterness and fear and hate as subconscious hostilities, and they bring evil into our world in opposition to that which we consciously desire.

Love or suffer; love or die; for the lack of love attracts evil, but the presence of love attracts good.

THE FRUSTRATION OF LOVE

Humanity strives for love from the cradle to the grave. Every moment of every day, every task we undertake, every word we utter, every opinion we have, every pose we assume are all aimed at achieving the feeling of being loved, or coping with the feeling that we are not loved. Each neurosis and psychosis has its roots in love frustration. Every disease, illness, accident, revolution, war, and disaster has its roots in love frustration. Blindly, all humanity searches for a love object. Sensitively, we recoil from each rebuff. Silently, we withdraw our love within the fortress of forgetfulness, and post sentinels of hostility, despair, ruthlessness, and cruelty at the gates to be sure that love will neither enter nor depart. And so we kill our hopes and our very lives.

How unattainable love seems to most of us; how complex our spiritual natures and our emotional drives. Yet the answer is appallingly simple. Lower the barriers! Love is God, is the Universal Subconscious Mind, and God dwells within each of us, constantly seeking expression and outlet. The perfect seed of love is within. Said Jesus, "Be thou perfect, even as thy heavenly Father is perfect." Said John, "Love lies in this, not in our love for him but in his love for us—and love for him is complete in us." Perfect love is in each of us, constantly seeking outlet. *All we have to do is let it!*

Banish false pride and vanity. You are neither better nor worse than anything that exists. We all depend on each other for our very existence. Men have not advanced by fighting and hating and competing, but by being brothers at labor toward a common goal. Love is the unfurled flag at the head of the ranks—by it we survive and progress—without it we perish!

We must love and we must accept love. If we fail in either, we defeat ourselves. If mankind fails in either, the purpose of life is defeated. Love is the power for good that surges heavenward all through the universe. It is forever trying to express infinite good through you.

Give over all things to the goodness and greatness of the perfect Self that dwells within you. Release all feelings of hatred, bitterness, unhappiness, and depression. Surrender your will and your guidance to God, Love, the Universal Subconscious Mind, with complete trust and perfect serenity. Look with the eyes of love, listen with the ears of love, speak with the tongue of love, think with the mind of love, feel with the heart of love. On all of life's pathways you walk hand in hand with God.

LOVE AND SEXUALITY

The most important love expression of mankind is sexuality. In this relation between a man and a woman, in the sexual act, is expressed the complete physical, psychic, and spiritual hunger of one being for another. No other activity or expression of mankind provides such a total outlet for love" as the sex act. Yet how little it is understood, and how abused!

Physical love provides the basis for most of our literature, art, music, drama, and has given birth to endless tomes of stilted and inhibited expositions on the place of sexuality in life. Humanity foists upon itself a false attitude toward sex, and each man is secretly ashamed that he varies sexually from what he assumes his fellows to be.

The end and aim of the sex act is not procreation—it is the expression of love! When the world has finally thrown out the window all sham and deceit and maliciousness and self-chastisement, it will finally come to understand that the conception and birth of offspring are incidental to love between a man and a woman and never the cause of it. It is indeed very obscure why mankind has saddled itself with the painful belief that the sex act is only morally right when it is for the purpose of procreation. Animals are bred that way! The emotional search of each man and each woman, to give and to receive, to possess and be possessed, is fully realized in the sex act when there is a free flow of unimpeded love between the partners. It is sexuality that provides us with a human outlet and a human expression of divine love. According to how a person is possessed by love, his sex life will be uplifting, indifferent, degrading, or agonizing. It will be an expression of love or it won't be. If it is not, he is out of tune with life, and his sexual dissatisfaction is but a symptom.

THE DESIRE FOR FUSION

Love is the recognition of our true being and the dim remembrance of the complete unity from which we all have sprung. Love is the great motivation to re-experience this unity. Love is the desire for fusion. We desire this fusion because it rewards us with pleasure. Thus there is an erotic basis for all love, whether expended on art, beauty, other persons, or even inanimate objects. All love is sexual in nature, for love is the desire to give pleasure and receive pleasure. No work of art, no bit of prose or poetry, no spellbinding speaker, no bridge or building, no scientific discovery or medical advance has ever inspired in a single human breast but a fraction of the pleasure that is known by millions of people daily through the simple act of sex. Thus it is again Nature which has provided the best mechanism of all for the understanding of love, but as always man sets about attempting to thwart Nature before he has the good sense to cooperate with her. Active and vigorous sex lives, unimpeded by inhibition and witch's tales, express the fullness of love that dwells within every human heart.

There is no such thing as licentiousness, debauchery, and lasciviousness when love is present. Sexual excesses are the product of the absence of love. Promiscuous sexual contacts are always the symptom of a person who is lost from love and is endlessly seeking fulfillment through varied sexual experiences. He is doomed to external disappointment until he discovers that satisfactory sexual experience is the result of love, and never the cause.

THE GREAT FULFILLMENT

Man is a monogamous creature because he needs an object for his love—an object that not only accepts his love but returns it as well. Because of the sexual nature of his body he fastens his affections on some person of the opposite sex. One of the great satisfactions of life is finding a mate and obtaining the great human expression of love through sexual union. Without this very primary love fulfillment a man pursues countless wraiths through all of his days in search of a fusion that has escaped him. He may turn his love to art, to business, to science, to endless numbers of activities, but in the end they all pall on him and he becomes sad and pessimistic and defeated, for he has denied his own humanity, which is physical, and thus his love has never been complete.

The poet Shelley wrote: "That profound and complicated sentiment which we call love is the universal thirst for a communion not merely of the senses, but of our whole nature, intellectual, imaginative and sensitive . . . The sexual impulse, which is only one, and often a small part of those claims, serves, from its obvious and external nature, as a kind of type of expression of the rest, a common basis, an acknowledged and visible link."

No one will deny that sexual intercourse can give pleasure. What unholy masochism prompts us ever to believe that such pleasure is sinful or wrong? We didn't make our bodies and couldn't if we tried. Do we presume to state that the great Creator made a mistake by accompanying sex relations with pleasurable sensations? It is just as sensible for us to say that it is sinful for eyes to see, and to set about forming organizations for the putting out of peoples' eyes.

Oh, the prophets of evil and shame and fear and hate have made their inroads when they have woven into our racial thinking the hideous tendency to believe that everything painful is good and everything pleasurable is evil. We have martyred ourselves too long.

SEX IS LIFE EXPRESSING LOVE

When people have learned to love, when they know that love is divine and fills the whole universe and themselves, when they realize there is no fulfillment in life when love is denied, the world will see an end to the failure of marriages. For when love is free to enter a man's world through his heart, it will pervade all the things he touches. It will find perfect expression in his sex life with his mate, for we are all of the same nature and all seek the same fulfillment, and we shall all find it through love, for love never fails.

Sex is an outlet of love, and left to love will be good and great and joyful. In the words of Havelock Ellis, "It is passion, more passion and fuller, that we need. The moralist who bans passion is not of our time; his place these many years is with the dead. For we know what happens in a world when those who ban passion have triumphed. When Love is suppressed, Hate takes its place. The least regulated orgies of Love grow innocent beside the orgies of Hate ... It is passion and ever more passion that we need if we are to undo the work of Hate, if we are to add gaiety and splendor to life, to the sum of human achievement, to the aspiration of human ecstasy."

The universe dances and sings and buds and blooms and builds. All of life clings one to the other, serves one another in a great common purpose. Love pervades all, love is behind all, love is the great goal. God is love, and there is nothing sinful or shameful about God. All the universe is caught up in the work of love, in the work of fusion, in the work of sex.

Sex is life expressing love!

Thus your sex life, your relationship with your mate, expresses always your own understanding of love. But love never proceeds into the understanding solely through the relationship of a man with his mate. The understanding of true love comes only from the relationship of man with his spirit, of man with the Universal Subconscious Mind, of man with God. No human being can truly love another unless he first knows of the love of God. The Kingdom of Love is the Kingdom of Heaven, and exists within each man and woman. A man who loves God loves life, loves himself, and the nature of his lovingness will eternally come back to him; his marriage will be a perfect fusion of his understanding of love, and all the things of this world will shower him with goodness. In the words of Emerson, "Love asks nothing but does all receive."

THE TRUTH ABOUT HATE

Ours is a world of many conflicts because we are still ignorant. On all sides of us we see the contending forces of good and evil. Many people would have us believe that evil is as much a reality as good; they would have us believe that there are two opposing forces at work in the universe—God and the devil. Such people are accepting opinion evolved during the darkest ages of mankind, when all things were judged by appearances. The slightest thought on the matter makes it apparent that both God and the devil could not exist. There can only be one Creator. God couldn't make the devil, and the devil couldn't make God; there is only one truth behind the universe. If you accept the devil as being this truth, you are forced into believing that truthful things are hate, violence, robbery, murder, war, ugliness, poverty, disease, and chaos, and all goodness is false. If you accept God as being this truth, you are perceiving that truthful things are love, peace, work, constructiveness, neighborliness, beauty, abundance, health, and order, and all evil is false. The choice is obvious. All evil is false, is illusion.

Then what is the truth about hate? The truth about hate is love. Hate is simply love moving in the wrong direction. Hate is simply love turned upon itself. In the ancient Dhammapada we find, "Hatred does not cease by hatred; hatred ceases by love." Thus it is that Jesus advised to "turn the other cheek" and to "love your enemies." Love always overcomes hatred, for love is the truth about hatred.

Find a man who hates and you will find a man who believes he is hatred. Find a man who resents and you will find a man who believes he is resented. Find a man who is bitter and you will find a man who believes life is treating him bitterly. Find a man who is hopeless and you will find a man who believes that no one cares for him. *The common belief of all who deny love is their conviction that life does not love them.* So it is that all evil is born of rejected love. So it is that a man must first know that he is beloved of God and of life before he allows love to operate through him.

Love creates, produces, heals, comforts, guides, illumines. *He who makes himself one with love makes himself one with with God, and God works through him.*

TRUST LOVE

We exist in a world which is striving to know and understand itself. Each of us is a miraculous manifestation of that world. There is a great and unknown spirit working in and through every man, woman, and child in the universe. This spirit is seeking to know. We serve the ends of Almighty God by living and loving and learning, by lifting up our eyes to the stars, by asking questions, by searching for answers. Life is the supreme adventure. The deathless, sleepless spirit within us leads us ever onward to a higher good. We cannot fail if we keep our hearts filled with love and faith.

Trust love, for when you trust love you trust God. We are all children sitting at the knee of a loving Father whose purpose we will fathom in time. What is going on is a great and good thing, and we are a part of it; we shall always be a part of it; we shall finally be one with it. We need not be perfectly happy every minute of every day, for perfect happiness only comes with perfect knowledge. But by trusting in the great and good ends of life and by knowing that the door to the mystery swings on the hinges of love, we shall never lose faith in our divinity and our ability to build a heaven here on earth.

Know that truth is always the great and the good and the Beautiful and the aspiring. Close your eyes, your ears, your mind, and your heart to all else; it is illusion. Says the Bhagavad-Gita, "There is no existence for that which is unreal; there is no nonexistence for that which is real."

THE ADVENTURE OF LIFE

One desire pervades the universe—the desire for love. Through this desire all things are created—our songs, our stories, our paintings, our engines and machines, our cities and schools, our churches and stores. The hunger of mankind is to know the love of the great Creator. In all lands men are supplicating God to join with them in some enterprise. Each of two warring nations calls on God to aid it in the fight. But men are beginning to realize that God doesn't join anybody— people join God. God is love moving according to law. We must move over on God's side rather than ask him to move over on ours. God's side is the side of love. When man moves toward love, he moves toward God, toward the foundation on earth of the brotherhood of man, peace, happiness, and knowledge.

This adventure of ours, this life we live, has caught us in the miracle of all creation. *We create by our thought and our desire.* How precious are the chambers of thought within us. Whatever we think is visited upon us in this world. Learning how to think and how to love, how to create through the use of Universal Mind are the main businesses of our lives. According to how we learn these laws all things come to us.

Every thought we think, every desire we have, every mood we invite, each emotion we undergo is projected into the great creative substance of the Universal Subconscious Mind to be manifested in the world about us. What a miracle! But also what a responsibility. We as easily visit evil upon ourselves as we visit good, for according to how we think and believe so is it done to us. Every minute of every day we are using the greatest power in the universe for good or for evil. Only a fool or a madman would *deliberately* use this power for evil.

God's will is love, and by following love as the guiding law of life, we follow God's will and thus have infinite power. Every thought attracted by love and accepted by faith will create good in your world.

THE MIGHTY MEDICINE

Society is love expressed by groups. Men living together, working together, building together, helping each other, seeking common goals, attaining knowledge, are all brought about through love. We depend on each other for our very lives, for we are all one in reality, and are nothing without each other. The cities and schools and institutions of our world have all been built through love, one man for the other, one neighbor for the other, husband for wife, parent for child. Every step we take toward the divinity that is ours is guided by the illumination of the love of God for man, and the love of God is complete in man through each step taken. Wondrous things ⌐ work in the universe, and we need not see into the reaches of infinity to grasp their mighty import. Wrote Nietzsche, "Behind thy thoughts and feelings, my brother, there is a mighty lord, an unknown sage—it is called Self; it dwelleth in thy body." What a vision of splendor, what a mighty fate awaits each of us when we have returned once again home, to know as we shall be known.

There is no limit to love in the universe, and all of it is available to you. Put this mighty medicine to work in your life, and you will see such a healing and prospering and peace as will dazzle your very eyes.

In your meditations, in the silent times at the center of your consciousness, remember to think all things with love, and negative thoughts will be banished from your mind. Love bars the door of mind to the evil and the negative, and opens the door to the good and the positive, and from mind all things proceed. Yet the heart rules, always has ruled, always will.

Whatever takes root in mind is first attracted by the heart, by love or hate, one or the other. Thus by letting love into your heart, you bring good into your mind and into your life. By letting love into your heart you banish hate; hate cannot live with love. Trust in love, trust all things to love, think all things with love, do all things with love; in this manner you will walk with God, in tune with the infinite power of the universe.

REVIEW

1. Love is the underlying unity of the universe.

2. Love is the supreme spiritual law. Love is God.

3. Humanity seeks love above all things.

4. True love is recognition of the spiritual unity of all life.

5. Frustrated love gives birth to fear and hate, gives birth to evil.

6. The absence of love is fear. The rejection of love is hate.

7. Love will cast out the Prompters of the Subconscious Mind, and never fails.

8. He who knows and believes in the love of God loves all things both great and small.

9. Complete and absolute love is within each of us.

10. All creation is but an expression of love.

11. On all sides of us we see the commands of the universe, "Love or suffer. Love or die."

12. Faith and knowledge are nothing without love.

13. By our fancied hurts, by our sensitive egos, we isolate ourselves, develop fear and hate, create evil in our lives.

14. All unhappiness, every neurosis, every psychosis, all illness, accident, disaster, all evil are born of rejected love.

15. Love works for all who surrender their hearts, and works only with surrender.

16. Spirit is always perfect and love is always perfect. The imperfect things of our world are the result of our imperfect knowledge of love. We are growing to perfect knowledge.

17. Sexuality is mankind's most complete expression of love.

18. A satisfactory sex life is the result of love and never the cause.

19. Throughout the universe sex is life expressing love.

20. Love of man for woman and woman for man is a manifestation of the love of God for all mankind.

21. Love creates, produces, heals, comforts, guides, and illumines.

22. Man creates through his thought and desire projecting into Universal Subconscious Mind. What he thinks and desires with love creates good. What he thinks and desires in the absence of love creates evil.

23. By becoming one with love we become one with the power of the Universal Subconscious Mind.

THE CONQUERING IDEA

These are the tools we deal with: we think; we love; and we believe. Through thought we attain knowledge. Through love we attune ourselves with Universal Mind. Through belief we transform thoughts into things. These three tools, understood and used, bring power.

Slowly the world is awakening to the truth. Gradually the light of man's spiritual splendor and destiny is penetrating into our schools and social institutions, into our business houses, into our governments. A common Father binds all men together in a great and irrevocable bond. Through love alone will we be guided to our destination, make our lives on earth great and good and abundant. This is the message that Jesus brought. It will win the universe for man!

In the words of Albert Schweitzer: "Sooner or later the idea here put forth will conquer the world, for with inexorable logic it carries with it both the heart and the head."

RECOMMENDED READING

Change Your Life Through Love by Stella Terrill Mann. Published by Dodd, Mead and Company.

EIGHTH MEDITATION

The truth about life is the infinite love of God for all things. Each man is my brother, bound to me by immortal and everlasting ties. I love all people; they dwell in my Father and my Father in them. I surrender my heart to humanity, and humanity serves me with love. I surrender my heart to God, and the love of God becomes complete in me. I am one with all the power and vigor and knowledge of the universe. I let go of fear and confusion; they are illusions and cannot live with truth, which is love, which is complete and fulfilled in me now. The great reality of Universal Subconscious Mind is forever present at the center of my being. I draw from it perfect intelligence, perfect health, perfect peace, perfect happiness, perfect love. I surrender all the built-up inhibitions that have been impressed upon me by the illusions of the world. I refuse to accept anything but truth, which is always the good and the positive. I move in accord with Divine Intelligence. I accept the will and the love of God, which I express in laughter and joy and pleasure and service. Only the good, the great, the significant, and the constructive do I add unto myself. Nothing else is allowed into the creative depths of my being. The surging desire of each man is to know the fulfillment of love. The way to this fulfillment is through contact with the center of consciousness, through communion with the silent dweller within. I surrender my doubts and confusions and fears. Universal love is complete in me. I am united with God, move with God. I am serene and sure, joyful and achieving, confident of ultimate splendor

Chapter 9 - SUCCESS

Follow the light that illumines thy soul
Nor fear if thy steps seem to plod
A man ever gains his most cherished goal
When he giveth his work up to God

MONEY—A MEDIUM OF EXCHANGE

Success is a constant vision in the mind of modern man, which envisages it always as a pinnacle of wealth where he sees himself surrounded by large homes, motor cars, yachts, servants trips abroad, and plenty of time to enjoy himself. "What obtains these things?" asks modern man, and he answers quickly "Money." So off he sets with his battle cry ringing, "Make money!" It is little wonder that from this absurdly false premise he scarcely is able to obtain enough to pay his bills.

The only people who *make* money are those employed in the various governmental minting houses; the rest of us earn it. We earn it by providing our fellow beings with services on products which are both needful and useful. Our fellows make a like effort in our behalf; we *exchange* goods and services Since it would be extremely difficult for a man to carry a steer to Detroit to exchange for an automobile, money ha; been devised to represent both of them. We go through our days exchanging our services for the services of our fellows and the exchange of money represents nothing more than the exchange of services.

Success is not the result of making money; making money is a result of success; and success is always the fulfillment of the individual in productive effort that betters the welfare of mankind. Modern man has got the cart before the horse. He lets out to make money when in truth he should set out to be of service. Create! Build! Serve! Those are the commands of nature. Follow them, and you will find there is no limit to the prosperity and abundance of the universe.

He who sets out simply to make money, sets out to accumulate money. Since acquisitiveness provides no noticeable service to mankind, our incipient money maker has defeated himself at the start. This is not to say that he may not, for some period of time, actually accumulate a certain amount of money; but he is certain not to be surrounded indefinitely with prosperity, for his premise is not to give but to get, and the law of mutual exchange will catch him sooner or later and exact the utmost farthing of his "getting."

Money has become a controversial subject. The possession or lack of it determines the sides in revolutions, in wars that set one country on another. In an age when the miracle of man's existence has been rudely shunted out of mind by reverence for matcrial possessions, man has replaced hope and love and peace of mind with despair and hate and confusion by switching his worship from God to dollars. Money has become an end in itself, and any means of accumulating wealth becomes justified because of that end. Bleak indeed is the prospect of the man who reaches the highest pinnacle of wealth and sees its futility. He cannot buy peace of mind, nor stay his body from aging, nor stop death; and he comes at last to wrestling with his soul, if indeed his years of ignoring that soul have not withered it away.

MYTHS OF MATERIALISM

Abundance and prosperity are true spiritual conditions and are desirable and just for all men, but the pursuit of money for money itself is both senseless and degrading to the spirit, for it ignores the destiny of man. Out modern social structure, of almost complete interdependence, causes each of us, to lean heavily on his daily supplies of money to provide food and shelter and the comforts of life, things that most of us are not equipped to obtain in any other fashion than through the use of money. Money becomes our staff of life; our security rests upon it; and we overlook the eternal truth that security always lies within.

In America we have foisted upon succeeding generations of children the myth of the "go-getter" and the legend of the millionaire, and we have done each generation a great disservice. The myth of the "go-getter" is rooted in the philosophy of "dog-eat-dog" and "survival of the fittest," and millionaires are all too often the product of an acquisitive society. The go-getter is a result of a materialism which believes there is limited supply and not enough to go around and each man has to provide for himself by taking from others. The millionaire is the product of the same materialism that attempts to create security through possessions. Each of these phenomena of our modern age defeats itself. A man whose premise for success is founded on "taking away" is inevitably visiting upon himself this same kind of treatment. A man whose security is founded on material possessions is doomed to see his security corrode and rust and wither away, leaving him with nothing but confusion.

Spake Jesus:

Lay not up treasures upon earth, where moth and rust doth corrupt, and where thieves break through and steal: But lay up treasures in heaven, where neither moth nor rust doth corrupt and where thieves do not break through and steal: For inhere your treasure is, there will your heart be also.

184

THE YARDSTICK OF SUCCESS

Let money measure your service. Let your thoughts be always on the further service you can be to your fellows, and you will find their gratitude coming back to you in the form of money; perhaps not from the persons you have served, but return it will, for that is the law. Take your satisfactions from service, constantly seek to expand and improve it; take no thought for the money, which is always the *result* of service; and you will find yourself involved in an abundance that is unshakeable for it comes from the roots of the soul.

Prosperity is founded on the law of mutual exchange; so is poverty. "Whatsoever ye would that men should do to you, do ye even so unto them," said Jesus, for he saw the great exchange of all life, and he knew that one who contributed to impoverishment must be impoverished in turn, and one who contributed to prosperity must prosper himself. So it is that what you give you must get, what you sell you must buy, what you think you must see; and all things return home once again.

If we want money it is because we want the service of others. If we want the service of others, we must provide them with equal service in return. Our success is measured always in the quality and quantity of service we render, and money is a yardstick for measuring this service, a very fallible one it is true, but a yardstick nonetheless.

Perhaps you are calling to mind instances of people who have been enriched through swindles and through violence and through false promises. Do not be tricked into believing this. Nothing is judged on the day of its appearance, and nothing corrupt can stand. Prosperity based on falsehood is false prosperity and will wither before many a sun. The lasting wealth of this world is rightfully won by those who have rendered service in equal measure. Such money is not "taken away" from anyone; it represents but a fraction of what has been created. The man who has surrounded himself with a lasting prosperity has enriched the whole world through his efforts. There is no limit to the abundance that can be created out of the limitless Universal Subconscious Mind, and such abundance is available to all. No man can enrich himself without enriching others, for the law of life is that we do not progress singly, but by twos and threes and groups. And who-, soever provides a great service cannot avoid a great reward, any more than one who provides no service at all can avoid a, condition of poverty.

POWER IS CREATIVENESS

Money then is never an end, never a means. Always it represents service only, for it is never more than a medium of exchange, and we can no more stop it coming our way when we are rendering service than we can start it coming our way when we are not rendering service.

Above all things, dispense with the idea of "getting the best" of people. Each of us is like a pole in the flow of electric current. We absolutely cannot receive more current than we transmit, and always get back exactly what we send out. For moments in our lives, days, even months, we may seem to be giving more than we are receiving, or receiving more than we are giving, but in the end the flow always balances. We never get the better of anything, nor are we ever dealt the worst. There are no bargains in living, nor is anyone duped except by himself.

Mutual exchange is always with us; it is life itself; and he who recognizes this will spend his hours developing his capacity to serve and build and create and give. "Whosoever compels thee to go a mile," said Jesus, "go with him twain." *No service that you perform can possibly go unrewarded.* And no disservice that you perform can possibly go unpunished. The law of mutual exchange is the law of morality, of sin and punishment, of righteousness and reward.

How best can we serve? The answer is by creating, never by competing. We serve neither ourselves nor humanity by competing for another man's job, another manufacturer's market, another man's business. We serve by creating *new* jobs, *new* markets, *new* means, *new* methods. The magic that makes each of us what he is springs from an inexhaustible source. We are creative creatures, umbilically tied to the creative power of God. We create by our thoughts, miraculously, each moment of every day. Beneath the level of our consciousness there lies an infinite pool of knowledge upon which we may draw for every project we have the courage to embark upon. Always "God gives threads to those who spin a web," and he smiles on those who dare and aspire. No man is denied this creative power. It is the foundation, the root, the very essence of each of us. By working with it we are carried to dazzling heights; by opposing it we wither our lives in endless rounds of futility.

The secret which every intellectual man quickly learns—that beyond the energies of his possessed and conscious intellect he is capable of a new energy (as of intellect doubled upon itself), by abandonment to the nature of things; that beside his privacy of power as an individual man, there is a great public power upon which he can draw, by unlocking, at all risks, his human doors, and suffering the ethereal tides to roll and circulate through him; then he is caught up into the life of the universe, his speech is thunder, his thought is law, and his words are universally intelligible to plants and animals.

—Emerson

THE WONDERFUL BANK

I often engage in buying and selling oil properties, and occasionally someone will ask, "How do you figure you are rendering creative service when people sometimes buy oil properties from you without realizing a return on their investment?"

I usually answer, "Everyone gains in some manner." All men benefit from the development of the petroleum industry—through heating, transportation, plastics, to name only a few—and the interchange of oil lands is an integral part in the creation of the vast reservoir of petroleum that is so essential to our modern life. True, there are those who prosper more than others, but this is a law of life, and nothing can alter it. No one fails but another forges ahead. Nothing is lost, nothing wasted. We all fulfill the fondest wish of God when we take part in activities that create new wealth, new methods, new gains for mankind.

During my years in the advertising business I once had a client who sought new customers in an intensely competitive market. His answer was to cut prices to the danger point and employ great hordes of salesmen who used every possible ruse to sell. Despite the most frantic of his energies, his sales continued to decline.

"Look here," he said, "I'm just as smart as my competitors. I work harder than any of them. Yet people buy their products, not mine. What's the answer?"

"Do you like cheap imitations?" he was asked.

"Of course not," he answered.

"Then, what leads you to believe your customers do?"

"I never said they did," he protested.

"But you act like it. You make a product just like Jones's, only not quite as good, so you can sell it cheaper. You don't expand because you don't aspire. You need something new— something you, yourself, have created."

"That's easy to say," he answered, "but what?"

"Only you can find the answer. There is a great creative power that will work through you. Try opening your heart and mind to your inner self."

"How?" he asked.

"Through prayer."

This man must have found a direct wire to God. Whenever a new product is introduced in the drug and grocery stores .of the nation, chances are it is his. Needless to say he is a leader in his field. Recently he was asked about the secret of his success.

"I have a wonderful bank," he replied. "All the deposits are ideas. Whenever I want one, I simply draw it out."

UNMASKING THE EGO

Life is seeking to achieve. By seeking for achievement in our own lives, we make ourselves one with the purposes of the universe and become caught up in enrolling tides of unlimited power. And always we achieve by creating. Always we achieve by cloistering ourselves with Universal Subconscious Mind, by seeking the center of consciousness, by becoming one with God and getting ourselves out of the way. The thing we believe ourselves to be is never ourselves at all, but merely a *papier maché* gown we have donned and pleased ourselves to call "I." This is ego, tricky, despoiling ego, product of the awakening consciousness, which is always attempting to isolate us, to separate us from our true being.

We wear a mask of vanity, this "I" of ours, and before we can truly learn to create, this mask must slip away, the ego must go, vanity must go. We must strip ourselves of all pretension, of all vain posturing and humbuggery, of all personal responsibility and conceit and pride. We must reduce ourselves to nothing so that we have eyes to see at last, eyes to see the towering dimensions of our true being, a thing of no vanity at all, where all things lie revealed, the center of consciousness, the Kingdom of Heaven. We must get ourselves out of the way so the power can flow through.

So success depends upon service, and service depends upon achievement, and achievement depends upon creation, and all creation springs from the Universal Subconscious Mind, which responds to us as we use it. How then shall we be creative?

We are, of course, all of us, already tied to the greatest creative power under the sun. We are using this creative power every moment of our lives. Indeed, we do little else than create. Yet all too often we are using the power in such manner as to bring evil and disaster into our lives, and more often than not we have become so mesmerized with fear and frustration that we reduce our existence to mockery. The question is not how we can be creative, but instead, how can we learn to create only good.

IMAGINATION AND CREATION

Universal Subconscious Mind protrudes through every Conscious Mind in the form of what we are pleased to call imagination. This play of imagery, which we may summon into our Conscious Minds, has absolutely no limit upon it except that which we ourselves impose. All creative impulses spring from imagination.

The imagination of Columbus allowed him to ask, "What if the world were round?" Universal Subconscious Mind did the rest, and one day Columbus found himself sailing westward on a sea which everyone said was flat.

"What if a man could fly?" asked Orville Wright, and Universal Mind provided him with the answer one day at Kitty-hawk.

It is the undreamed, the undone, the impossible, which like itself is constantly striving to achieve. Only an unfettered mind, where imagination has full play, has the audacity to challenge the impossible. What if I could make it cheaper? What if I could do it better? The imagination conceives, and Universal Subconscious Mind delivers. Men conquer disease, build great towers and bridges, provide transport by gasoline and Diesel engine, light cities with invisible power, send pictures and voices through the air, whizz from one continent to the other via machines that travel through space; and all because the audacious imagination has dared to suppose these things were possible. All of them, every major advance made by humanity when first conceived, inspired laughter and derision on the part of vast numbers of people who would rather be little and blind and smug than big and humble and visionary.

It matters not what your job is, whether you dig ditches or rule nations, the same power is available to you as is available to anyone, and even the most exalted of the earth use but a tiny fraction of it. If you will discard the false notion that security rests with material things, and place your faith and trust in Universal Subconscious Mind, the power will go to work for you, creating in your life those very things which you allow yourself to imagine and accept. "Consider the lilies of the field," said Jesus, "they toil not, neither do they spin." Vain striving made them not nor will worry hurry their bloom. They spring well formed from the power that governs all; and man may pursue his ends on earth with the same composure as a lily nestles in the field, with trust in God and faith in tomorrow.

JOIN THE POWER

Nothing remains static. The great rhythms of life, of birth and death, of ebb and flow, of bud and bloom, are all reaching, searching, building, expanding. God seeks to know—through man he seeks an ever greater self-awareness. He who attunes himself with the expanding nature of life makes himself one with the purposes of God, and success will surely come to him.

Success, then, comes to him whose life is creative, and true creation brings forth into the material world the physical counterparts of thoughts, ideas, and conceptions aimed at the benefit of the human race. Through opening the channels by which Universal Subconscious may operate through us, we arrange all things in our world. Said Lao Tze, "These two things, the spiritual and the material, though we call them by different names, in their origin are one and the same." To be successful, we must think success. To be surrounded by prosperity, we must think prosperity. But the prerequisite of both these conditions is to put our great creative power to use through the love of God and the love of humanity. Thus we benefit others and life itself, and our good works return home to us in the form of success and prosperity.

Nothing is done by man alone; all things are done by Universal Subconscious Mind in answer to thought and conception. What you think returns to you in physical reality, and when your thoughts are guided by love, good inevitably returns to you. Turning your work over to God, letting love into your heart through perceiving the unity of all life, guarding the bastions of the mind so as to think only positively—these are the elements of success.

> *With the key to the secret he marches faster*
> *From strength to strength, and for night brings day;*
> *While classes and tribes too weak to master*
> *The flowing conditions of life give way.*
> —Emerson

THE SOURCE OF ALL IDEA

Primary on the ladder of achievement is the first rung—getting the idea. How often we are witness in this modern age to a new invention, a sweeping novel, revolutionary businesses, new forms of entertainment, education, and convenience. How often most of us say to ourselves, "If only I could have thought of that," and how often we believe we might! have if only chance had directed the idea our way.

Chance has nothing to do with directing great ideas to the people who have them. The idea finds its owner because the owner *attracts* it. He attracts it by placing himself in a mental position where the idea must come to him. He does this by removing from his mind all barriers as to what can or can't be done, all negative thoughts concerning limitation and lack, and he puts his trust in Universal Subconscious Mind, confident that it will deliver the answer if he has but the courage to pose the question. Something better, greater, finer, more useful—those are the creative aims of all of us, but we spend most of our hours placing ourselves in mental positions that attract the very opposite ideas, so firm is our faith in limitation, lack, and suffering.

The greatest men in the world use the exact same power as the aborigine in darkest

Africa, and the great man has no more claim on this power than the aborigine. The power is equally available to all, and it works in the life of each man according to his vision and understanding. Be assured that Einstein has no more access to this power than you, nor did Jesus. You need only open your heart, become possessed by love, free yourself from the limits of racial thinking and pain remembrance, and the power will flow through. It will deliver to you anything you can ask for with faith and courage and clear conception.

Free yourself to ask the aspiring question, with complete confidence that the answer will come. Will you write a book, build a bridge, develop a new market, start your own business, attain a better job, develop your capability for rendering increased service? Ask Universal Subconscious Mind, "How can I do this thing?" Rest assured that the answer will come. Don't struggle with it. Don't snarl and doubt and wonder and fret. Simply have confidence. In a day, a week, a month, the answer will come, clearly, as if a voice had spoken in your soul. Some little thing, perfectly matter-of-fact, will lead to its being revealed to you; and it will be easy to say that pure chance delivered it or that it would have come anyway, so natural will it seem. But don't be fooled. What Universal Subconscious Mind manifests in this world is always easily attributable to physical causes, but no one has ever been able to trace such a chain of cause and effect to anything other than the eternal source. When the answer comes to your question, and a fine idea has been delivered into your life, you are witness to the handiwork of God. If you are wise you will take a moment to regard this miracle with awe and humbleness.

Getting the idea simply involves opening your mind and heart to attract it, with complete trust that it will be delivered to you by Universal Subconscious Mind. Remain steadfast in your faith. The idea will come.

UNLOOSING THE DELUGE

Don't make the mistake of expecting that the idea will be delivered to you refined and tooled and ready for instant use. When the idea comes it will be rough-hewed, general, and will require patient examination and refinement. Your purpose, then, must be to reduce the idea to its leanest, most beautiful, most utilitarian form. Come to complete understanding of the aim of the idea and you will see the form take shape. Such mental vision was possessed by Michelangelo when he said, "In every block of stone there lurks a perfect form." And in every idea, rough-hewed though it be, there lies a perfect expression. Seek for this perfect expression, and it will come to you. Do not be satisfied with less.

Through examination, meditation, your conception will become clear and gradually will filter down below the level of consciousness, impregnating Universal

Subconscious Mind. The greater your faith, the clearer your image, the more readily it is impressed upon the Subconscious, and the sooner it will be returned to you in the physical world. If your idea was conceived in love, for service, for advancement, for building, for creating, then abundance and success will be yours when it becomes manifest. You need not drive yourself, rush about, hurry or worry. Your action will be guided by Universal Mind, and all the things that you need for final success will be directed into your path, even as you are directed toward them. So your tools will come, so will your workers, so finally will all the organization and help you need. Opportunity will eventually knock on your door, ring your telephone, greet you in the mails, visit you in the lunch room, seek you at work and play and rest, so that you will wonder what deluge has been unloosed. Those who work in tune with God have an unseen army aiding them.

> *Draw if thou canst the mystic line*
> *Severing rightly His from thine*
> *Which is human, which divine.*
>   —Emerson

EVERY MAN'S ASSET—WORK

Whatever we set out to do, whether in the arts or sciences, whether in manufacturing, farming, distribution, or education, must aid in the production and dissemination of goods and services that benefit the physical, mental, and spiritual welfare of society. Any other aim is error, is illusion, is therefore evil, and will return evil to us sooner or later. Thus a man who aspires to success must set out to benefit others. According to how he succeeds in this, both achievement and prosperity are his.

In the complex economics of our modern world the common asset of every man is his work, and he is rewarded according to how his labors benefit society. A great benefit has a great reward; a small benefit has a small reward. Realizing that productive land is limited and must eventually fall into the hands of the few, the benevolent state increasingly strives to place the premium on labor instead of ownership. Depending on how fairly this is done, economic freedom continues to be enjoyed even when land frontiers cease to expand. It is such a society that we live in today, one which is gradually achieving a fine moral temper by de-emphasizing acquisitiveness and emphasizing productivity. Today the premium is on labor, the capacity to produce. Outside the arts and sciences and personal services, most of us take our part in the production and distribution of goods. Work and the enjoyment of the fruits of our labors—such is the cycle of our material lives; and by developing our capacities for creation and production and service our labors bear us increasing fruits.

No one was ever successful at an undertaking when driven into it against his will. No one can rise to the pinnacle of his profession if he detests his job and begrudges every hour spent at it. But don't start casting around for a different job or a change of scenery. No matter how far you travel or what changes of scenery you encounter, you still take yourself with you. The seed of success blossoms as well in any surrounding, provided a man knows himself and the power of Universal Subconscious Mind. It is never the job that needs to be changed; it is the person holding it. He needs to change his attitude, his mental outlook, to start thinking positively and creatively instead of negatively and begrudgingly. All of us, wherever we are, whatever our jobs, are sitting atop great opportunities this very day, but they assuredly will pass us by if we keep our minds closed to them. We need to get rid of negation, to open our hearts and our minds, to realize that the entire universe is moving forward at a great pace. We have only to hitch a ride and let the power carry us along. We have only to get our fears and doubts and negations and timidities out of the way, and burgeoning forces will carry us onward.

Quoth Shakespeare:

> *There is a tide in the affairs of men*
> *Which taken at the flood leads on to fortune;*
> *Omitted, all the voyage of their life*
> *Is bound in shallows and in miseries.*

Such a tide does not come but once like proverbial opportunity, but rolls forever through all life and all nature, and is always at the flood. It may be omitted through the major years of a man's life, but will never turn away from him once he appeals to it. It is the tide of power that flows forever from Universal Subconscious Mind.

It is never too late. Never! The most prodigal and tardy of sons is always welcome to the Father who dwelleth within. Young, middle-aged, three score and ten, the power will go to work for you this very day. You need only let it.

THE HOBGOBLIN OF FAILURE

As with all things, prosperity and achievement are mental conditions, and their physical existence is merely a result of the cause that exists within mind. In order to achieve, you must first think achievement. In order to create you must first think creatively. In order to prosper you must first think prosperity. Since few of us are in the situations we most desire, we have no alternative, if we would achieve our goals, than to rise above our circumstances. *We must not allow our thinking to be governed by the conditions that surround us.*

Confusion is the hobgoblin of all failure—confusion between what constitutes a cause and what constitutes a result. Our racial Prompters, our national Prompters, our social

Prompters, our individual pain-remembrance Prompters would have us believe that cause lies in the physical world. When we are surrounded by poverty we think poverty; when we are surrounded by disease we think disease; when we are surrounded by failure we think failure; when we are surrounded by hate we think hate. Thus we become automatons, victims of circumstance, reflexive organisms instead of self-determining souls.

Do not be confused between the physical, which is always a result, and the mental, which is always a cause. Refuse to let circumstance alter your thinking, and you will see circumstance grow into the image of your thought. He who discovers the center of consciousness, the Kingdom of Heaven, always remains untouched by the world about him. His foundations rest in eternity, and the apparent disasters and evils of the world brush lightly from him. The words of Jesus are his: "Before Abraham was, I am."

DESIRE AND DESTINY

It is a difficult thing to convince people that destiny and desire are the same thing, but there remains not the slightest doubt that this is so. Confusion comes because people believe that desire is wishing, or hoping, or envying. A man will say, "Why, I've desired to be a writer all my life, and I've never had anything published, nor even come close to it." We might ask then, "What have you written?" and be assured that his answer will be, "Well, I've started quite a few things, but I can't ever seem to finish them."

He doesn't *desire* to be a writer. He actually desires not to be a writer. He is so convinced of failure that his escape mechanism prompts him never to finish anything so that he won't have to suffer the fear of having it rejected.

Desire always springs from emotion, and emotion is what impresses a conception on Universal Subconscious Mind. People are forever adopting attitudes that are in direct contradiction to their emotions, simply because they want another face to present to the world. They go to great lengths to preserved this face, some of them even winding up in institutions for the insane, but they do absolutely nothing about changing their feelings. Beneath the level of consciousness their desires are all aimed at negative things, through fear, hate, or insecurity, even though the face they show to the world seems pleasant and aspiring. We know them and find them wherever we go. They are our brave little martyrs, long suffering, our "good" people whom fate seems to delight in dealing blow after blow. They are not to be chastised or scorned. They would help themselves if they could. They simply do not know how.

Do not confuse true desire with the defensive mechanisms of your Conscious Mind.

Know yourself. Lay bare the bones of your feelings, expose them, no matter the pain or suffering or humility involved. For only when your hurts and griefs and torments and fears have been cast away can you find your true being and see the nature of the power that flows forever through the depths of your soul.

Individuality is founded in feeling; and the recesses of feeling, the darker, blinder strata of character, are the only places in the world in which we catch real fact in the making, and directly perceive how events happen, and how work is actually done.

—William James

THE FALSE FACE

Desire and destiny, mind and matter, the thought and the circumstance, are all one and the same. What you truly desire to be beneath the level of consciousness, you will be. Nothing in the world can change this fact except changing your subconscious desire—by meditation, by positive thinking, by coming finally to full recognition of how you inevitably shape your own fate.

By the very nature of your affinity with Universal Subconscious Mind it is impossible for you to have a true desire that does not manifest in your life. No man can know himself by examining the surface of his mind, for this is his "front," the face he shows the world, the mask he has donned to hide his hurts and sufferings and shames and fears and chastisements. To truly know yourself you must look first at your life, objectively. The things that surround you, the circumstances you are involved in, these have sprung from your subconscious desires. It will avail you nothing to protest that this is not so. Facing this irrevocable fact requires humility and very often considerable emotional suffering. But face it you must if you are to change your subconscious desires and thus change the
world about you.

Take the case of the man who had failed three times in business. "I can't make a go of it, and I can't understand it," he said. "Each time people have been clamoring for the product, the product has been a good one, I've been one of the first in the field, but each time I've fallen by the wayside while others have gone on to fortunes."

"Did your failure surprise you?" he was asked.

"No," he answered immediately, "I've never been able to make a success of anything."

It would have been unkind at that moment to point out to this man that he actually desired failure, but that was his situation exactly. A little probing at his family history revealed that his father had been a very successful man, a particularly stern and violent man, who had terrified his son in infancy. The son's entire life had been an

195

attempt to escape competition with his father. He was subconsciously afraid of his father, afraid of incurring his wrath if he met him on an equal plane. Thus he was afraid to succeed in business, desired failure as a subconscious means of soothing what he fancied would be his father's displeasure if he were to succeed.

Psychiatry might have set him straight on this aspect of his life, and indeed it was considered, for he had a difficult time with meditation and was almost incapable of any prolonged period of positive thinking. But he persevered. Today he heads one of the most promising firms in the country, takes on innumerable tasks, all successfully, and no longer seems able to understand the man he was three years before.

"I've got it now," he says. "It's viewpoint. All a matter of the way you look at it."

We might smile at this apparent over-simplification, but the truth is always simple to one who understands.

SLAVES AND MASTERS

The world is full of people who put the power of the Subconscious to beneficial work in one aspect of their lives, but use it destructively in all others. Men are healthy but poor, wealthy but sick, creative but unhappy, powerful but unloved; and always, in such cases, they use the power unknowingly, without control, having built habit patterns of positive thinking in certain lines and patterns of negative thinking in others. Only in one tiny orbit of their lives are they masters; in all others they are slaves.

The power must work in all aspects of a man's life before he finds peace of mind and security. It is a small thing when it works in the realm of prosperity alone. Said Jesus, "What is a man profited, if he gain the whole world, and never find his own soul?" Indeed, the vanity and egocentricity that usually accompany wealth and social position make it increasingly difficult for a man to attain the humility and lovingness necessary for the discovery of the center of consciousness. Jesus pointed this out when he said, "It is easier for a camel to go through the eye of a needle than for a rich man to enter the Kingdom of Heaven." Riches beget vanity, and vanity is a bar on the door. Yet if a man will first discover the center of consciousness, abundance and achievement will fill his life, and he will truly understand that it has not been produced by his inconceivably small "I," but by the power of Universal Subconscious Mind. Seek first for the center of consciousness—all else will follow.

Success comes from successful thinking, which comes from inner poise and spiritual courage, which comes from a man's discovery of the eternal Self that dwells within his body. "Wist ye not I must be about my Father's business?" becomes the motivation of his life. No aspiration is too high, no task too great, for he sees the grandeur he is caught up in, understands all things are possible to the power that dwells within.

THE SEED AND THE HARVEST

Hard work is the bugaboo of success for most of us. We see the immensity of our contemplated tasks even before we begin them. Imagination is both our blessing and our curse. Through it we perceive our aspiration, and through it is revealed the long road that sets us to despair. We have not yet learned that all paths must be trod step by step, whether they lead to the pinnacle of the highest mountain or to the top of a gentle slope; nor have we learned that the fruits of today are always the seeds of yesterday.

Dink Templeton, now an outstanding radio and newspaper sports commentator, once led Stanford University to some of its greatest victories in track and field, both as competitor and coach. Dink used to say to his teams, "It doesn't matter what you do the night before a track meet—what matters is what you've done the six months before." Dink made certain his teams were prepared when they took the field. His remarkable record was no accident!

Each day of your life you are sowing seeds that one day you must harvest. When you have come to truly understand this, you will take your satisfaction from your work and never from your harvest. For the sowing of the seed is all any of us does in this life. The shoot, the bud, and the flower are all the work of the Universal Subconscious Mind.

No goal is too distant, no path too arduous when we take the journey step by 'step. Withdraw your mind from the seemingly impossible summit and turn your attention to the step to be taken today. Our steps through life are chains of cause and effect, and each step successfully taken delivers the next one to us with greater ease until in the end the final goal is ours.

No man can be happy, efficient, creative at his work when he is unhappy with his situation and lives for another day. All of us are too prone to postpone our living until some nebulous time when "our ship will come in." Nothing is so apt to inject dissatisfaction into our lives as this wasteful attitude toward the most perishable of all things we know—time. Today, this very day, is the most important time of all, for what we do today determines what we will be tomorrow. Therefore turn all your attention to your labors of the moment, absorb yourself, take your satisfactions from each thing you do, however humble in your own mind. Nothing is small or petty in this life. The massive door of a vault swings on the apex of a tiny jewel, and men have become great through learning how to do well the lowliest of jobs.

MAKING HARD WORK EASY

There are no such things as hard work and easy work. There are only repugnant work and enjoyable work. If you would make work easy, then enjoy it. Whatever you enjoy unlooses a creative power that enables you to do it well. A job done well leads to a greater job, and then still a greater, until your dream springs from mind to join you in the world. Success comes to him who builds his house with unremitting purpose, stone by stone, taking as great care with the first as he does with the last, knowing always that the most important stone is the one he lays at the moment.

Inherent in every cause is its exact result, for effect is nothing but cause moving through space and time. When we have learned life's great lesson that cause and effect are one, we have achieved that pinnacle of serenity where our labors always bear fruits of enjoyment. Anxiety, worry, fear, and doubt can no longer tempt us, for having set cause in motion we art assured of effect.

Hard work is made easy work through knowing that none of our labors is wasted. The universe exacts the utmost farthing but also returns the utmost farthing, for mutual exchange is the law. No matter the apparent thanklessness of your tasks, you can be assured that they are part -of a purpose that will one day be fully revealed, a purpose grand and aspiring, which you become a part of when you keep faith and persevere. As Emerson wrote, "No fate save by the victim's fault is low." No man is deterred from the great and good ends of life unless he warps his own God-expression through negative thinking and fear.

No task is too great for one who leaves his plan in the hands of Universal Subconscious Mind and concerns himself solely with his day's work. Inch by inch, foot by foot, step by step is the kind of progress life itself makes. Lasting success is evolved slowly, just as it requires a longer time to lay the foundations of a building that will tower into the sky. The satisfactions of the journey are always to be found on the way and never at the destination. He who has learned this has learned the secret of peace of mind.

Let your work be an expression of your love; thus will you render true service.

Wrote Kahlil Gibran:

> *And I say that life, is indeed darkness save when there is urge,*
> *And all urge is blind save when there is knowledge,*
> *And all knowledge is vain save when there is work,*
> *And when you work with love you bind yourself to yourself, and*
> *   to one another, and to God.*

All labor of love is not labor at all, but joyous self-fulfillment. Good works are simply

ﾉve expressing itself, and a man whose heart is full oE love reckons not the support of the flesh in the sweat of his brow, nor does he curse his hours of labor nor begrudge his appointed tasks. Through his love of life he sees in all work the opportunity to serve, and serve he does, and fulfills himself, and God.

THE RECKONING SCALES

The universe commands self-fulfillment and never self-sacrifice. He who destroys his own life for some fancied thing, acts through vanity, and destroys a work that God has wrought. Through each of us God has become a unique thing, and by following the nature of our being to fulfillment we have fulfilled the fondest commandment of life. We have neither the knowledge nor the authority to decide that anything merits our own destruction, for it is no less evil to destroy ourselves than it is to destroy another. Self-sacrifice of our immortal soul, the universal Self, we can never do without acting against the purposes of life; but self-sacrifice of the vain "I," the ego, the isolated self we all must do eventually, for only when the ego goes can the immortal Self peer through.

Wise is the man who strives for fulfillment of the great Self that dwells within him. To this end he will make any sacrifice, but he will never sacrifice the Self, or his knowledge of the Self. All his aims will be at ridding himself of ego, at achieving unity with Universal Subconscious Mind, at communion with the center of consciousness. Thus success will come, thus prosperity.

REVIEW

1. Success is not the result of making money; making money is the result of success.

2. Abundance and prosperity are spiritual conditions.

3. Success is service, and money is a measure of it.

4. The Law of Mutual Exchange is the law of receiving what we give.

5. We serve best by creating and never by competing.

6. All creation springs from Universal Subconscious Mind, which responds to us as we use it.

7. Imagination is a projection of Universal Mind, is therefore creative.

8. To use the creative power of Universal Subconscious Mind with love is the

foundation of success.

9. All ideas spring from Universal Mind and are delivered to him who seeks them; he has only to ask the aspiring question and listen patiently for the answer.

10. Accepted ideas filter down into the Subconscious, move it to creation, become manifest in the world.

11. Productivity is the true measure of success. Acquisitiveness belongs to the materialist, who deludes himself.

12. All successful labor is performed with love.

13. The successful man refuses to be discouraged by circumstance; he knows that first cause lies within and never.
outside.

14. Subconscious desire determines our fate, and we may change subconscious desire by positive thinking and faith.

15. All things come to a man who knows his center of consciousness.

16. Hard work is work performed without love. With love, all work is easy.

17. A tower must be built stone by stone; so must a man's life.

18. Success lies in this: in fulfilling the Self that dwells within.

Free your mind from all limitation, lack, and pain remembrance. God, who dwells within you, is working out a plan of: grandeur. When you allow his plan to work through you, creation, achievement, prosperity, and success are yours, and peace of mind, which no mortal goods can buy.

RECOMMENDED READING

The Prophet by Kahlil Gibran. Published by Alfred A. Knopf.

NINTH MEDITATION

The infinite creative power of Universal Subconscious Mind lies within me. I attune myself, remove all barriers from my thought, become receptive to the purposes of God. I know that my life is great and good when I perform service with love. The right ideas are delivered to me, I accept them, and Subconscious Mind provides me with the means of bringing them into my world. I know that all things spring from Universal Mind, which is infinitely abundant. Lack and limitation are errors of thinking, and I banish them from my consciousness, There can be no lack. I need only let Universal Mind express itself through me, and my world is filled with creativeness and achievement and prosperity; my goals will be delivered to me, for they will be the goals of God, who never fails. Whatever my task I perform it with love, for I know that when I serve another I serve the purposes of a greater design. All about me I see the law of mutual exchange; therefore I give as I would receive. I know that abundance and prosperity are mental conditions; I create them on the plane of mind with complete trust and confidence that they will manifest in my life. I refuse to accept undesirable circumstance as having final reality. First cause is mental and is never found in the world about me. A mighty truth is at the center of my consciousness, where no work is difficult, where peace always reigns, where all things are possible. I know that life is a journey which must be traveled step by step, and I am patient, enjoying the wonder of the way, with unshakable faith in my destination. I submit my will, knowing that success will come when I fulfill the indwelling Self.

Chapter 10 - HEALTH

By perceiving thy inner perfection
Thou attaineth a vigorous health
For thy body is but a projection
Of thy view of the indwelling Self

THE ORIGIN OF DISEASE

Health and well-being are the natural states of every form o£ life, for all things are rooted in Universal Subconscious Mind which is perfect. Every living thing is but an idea held in Universal Mind, made manifest in space and time, gifted with consciousness which seeks ever to know more about itself. There is only one intelligence, one mind in all creation, and all things are made from it. According as each thing realizes the perfection in which it is rooted, it attains to perfection itself. *Thus physical health proceeds from mental peace, and disease and corruption proceed from mental confusion.*

Disease is a product of the confusion attendant upon growing self-consciousness. So it is that man, the most intelligent of all forms of life, falls constant prey to disease and illness, while the lower forms of life exist in physical perfection, unburdened by mental confusion. The lower we go on the scale of life the scarcer become the evidences of disease until at last we are forced to the conclusion that disease is a product of mental development, most certainly a product of evolving consciousness. Evolving consciousness carries with it an increasing number of conflicts, which project themselves into Universal Mind, which manifests them physically in the form of disease and corruption of the body. Man, who has come the full scale of self-consciousness but has not as yet evolved the greater consciousness of immortal Self, sees himself as an insignificant dot in a gigantic universe where he has not ordered his existence and cannot stay his death. His highly developed little ego cuts him off from the roots of his being, and he knows fear and futility and hate and bitterness, all of which set up conflicts between his emotions and his mind, project into universal intelligence, cast his concept of himself from perfection, and return to him as gallstones, kidney-stones, ulcers, high blood pressure, hardening of the arteries, cancer, leprosy, deafness, and so on, ad infinitum.

Psychology and psychiatry have unmasked this chain of cause and effect so clearly that medical science, devised to treat disease as a physical thing only, now freely admits that eighty per cent of all disease is of mental origin. It will not be much longer before this admission is enlarged to one hundred per cent where it should be. A truth cannot be partly right, and it is obvious that all things have their origin in something greater than the physical world around us. The bacterial concept of disease is satisfactory for the chain of effects that exists on the physical plane, but why do such bacteria enter one body and not another? And why are they harmless in some bodies and yet deadly in others? Indeed, why do they exist at all? Any man who considers the origin of anything must come at last to the invisible but very apparent intelligence from which all things have sprung, and concede it to be first cause. Since this intelligence would scarcely be intelligent at all if its normal procedure were to attack itself (such as in microbes attacking the human body), then it must be conceded that it is creating disease in response to *something*. That something is a conception, formed by the Conscious Mind and projected into Universal Subconscious Mind, whence it manifests in the physical world.

THE POWER THAT HEALS

It is a rare person who *consciously* desires to be sick, though it is certainly true that a few unhappy people have so completely cut themselves off from the spiritual unity of life that nothing further appeals to them than this form of slow suicide. The vast majority of people fall prey to disease through negative thinking habits and through coping mechanisms established in answer to buried pain remembrances or Prompters. A person who is chronically ill has a subconscious desire to be sick, though to confront him with such a thesis would be to inspire the most vehement denial. And even those of us who are sick only occasionally become so because it is a way of coping with a situation that confronts us. Since we do not know ourselves or even who we are, we do not understand the dynamically creative energy in which we live, nor do we understand our subconscious desires, nor do we understand that each of these desires is delivered to us in reality. So it is that all disease, all warping of the body from its natural physical perfection, comes because a person holds subconscious feelings of hate, bitterness, resentment, envy, jealousy, greed, self-pity, maliciousness, or any number of the countless abortions that corrupt the natural expression of the universe—love.

If a man does not love, he hates, or projects one of hate's deformed brothers, for love is the power of Universal Mind and flows through each person who lives, whether he uses it positively or negatively. If he uses it negatively, as in hate, it is a corrupting power, aimed at evil, and it weakens and decays and withers the body. Instead of the power for life, it becomes the power for death.

Once again we see that the commands of the universe are: "Love or suffer! Love or die!"

Love is the power that heals!

Love banishes confusion, roots out the Prompters, brings peace of mind, bars the door to negative thinking, reveals the indwelling perfection of the human soul—not the love of man for woman, or one person for another, but the love of man for God and the love of God for man, which is complete in man when he knows his love for God.

BODY IS ROOTED IN SPIRIT

Psychiatry is now only a skip and a jump away from being able to put its finger on the various negative emotions that bring on specific diseases. The day is not too far distant when medical text books shall list after hate, bitterness, frustration, repression, envy, and loneliness their resultant physical debilities; and mankind will guard its emotions with the same care it now bestows on its physical well-being, pills and potions being replaced by healthy habits of thought.

Writes Edward Carpenter:

Every organ and center of the body is the seat of some great emotion, which in its proper activity and due proportion is truly divine.

Body is rooted in pure spirit, in Universal Subconscious Mind, which is perfect. Body may be cast from perfection only by concepts held in Conscious Mind, which project into the Subconscious and are returned as physical ailments. We do not cause our hearts to beat, nor do we direct the flow of blood to our various organs, nor the acids of the stomach to perform the miracle of digestion, nor the intestines and the kidneys to go about the process of eliminating waste matter. The dynamic source from which our bodies have sprung has inculcated in them these reflexive actions.

The functions of a body represent the movement and concept of intelligence, and when we get our fears and negative desires out of the way, our bodies function perfectly. But every concept we hold of lack, limitation, acquisitiveness, repression, and despair performs its restricting influence on our bodies so that the blood does not circulate freely, the digestion does not assimilate properly, elimination is poor, congestion develops, strange growths appear and represent the distortion of our thinking. Thus our self-awareness with its attendant doubts and fears and frustrations limits the condition of our health and our lives. We must let go our little egos, take unto ourselves the God-consciousness which is our true being; then body becomes perfect, for we have become one with that which is perfect itself.

Body is only a manifestation of God's knowledge of himself. It is an idea held in Universal Subconscious Mind, an evolving idea which constantly changes. All about us we see the cycle of life's expression—seed, bud, bloom, decay, the giving way to new life. Form must change as knowledge and ideation advances. Thus body is that which changes, that which manifests idea, form within the formless, a complete and perfect expression of an idea held in Universal Subconscious Mind, destined to express the idea and give way to a more perfect idea. Birth and death, infancy, youth, middle age, old age, all are absolute essentials in the progress of evolution by which God seeks to know himself, and death will not be stayed until the journey is complete, for to stop death would be to stop the progress of evolution.

SPIRIT IS PERFECT

Jesus was the first great healer because he saw that body and mind were one, and he knew that body was only a visible result of an invisible cause. So highly developed was his consciousness that he perceived the spiritual perfection in which every living thing is rooted, and he realized that disease could be healed by revealing to an afflicted person the perfection from which he had come. When he met with leper, lame, halt, or blind, he knew at once that some buried pain remembrance within the mind of the unfortunate man had manifested itself in the man's physical condition. Jesus knew that he and the afflicted man were using the same mind, the Universal Subconscious Mind, the Father. So close was his unity with this Mind that he was able to effect instantaneous healing by removing his patient's negative Prompters- "Dost thou believe?" he asked, thus removing the concept of limitation from his patient's Conscious Mind. "Lord, I believe," his patient answered, and receptivity was established. "Thy sins be forgiven thee," said Jesus. "Take up thy bed and walk." The healing was effected.

When Jesus banished sins, he was not erasing from a ledger held in some ethereal realm by a God who kept records for a judgment day when He would reward the do-gooder and punish the evil-doer. The sins that Jesus spoke of were the buried Prompters of the Subconscious that were manifesting themselves as bodily ailments. His forgiveness of them was simply assurance to his patient that as soon as such buried guilts and hostilities and rejections were forgotten he would be healed. What Jesus was saying was, "The real you is great and good and perfect. Acknowledge this perfection, and your body will become perfect also."

There is no such thing as an imperfect body, for body is always a perfect manifestation of an idea. There are only imperfect ideas. They are imperfect because they are in error, and they may be changed by simply accepting the idea of change. A man who has stifled his divinity in the belief that physical things are first causes is incapable of healing himself until he has changed his belief. If his joints are stiff and his digestion poor, he spends a good portion of each day acknowledging the fact that his joints are stiff and his digestion poor, and he himself is thrusting his body into these very conditions by his concept. He is deluded into believing that he thinks these things *because* he has stiff joints and poor digestion, and cannot see that he has stiff joints and poor digestion because he *thinks* them. Place him under deep hypnosis and assure him that he can get about like an athlete and has the digestion of a lumberjack, and after he is awakened his afflictions will have flown. Alas, they will not be gone permanently, for patterns of negative thinking are his still and will shortly bring back his poor condition. But the marvelous illustration will not be denied.

The Intelligence that inhabits a man's body will become anything that is projected into it. It will make a healthy body if health is projected, and it will make a sickly body if limitation or hate or bitterness is projected. Thus a healthy body is always a result of a healthy mind, and a sickly body is always the result of a blocked and unhappy mind. If we would heal our bodies, we must first heal our minds, with love, with recognition of our true being, with meditation at the center o£ consciousness.

LET GO OF EGO

Worry and tension, guilt and hostility, resentment and vanity lay the foundations for all of our physical afflictions. They spring like growths from our over-developed little egos, which are forever being hurt and frustrated in a world which we set out to beat instead of cooperate with. Victory seems to be all we can think of. We have to outshine somebody, get the better of someone, make more money, be better looking, wear better clothes. How transient such victories are, and how unrewarding. Find a champion and you will see behind him the shadow of the man who will replace him. There is no victory for the hounded little ego, for it is nothing by itself, and it cannot see the larger dimensions of the being in which it is rooted. So it is hurt and sad and lonely and frustrated, and is forever turning upon itself and rending itself, as if by the self-affliction of pain it confirms the poor opinion it has oE life. Turn to the gigantic Self that dwells within, and you will cease to be concerned with the pains of your ego, which will immerse itself in an untroubled sea and bother you no more.

> *Some of your hurts you have cured*
> *And the sharpest you still have survived*
> *But what torments of grief you endured*
> *For evils which never arrived.*
> —Emerson

The entire miracle of existence and creation lies at our fingertips, yet most of us fill the pathways of our lives with wails of fear for what lies around the corner; we bemoan past mistakes, or dwell forever on the saddest words of tongue or pen—it might have been. Each day is a new birth, unlimited with miraculous possibilities for each man who lives. No matter what your age, situation, clime or time, you need only awaken to know with Kahlil Gibran that "That which sings and contemplates in you is still dwelling within the bounds of that first moment which scattered the stars into space."

FIND A MOTIVATING PURPOSE

Idea is a complete thing, aimed at a purpose, and the body made manifest from such an idea is also a complete thing, aimed at a purpose. It is this purpose which holds together the many interrelated functions of the body, and when purpose disappears from our lives our bodies disintegrate, even as the idea which manifested them is disintegrating. We often are witness to the vigorous business man who, at a mature age, decides to retire to a life of leisure. Seldom is he embarked many months upon this life before all sorts of symptoms of bad health begin to overtake him. A motivating purpose is absolutely essential to good health, for the organs and functions of the body respond to the goal set in mind. When the goal is removed, sluggishness and irresponsibility overtake the body, and it decays and breaks down. No body can be whole and vigorous unless the mind that inhabits it is whole and vigorous, for the ideas we hold in mind are made visible through our bodies and the circumstances that surround us. The first step to health is always the creation of interest and enthusiasm on the plane of mind. Aspiring and dynamic thoughts make vigorous bodies, and we must think health in order to be healthy.

Exercise is a case in point. Our physical culturists would have us believe that running, bending, squatting, lifting, and flailing the arms will bring health, and they point with pardonable pride to various outstanding physical specimens as examples of what comes from exercise. But once again we are witness to materialists who point to results and never causes. For the well-conditioned body is not a *direct* result of exercise but only a secondary result. True cause exists in the mind, as always, and a body is conditioned because of mental purpose, which causes purposeful exercise, which results in a vigorous body.

EXERCISE AND HEALTH

Some of the healthiest people of our age get little more exercise than walking from bed to dinner table, and many of our shortest-lived people are our athletes. It becomes increasingly obvious that exercise alone produces neither health nor longevity. Yet the evidence is all about us that men of great purpose live to ripe old ages, so that it becomes an inescapable fact that interest and desire and aspiration are mental conditions that are *always* found in those who are healthy and vigorous. Our materialists may argue that such people have interest and desire and aspiration because they are healthy. But many a healthy man has been led into illness when his interest and joy in life waned, and many a sick man has been led back to vigor and health simply through developing a consuming interest and purpose. All things proceed from mind, which is always first cause.

Physical vigor is the result of vigorous thoughts, and physical weakness is the result of confusion. Therefore a man who accepts the perfection and power of the indwelling Self will find such perfection and power mirrored in his body. Health comes from within, and never from outside.

By all means take exercise if it is fun, but there is no point in taking it if it is distasteful. Exercise merely conditions the body for more exercise. If you lift a hundred-pound weight ten times every day, eventually you will be able to lift it twenty times every day, but the lifting of the weight will not prevent your arteries from hardening, your nerves from fraying or your digestion from going awry. A man may as simply attain health through wielding a pencil with the purpose in mind of completing a book as he may through running the measured mile each day; in fact, more easily, if it gives him more pleasure to write the book than it does to run the mile. Our bodies are always perfect instruments of our thoughts, and perfect health may be ours whether we are athletes, professors, lumberjacks, clerks, or housewives, if our thinking is clear with purpose and our hearts are free to love. Exercise makes not the slightest difference.

Physical strength and endurance may be increased through exercise, but lasting health is as much a prerogative of the sedentary life as the athletic life.

PAIN IS A SIGNPOST

The spiritual unrest of the world is evidenced by increasing orgies of over-eating, over-drinking, over-working, overplaying, and under-sleeping. We undertake such a chain of neurotic activity as an escape from the gnawing doubts and fears and frustrations that lay at the crux of our Subconscious. Abuses of the body are always results of confusions in mind, so that a subconscious sense of insecurity may lead a person into eating far too much, or a sense of being unloved may turn a person to alcohol. We sometimes play too hard, seeking to forget the issues of life and death by burying our heads in the sand like ostriches. We often work too hard, seeking to amass a mountain of material gain to provide for our security, but it stays not death, and we cannot take it with us when the transition comes. We seek constantly for the pleasures of the senses, and by surfeiting ourselves, we dull the mystical creativeness of our true being; and when our bodies grow old and physical sensation wanes, the pygmy of our undeveloped soul plagues us with gnawing doubts and uncertainties. Truly, we cannot be whole men, either spiritually or physically, until we have recognized that the roots of our being rest in eternity.

We learn slowly, mostly by pain, and each of our gains in knowledge and awareness is hard won. Pain is that which visits us when we are in error, and through suffering we are turned back to the path of truth. Writes Kahlil Gibran:

Much of your pain is self-chosen. It is the bitter potion by which the physician within you heals your sick self. Therefore trust the physician, and drink his remedy in silence and tranquility.

Until we have learned the great lesson that pain is merely a signpost indicating that we have wandered off the track of truth, we shall continue to fight it and struggle with it, to lend reality to it, and thus to bring more of it into our experience. But once we have come far enough to realize that all pain—physical, mental, and emotional—proceeds from errors in thinking, we are well on the way to filling our lives with vigor, abundance, and joy; and have come a great step toward unity of consciousness with Universal Subconscious Mind. *The ordinary man learns by his own mistakes; the wise man learns by the mistakes of others.*

Over-indulgence in physical things marks an imbalance of the emotions. Fear, hate, and insecurity rest in the Subconscious of every person who flees his demon down the murky roads of alcoholism, over-eating, or frenetic searches for pleasure and acquisition. Moderation attends all things to him who has been introduced to the center of consciousness. No violent emotions constrict his soul, for he is secure in the consciousness of God. No uncertainties gnaw at the foundations of his being, for they rest in eternity. Confusion has no place in his mind, because he sees the goal of all life, becomes one with it, takes it unto himself as his own purpose. Should disease or illness become manifest in his body, he turns his gaze within, to the perfection and wonder of his true being, and his body is made whole.

> *And since he kept his mind on one sole aim,*
> *Nor ever touched fierce wine, nor tasted flesh.*
> *Nor owned a sensual wish—to him the wall*
>
> *That sounders ghosts and shadow-casting men*
> *Became a crystal, and he saw them thro' it*
> *And heard their voices talk behind the wall*
> *And learned their elemental secrets, powers, and forces.*
>
> —Alfred Tennyson

DISEASE IS NEVER INCURABLE

An infinite law is at work in the universe; it is the law of ideas becoming things. Since this law is the movement Universal Mind, it has absolutely no limitation. Therefore there is no such thing as an incurable disease. A law must work all the time in order to be a law, and the law that governs the intelligence in which we are rooted is the foundation of all things. Disease itself springs from an idea impregnated upon Universal Mind, and will be banished when the idea is banished. Whatever disease

209

science has been unable to find a cure for is not *incurable*. Something causes it; that something may be discovered and removed. Both medical science and psychiatry are learning that the root of all things exists in mind, springs from idea, and idea can be changed. Since there is no limit to idea and to the inexhaustible power of Universal Subconscious Mind, there absolutely cannot be any such thing as an incurable disease.

We must realize that the universe always turns out to be exactly what we think it to be, even as do our bodies. As we reach higher levels of consciousness, we take unto ourselves more perfect ideas, casting off the shackles of limitation, becoming aware that all things are possible. The moment we say something is *impossible,* we make it impossible for God to manifest it through us. And another man with a greater vision and a greater faith will bring it forth, for he will allow God to work through him. None of us has the right to say a thing is impossible, unless he is foolish enough to place limitations on God.

Perfect spirit is within us, willing to manifest perfect health for us if we but call upon it with faith. All disease may be healed by mental and spiritual treatment, by expanding consciousness to encompass Universal Self.

MENTAL HEALING

Each person who suffers from ill health has usually fallen victim to a specific ailment. This specific ailment is the result of some obstruction in mind; some false idea, some erroneous conception. When we heal the body by mental and spiritual treatment, we do not treat the body, *we treat the mind.* This is very important. One cannot get rid of result without first getting rid of cause. Cause is always in mind; bodily ailments are the *result.*

A lifetime of study would be unlikely to reveal the specific mental disturbances that cause each disease, but no table of mental and emotional disturbances with resultant physical debilities is needed to successfully conduct mental healing. All things spring from a perfect source, and we need only contact this source and allow it to manifest its perfection through our bodies. Said the Great Healer, "Be thou perfect, even as thy Father in heaven is perfect." In so saying he pointed the way to the healing of all disease: *Recognize your spiritual perfection.*

There is nothing in Universal Subconscious Mind that desires our bodies to be warped away from the purposeful functioning for which they were intended. It is our conception o£ ourselves that visits disease upon us, and when we have conceived ourselves to be spiritually perfect, we become physically perfect. The real you is not your body. Your body is but an infinitesimal extension in time and space. The real you is mental and spiritual, free of the confines of space and time, limitless in power and the capacity to understand and create. When you have recognized your true spiritual self you have become identified with immortal Self, and disease cannot exist in your body, for there is no limitation in Universal Subconscious Mind.

Therefore all disease may be treated as one disease, which is not disease at all, but simply limited thinking, errors projected into Universal Subconscious Mind. We treat disease by refusing to accept it as having any true existence, by affirming the spiritual perfection in which we are rooted. "Perfect love casteth out fear," and perfect faith casts out physical imperfection.

Yet rare is the man who has perfect love or perfect understanding or even perfect faith. We are all neophytes on the great adventure of expanding consciousness, and by the very nature of this adventure we are unable to go beyond our understanding. We stand at the crossroads, peering into the infinite reaches of space and time, exclaiming yet over one grain of sand on the gigantic beach of existence. But the veil is rent and light pours through with great revelation that mind and spirit are immortal and infinite and are always first cause of everything. If aeons of time are yet to elapse before man completes his journey to a oneness with God, what does it matter? We all are part of One Mind and truly exist in a place where space and time are nothing. We may call upon Universal Subconscious Mind with the understanding that now is in us, and the Great Creator will respond by creating for us the image of our understanding. If we can find it in ourselves to accept spiritual perfection, Universal Mind will manifest this perfection in our bodies.

Thus the basis of spiritual and mental healing is affirmation. We deny nothing, waste no time dwelling on that which we do not desire. Our moments of consciousness are directed inward, at our spiritual selves, and are aimed at perceiving the perfection that gives us consciousness. What we see is returned to us. Awareness of the center of consciousness, perception of the Kingdom of Heaven, brings health.

WE CANNOT GO BEYOND UNDERSTANDING

The objection that is usually raised against mental healing is that nobody seems able to set a broken bone mentally so the whole aspect of mental healing is in error. *It is not impossible mentally to set a broken bone!* The fact that it has not been done simply means that we have not yet arrived at sufficient spiritual understanding. Lacking the understanding, we call a surgeon, which is as it should be. N either do we have enough understanding to heal a ruptured appendix or dissolve a critical case of cancer, so again we call upon the surgeon. Yet these things and all others of the so-called incurable diseases are possible of mental healing, and the day will arrive when evolution will have brought man's consciousness and understanding to the point where disease will be banished from the face of the earth.

Another argument often used against mental healing is advanced by the school of materialists who see life as species preying on species and survival of the fittest. Their theory is that all organisms by their very natures must feed upon each other, that microbes must feed upon the human body; thus life is disease itself. This hopeless outlook on the miracle of creation keeps God imbedded in the slime of the amoeba, sees nothing but a screaming insanity in life, and projects a tooth-and-fang existence for even the most enlightened of men.

Evolution is the process of individualized consciousness expanding in search of God. The first result of individualized existence is the struggle to maintain life, with its natural outcome of survival of the fittest. The second result is consciousness of self, the identification of one self with another, and the birth of love and cooperation as opposed to competition and. preying on the weaker. The third result is the expansion of the consciousness of self to encompass the consciousness of Universal Subconscious Mind, and it is this step that mankind is preparing to take now. Once it is fully taken, men will see through the illusions of space and time and perceive that material things are but tiny extensions o£ a far greater reality that has its roots in infinity. Such a consciousness orders the universe, for the universe turns out to be exactly what it perceives. Microbes, which have their roots in Universal Mind, may be banished by banishing the conception. "Hold out thy hand," said Jesus to the man with the withered limb. The man did; Jesus saw a whole hand; the same became whole.

PERCEIVING THE TRUTH

It is sometimes difficult for us to believe that a man who lived two thousand years ago in the rude agrarian life of primitive Palestine could have attained the universal consciousness for which mankind seeks so desperately in this so-called enlightened age. Yet there can be no doubt that the veil was lifted for Jesus. Every word he spoke, every action he undertook, is fraught with his knowledge of universal consciousness. By parable and deed he sought to convey the mighty truth which he held in the palm of his hand, but he spoke to a political-minded people engaged in revolutionary activity, unready for his spiritual perceptions. Only the enlightened power of Jesus has preserved his dialogues for us to marvel at today. He had achieved unity with Universal Subconscious Mind. When he looked at a withered hand and perceived it to be whole, the hand became whole. Whatever is perceived by Universal Subconscious Mind becomes a physical manifestation, and it is always Conscious Mind that forwards the perception to Universal Subconscious Mind. Though our consciousness does not attain to that of Jesus, we may approach his healing power through faith in our spiritual perfection and an abiding sense of love.

Disease is a negative thought-force, is false, is therefore an illusion of the mind. In mental healing, we simply separate false thoughts from the true, consciously, and by allowing our faith and affirmation to sink down into the Subconscious we admit physical vigor and health into our lives. The principle of existence is the principle of thoughts becoming things. Since this is a law, we do not argue or struggle with it. Some well-meaning friend may ask you why you don't try walking upon the water since you are so all-fired convinced of this mind stuff. All you can do is assure him that it is toward such a goal that you aspire, for we either walk on the water or drown in it; we either master life or defeat ourselves.

RELY ON THE LAW

Mental treatment entails no personal responsibility other than for the idea and its affirmation. All else depends upon the principle of creation that underlies the universe; and this principle never fails. When you affirm your spiritual perfection you are setting universal law in motion, which accepts your conception and the power of your affirmation, and manifests it in the physical world. There is nothing superstitious or occult about this. The law we are dealing with is infallible; it is true reality, beside which all else pales to nothingness.

Since disease is caused by a mental condition, before it can be healed the mental condition must be surrendered. A man must first surrender himself to God, to Universal Subconscious Mind; he must let go, give up the struggle, trust in the invisible roots of his being, so that God-consciousness may engulf him and make him whole. You cannot successfully treat yourself or another person until you are willing to surrender your doubts and fears and hates and hurts. The nagging, gnawing emotional hurts we bottle up inside ourselves are like time bombs laid within. They explode in tumors, cancers, high blood pressure, hardening of the arteries, diabetes, heart trouble, lung trouble, literally riddle our bodies with poisonous thoughts that impregnate Universal Subconscious Mind. We must surrender our fears and frustrations and guilts, lay aside our vanities and our little egos, place all our hurts on the shoulders of the Atlas of Eternity, then we shall be free—free to partake of the beauty and perfection and abundance of the universe.

God is always right where we are, responding to us exactly as we conceive of Him. He is our infinite invisible dimension, of which our physical bodies are but a negligible projection. The power for physical perfection is running over inside of us; we need only surrender to it, accept it, trust ourselves completely to it, and health is ours.

When you treat yourself or someone else for a physical ailment, remember that you are treating mind and not body. You are assuring yourself of mental and spiritual perfection, you are affirming it, you are projecting it into Universal Subconscious Mind with complete faith and trust. When you treat someone else you still deal with the same Mind. You treat *yourself* to think perfection of the person you are treating. Do not try to change the other person's thinking by the power of your own thought. Simply treat *yourself* for your conception of him. You move Universal Subconscious Mind; Universal Subconscious Mind moves *him*. Therefore whether you are treating yourself or another, the treatment is always the same, though of course in the latter case you will substitute "he" or "she" where you would normally use "I." But always you are treating yourself, your own conception, and projecting it into Universal Mind. When you heal another, you must first be able to completely accept in your own mind his spiritual perfection. When you have done that, the healing will be effected.

THE MENTAL CAUSES OF DISEASE

A partial list of common physical ills follows, with the underlying mental cause for each, so that you may be guided more easily into directing your treatments at mental conditions rather than physical.

Headache:

Confusion is the predominant condition attendant upon headache. Most generally this is brought about by the suppression of some emotion which revolves around the affections. When headache is attended by dizzy spells it is a sign of a basic insecurity. Treat for peace, the clarity of the Subconscious, the love that pervades the universe, and the consciousness of immortal Self.

Fatigue:

When enthusiasm and joy desert us, fatigue enmeshes us in its enervating grasp. Joy and enthusiasm are results of mental and spiritual expansion. We cease to expand when we place limits on our thinking and on our conceptions; our goals disappear or seem unobtainable and we accept defeat and its attendant feeling of lethargy and tiredness. Treat for awareness of life and movement and joy and expansion. There are no limitations on God, and God is expressing Himself through you.

Indigestion:

An intense sense of personal responsibility usually manifests itself in digestive upsets. People who work at high speeds and feel they must do everything by themselves often fall victim to excess stomach acidity and stomach ulcers. Their refusal to assimilate on the plane of mind a unity with the underlying Self becomes symptomatic in the difficulty they have assimilating food. Treat for peace and perception of how God is the only doer. Treat for relaxation and trust in Universal

Subconscious Mind. Learn how to let go and leave it to God. There is perfect assimilation in perfect spirit.

Constipation:

Fear causes immobility, which brings inaction into life, freezing and constricting, often manifesting itself in constipation. Fear is the basic cause of greed, acquisitive tendencies, unwillingness to let go. Very often fear comes from belief in limitation, in lack, in burden. It brings on excessive tensions, constricts and binds the muscles and the movements of the body. Fear is faith used negatively. Treat for positive thinking, assurance, confidence, the knowledge that you are one with God and God is right where you are, guiding you unerringly to your goals. Banish negative thoughts. Whatever you refuse to accept in mind can never touch you in the physical world.

Obesity:

We become fat because we eat too much, and we eat too much because certain of our desires and longings are frustrated. Seeking solace, we find it in food, for the pleasure of taste and the comfort it gives us. Our frustrations are caused because we have taken unto ourselves false ideas of our personal unworthiness and no longer believe we can achieve our goals. We have lost confidence in our divine roots, and our energies are directed at sensual pleasures rather than at achievement and service. Treat for knowledge of the center of consciousness wherein there is perfect order, perfect beauty, and perfect symmetry. Food is a symbol of love and should be eaten with moderation lest gluttony turn love to greed. God is love, and the perfect seed of love lies within you.

Insomnia:

When we sleep we become immersed in Universal Subconscious Mind. If we cannot sleep it is because we are over-concerned with the material world, and our Conscious Minds have over-ridden the Subconscious and refuse to let go. The physical world is simply a series of manifested results which have all proceeded from Subconscious Mind. We cannot change these results by fighting them, but only by dealing with them in mind where they originate. Thus holding onto your cares and worries is the worst possible way to overcome them. Seek your center of consciousness before going to bed. Treat for peace and relaxation. Real truth is of the spirit and lies inward. Turn your eyes away from the world and look within.

Intemperance:

Alcohol provides a tortuous trap for those who seek escape from an unwanted belief. It is always some unwholesome or painful picture gnawing on the Subconscious that turns a person to drink. He himself has created this image, and he might change it by creating another, but he lends reality to his self-made monster and flees it down the avenues of alcoholism or drug addiction or senseless pursuits of pleasure. Treat for the dissolution of guilt and personal responsibility. God is in you, and God is not guilty. Mistakes are for learning, and each day is a fresh start with a clean slate when you learn to forgive yourself.

Colds and similar congestions:

Mental conflicts and repressions attract congestions of the body such as the common cold. Such conflicts are usually first evidenced by depression of the spirits, a bleakness in outlook. Our creative nature demands that we either make a decision on a problem or put it out of mind. When we hold a problem in mind and are unable to come to a decision, we set up congestion in the forces that flow through us from the Subconscious. This reduces our energy and activity, depresses the spirit, brings on bodily congestions and colds. Also our racial conviction that colds are "catching" and caused by exposure to wind and low temperatures sets up creative impulses to manifest them when we encounter such situations. Treat for harmony and the knowledge of the perfection of Universal Subconscious Mind. Each of your problems will be perfectly answered if you will only let go and leave the solution to your greater Self. Treat for poise and assurance and calmness. There is no congestion in perfect spirit.

False growths:

A seed buried within grows in darkness, and so we carry our guilts around with us. They block us from knowledge of the great Self, warp and distort our consciousness, manifest their falseness by false growths in and on the body. Treat for unity with Universal Subconscious Mind. Let go of your guilts and sins and give them over to God.

Paralysis:

Ideas of restriction and limitation may manifest themselves in paralysis or the malfunctioning of the senses. There is no restriction and no inaction in the mind of God, which you may take unto yourself by meditation at the center of consciousness.

Heart trouble and organic disturbances:

The heart is the seat of purpose, and when purpose is centered in spirit and not in the material world, the heart is rooted in perfection. Organic disturbances always come from a man being out of tune with his spiritual nature. Heart trouble and attendant disorders visit our materialists, those who seek their goals, purposes, and pleasures in the physical world. Treat by meditation on the birthless, deathless, ageless spirit from which man springs. Take unto yourself the mantle of God, become one with him, and

His purpose will energize your heart.

There is only one mind, one spirit, one power pervading the entire universe, and it is perfect. It is constantly attempting to express itself perfectly through each of us. Because we are newly arrived at the consciousness of our own little egos and have not yet taken unto ourselves the consciousness of the greater Self, we see neither from where we have come nor where we are going, and the gigantic universe seems to threaten and frustrate us on all sides. Our limited vision causes us to create fear and hate and bitterness and apathy which manifest imperfections in our bodies. All disease and distortion of the body may be healed by meditation at the center of consciousness, by knowledge of the love of God, by awareness and use of the unlimited power and perfection of Universal Subconscious Mind.

REVIEW

1. Disease proceeds from mind and is the result of confusion.

2. Spirit is perfect; and body, which is the result of spirit, is perfect also, unless it is distorted by an idea of imperfect spirit.

3. Love is the eternal healer.

4. Body is idea implanted in Universal Subconscious Mind. There are no imperfect bodies; only imperfect ideas.

5. From the wounds of the little ego arise the negative emotions which lay the foundation for disease.

6. Mental purpose is necessary to health, for such purpose co-ordinates the many inter-related functions of the body.

7. Exercise of itself will not produce health, which comes always from interest, desire, and aspiration in the mind and heart.

8. Over-indulgence is a mark of imbalance of the emotions.

9. Pain is punishment for mistakes, is therefore a teacher; but the wise man learns by the mistakes of others.

10. Focus your attention on the world within and let moderation attend you in all things.

11. Mental healing does not treat the body, but treats the mind.

12. All disease is treated by affirming the spiritual perfection in which we are root

13. Since it is beyond our understanding to mentally set a broken bone or heal a ruptured appendix, we sensibly call a surgeon.

14. Mental healing is the use of a principle that is law. It is never ourselves who do the healing. We simply call upon the law of thoughts becoming things by affirming the perfection of spirit. Body, manifesting the spirit, then becomes perfect also.

15. You heal another by treating your own mind for knowledge of his spiritual perfection. Thus you don't treat him; you treat yourself for your knowledge of him.

16. Behind every distortion ot the body lies a distorted concept in mind, for from mind all things proceed. Contemplate perfect spirit; health will follow.

All barriers are those created by Conscious Mind, by limited thinking, by ingrained racial prejudice, by buried pain remembrances. Universal Subconscious Mind is unlimited in both scope and power. Peace and perfection await him who surrenders his ego to the immortal Self that dwells within. Love is the great healer, for with love the foundations o£ the universe are perceived.

RECOMMENDED READING

The Art of Creation by Edward Carpenter. Published by George Allen and Co.

TENTH MEDITATION

My body is a manifestation of my knowledge of myself, and my true self is spirit, is consciousness only, and is invisible. Other people see me not; they see but my body. It is only I who know myself, and this knowledge returns to me in my health and in the things of my life. Therefore I affirm that my spirit is perfect, that I am one with the great Self of the universe. The energy of this great Self permeates my being, cleanses me of all impurities of the flesh, restores every function of my body to harmony. There is perfect elimination, perfect assimilation. My entire being is spiritual, and my body is quickened into new life with the perception of this great truth. I surrender myself to the wisdom and guidance of Universal Subconscious Mind. I become one with the purpose of God, and this mighty purpose animates my body, projects into every aspect of my life. There is no obstruction, no barrier, no limitation in my mind. I see only peace, power, vigor, and plenty. I open my heart to love, and love flows through every atom and pore of my body, energizing, molding, coordinating. By healing my mind of limitation and lack and negative thinking, I automatically heal my body. At the center of my being I perceive limitless, deathless, ageless spirit, perfect in beauty, perfect in function; this spirit becomes manifest in my body and in my affairs. When I am faced with apparent confusion, I surrender it, give over each of my problems and worries to that which has the perfect solution and in which there is absolute clarity. I take my thoughts from the limitless reaches of Universal Subconscious Mind, never from the world around me. I do not think responsively, I think originally; I do not react, I act. I am never a victim of circumstances, for each thing of my life proceeds from out of my thoughts, which move always in accord with God.

Chapter 11

IMMORTALITY

Each soul slumbers a little while
On this shadowy side of the stream
And waking remembers life with a smile
As a tale once told in a dream

SPIRIT NEVER DIES

All too often those who search for the soul's immortality do so in answer to the question, "Will a man live again?" and they cloud the issue, for if a man be immortal he never dies; nor is he ever born; he simply *is*. That which has no ending can have no beginning, and that which has no beginning or ending is timeless and infinite, is pure being, exists forever.

It is apparent that the body is not immortal; it has an obvious beginning and an obvious end. What we expect to be immortal in man is thus invisible, is spirit, a mysterious presence that animates body with consciousness. Each of us knows this presence very well, for it is what we feel ourselves to be; it is what we refer to when we say "I," This "I" then, this consciousness we know to be ourselves, is what we expect to be perpetuated after the death of the body.

What and who is this "I"? Is it the accumulated memories of a lifetime? Is it the knowledge each of us has attained? Is it some central perception station at the nerve endings of the five senses? Perhaps it is all of these, but it is a certainty that it is consciousness, for only that which is conscious is capable of referring to itself as "I." *And consciousness is invisible!*

True, we mark consciousness in another being by observing that it is animated, but we never see this consciousness, never touch or hear it. It exists within the very depths of the creature, and we understand it at all only by understanding the consciousness in ourselves. There are not different *kinds* of consciousness. Consciousness is consciousness. The sense of self that peers from behind your eyes is the same sense of self that peers from behind the eyes of your neighbor. Though this awareness is never at the same identical stage of development in any two beings, the difference is always one of degree and never of kind. One self pervades the universe, and differentiating in an attempt to know itself better, it attains to finiteness and uniqueness by becoming multiplicity instead of unity. Each creature is thus an expression of the immortal self. There is that within it which was never born and which will never die.

THE FALSE "I"

What is this deathless, ageless spirit that each of us senses within himself? How ephemeral it seems and how difficult to understand. Like mercury it slithers from under our fingers the minute we try to grasp it. For a second, a moment, we have a flash of insight, so that we seem right on the verge of discovering some mighty secret, then we begin to think about it and it disappears, leaving us wondering if we haven't imagined it. Something blocks us away from the discovery. Some false habit of thought bars us from true knowledge of self. *The culprit is the ego, the erroneous sense of self which we accumulate during our lifetimes. The death of the ego, which we fear so much, is the very thing we must achieve before we take unto ourselves the consciousness of immortal self.*

Let us reconsider the timeless, spaceless qualities of Universal Subconscious Mind, which has no beginning and no end, which is conscious but not self-conscious, and which is immortal being. Self without beginning or end incarnates and in so doing becomes something with a beginning. Anything with a beginning must have an end, and so the cycle of birth and death of physical bodies is established. With the birth of the physical body there is gradually built up something subtle and deluding, the accumulated experience undergone by Self within body, which gives rise to a sense of separateness and isolation, and is ego. This is memory of the beginning of physical experience, and we are deluded into calling it "I." In this manner we fail to perceive our true being, identify ourselves with the shallow and transitory little ego, and are shut away from the infinite and immortal intelligence from which we have sprung.

Nearly everyone considers his ego to be his true self, and as a result is totally unable to comprehend a life after the death of the physical body. He remembers the birth of his ego, in his first experiences and thoughts, and thus he senses the ego's inevitable end. Since he identifies himself with ego, he either looks forward with fear to undesirable oblivion or refuses to consider the matter of eventual death at all. If fear has been sufficiently ingrained in him by the practitioners of masochism, he even fancies himself faced by the possibility of providing an eternal roast for the fires of hell.

REBIRTH OF CONSCIOUSNESS

Ego, the tinsel trapping of self-awareness, is the undoing of us all. It bars us from consciousness of universal Self. It perceives all things as existing outside of consciousness and thus deludes us into believing that things originate on the physical plane. It loads us with a sense of personal responsibility, engenders bitterness and hate by its fancied wounds, sees itself as a speck in a limitless universe and blows itself up all the bigger in an hopeless attempt to fill infinity. The question is not how the ego shall live, but how the ego shall die. For only when the ego dies do we truly begin to live.

The ego is mortal. It has its beginning and it has its end. When death overtakes the body, it overtakes the ego also. Freed at last from delusion, self knows Self and sees its immortality.

The fear of death, then, springs from the ego's fear of dissolution, but only because we cling to the ego as our true selves. He who perceives at the center of consciousness the Great Self which is buried there, lets go of the ego forever and moves in tune with the infinite. The death of the physical body frees us all from the bonds of the ego, but the unshackling of these bonds during our lifetime brings power.

The death of the ego, then, is not a thing to be avoided, but a thing to be welcomed, a spiritual awakening that illumines all things, a transfiguration wherein the soul becomes fused with immortal Self. It is attained through humility, through love, through non-resistance, through fusion with Universal Subconscious Mind at the center of consciousness. Who achieves this consciousness perceives immortality.

Walt Whitman:

Afar down I see the huge first Nothing, I know I was even there. I walked unseen and always, and slept through the lethargic mist.

And took my time, and took no hurt from the fetid carbon. Long ago I was hugged close—long and long. Immense have been the preparations for me. Cycles ferried my cradle, rowing and rowing like cheerful boatmen.

For room to me stars kept aside in their own rings. It avails not, time nor place,— distance avails not. I am with you men and women of a generation, or ever so many generations hence.

Jesus:

Lo, I am with you alway, even unto the end of the world.

IMMORTAL SELF

One mind, one spirit, one Self pervades the universe, and its purpose is to know itself. It is primal stuff, first cause of all things, and is engaged in a work of expanding consciousness. Neither space nor time exist in it, for it is infinite, nor does it adhere to any form, for it is all form. It is becoming things; it becomes *all* things; and each form it creates is an expression of its knowledge of itself. It is eternal now, which is all times, past, present, and future. It is one place which is all places and anyplace. It is invisible. It is spirit. It is intelligence. It is mind. It is God. Incarnating into form, it becomes that form, and when the form dissolves, the spirit again becomes universal. It is this in man which is immortal, not the body, not the ego, not the personality, but the Self. He who attains to awareness of the Self in life, attains to power.

From the Upanishads:

The one Self within all beings becomes different, according to what it enters, and exists also without.

Self is Universal Subconscious Mind, which is infinite. All of it exists within each of us, and all of it exists without, for infinity is absolute unity and cannot be divided. It is this that Jesus meant when he said, "The Father in me, and I in the Father." Therefore if we would perceive our immortality, we must perceive the timeless being that exists at the center of our consciousness. But whether we attain to this illumination or not, we are immortal still. Everlasting life is not given to some and taken from others, for we are all one in reality. To him who is held firm in the bonds of ego, the veil will yet be lifted when the physical body dies and the ego ceases its delusion. Then he shall know as he is known, shall see self in Self, shall perceive in an instant the vast reaches of infinity. But a degree of this power and perception can be ours in this life if we can only forsake the ego and take unto ourselves the mantle of God.

FORSAKING THE EGO

Ego proceeds from Conscious Mind, though they are not identical. Conscious Mind is the reception station at the nerve endings of the five senses. It is a classifying, tabulating, analyzing machine governed solely by sensory stimuli and perceiving all things as existing outside it. It builds habit patterns of work and a mass of experience and perceives the movement of time. Thus the ego is compounded of memory, and prompts us to act always in the light of experience. According to the ego's conception so our lives become. This thing we falsely call "I," this ego, sees its limitations and brings those limitations into our lives. It fears and hates and envies, for it seeks constantly to puff itself up, by vain posturing, by blind attitude, and it brings into our lives the physical results of these mental causes, and keeps us constantly in chains.

So it is that a man must first be meek and humble before he can enter the Kingdom of Heaven, before he can become fused with immortal Self. Sometimes he comes to it through great suffering, sometimes through despair, sometimes through pain, but always the ego is reduced to nothingness before the portal swings open. And the ego does not surrender lightly. This posturing little elf with its blind delusions would have us believe it is our true self, and when we attempt to cast it aside, we feel its struggles in the very depths of our souls. So great is its resistance that men mortify the flesh, practice celibacy, abstain from all sensual pleasure in an attempt to ignore the evidence of the senses so that the ego might leave and the center of consciousness be revealed.

The ego is what we *seem* to be; the knowledge of what we truly are lies at the center of .consciousness. Such knowledge is perceived only by him who strips the ego bare, casts it aside like a worn-out garment. There is a kind of death in this, because we are accustomed to regard the ego as our true self, but the ego shall die anyway, and he who achieves its death in life attains power. Said Jesus, "Unless a man be born again, he shall not enter the Kingdom Of Heaven."

Seek the death of the ego, and be born anew in the knowledge of Self.

It is the Self that is immortal. It is the Self, Universal Subconscious Mind, which we truly are. All men have everlasting life, and it is not a question of whether we shall live again, but the insistent and glorious fact is that our real selves shall never die, just as they are never born. The spirit is birthless and deathless and changeless.

THE AFTERLIFE

What will the afterlife be like? It will be like stepping from the consciousness of a gnat into the consciousness of infinity. With the death of the physical body we shrug off the bonds of Conscious Mind and ego, lay aside the limitations of flesh, and become one with Universal Subconscious Mind, pervading all times and places. We shall have no bodies in the hereafter, for we shall be all bodies. We shall be in no specific place in the hereafter, for we shall be in all places. We shall not meet old friends and loved ones in the hereafter, for we shall all be one, unified and indivisible, one Self, one mind, one eternal "I."

The question is sometimes asked, "What good is a hereafter like that? Unless a man have a body and five senses and things to accomplish and friends to meet with, what good is it? Wouldn't oblivion be better?" And the only answer possible to this question is that oblivion is inevitable for the part of any man that asks this question, for it is the ego that poses it. It is Conscious Mind, built up of the experience of the five senses, that seeks to perpetuate itself, and it is no more than a flower, a bud on the everlasting shoot, flowering in season and withering out of season. Life with its give and take, serve and be served, strive and accomplish, cannot in any manner be compared with existence in the hereafter. Life is the ego's day in the sun; the hereafter is the eternity of the Self.

MOMENTS OF MYSTICAL EXPERIENCE

Space and time and body are the means by which Universal Subconscious Mind seeks an ever greater self-awareness. From infinity immortal Self incarnates in space and time, and what it becomes is an expression of its knowledge of itself. As its idea of self enlarges, it withdraws from body and incarnates again in a higher expression. All evolution follows this path, constantly upward, always increasing in self-awareness.

To everyone at some time in his life has come the startling magnitude of his own consciousness, perhaps for a second only, and he has been overcome by the question, "Why do I live at this particular time, in this particular place, in these particular circumstances? Indeed, what miracle has caused me to exist at all?" And at that moment he stands very close to the veil, almost sees through it, but not quite, almost understands what is beyond it, but not quite. He is startled, and a little uncomfortable, seized by a strange sense of vertigo, wondering whether life itself is not die dream, a sleep he has fallen into at some dimly remembered place, from which he will awaken at any moment. But usually he shunts aside this rare moment of mystical experience and concerns himself again with the workaday material world, taking assurance from the solidity of physical objects and the sharp definition of sensory perception. Thus he lives like an ostrich, burying his head in the sands of life and refusing to examine the most miraculous thing of all—his own consciousness—where it has come from and where it is going.

> *Our birth is but a sleep and a forgetting.*
> *Heaven lies about us in our infancy*
> *Shades of the prison-house begin to close*
> *About the growing boy.*
> —William Wordsworth

Sprung from the everlasting Self into life, there is in each child the remembrance of Universal Subconscious Mind. But as his ego develops, as he attains memory of sensory experience and the Conscious Mind grows, the memory becomes dimmer and dimmer, until at last he can recall it no longer, blocked from its view by the posturing ego which clutters the vision of the spirit. So it was that Jesus said, "Unless ye become as little children, ye shall not enter the Kingdom of Heaven."

THE ANIMATING PRESENCE

That which is, was never born and shall never die, is the very being of each of us. One Self, one mind, one life is in everyone. There is no difference between your neighbor and yourself except that of ego, of Conscious Mind. The difference you perceive is the difference brought about through thought, for your neighbor is a product of every thought he has ever had, even as you are. Since it is impossible for two reactive beings ever to have the exact same kind and sequence of thought, there never has been nor will there ever be two identical humans, short of union with God. And union with God is achieved by all when the worn house of the body is laid aside at last. It may be achieved in life only when the individual ceases to think in response to the stimuli of the senses and originates thought at the center of consciousness. Then free of the bondage of the flesh, he achieves power, control over all the circumstances of his life.

Everyone knows that he exists, and not simply because he observes other individuals responding to him. That which he feels himself to be he knows as consciousness, lying within his body, yet not his body. He observes other animated beings around him and correctly supposes them to be possessed of the same kind of consciousness as he; and he further observes death overtake the bodies of a few of these beings, and notes that the animating presence has departed. He does not see where the presence has gone and is mystified, for he does not know if it has simply left or has suddenly ceased to be. He further observes that this condition of death, or departure of the animating presence of the body, is inevitable to all forms of life and thus is inevitable to him, and he vainly tries to peer beyond that event in order to determine if he might not still continue to exist after his body has ceased to function.

Alas, the veil is too great for him, for he cannot imagine an existence without his body, and so at last he throws up his hands in despair and decides that his consciousness resulted from the fantastic array of circumstances that produced his particular body and that on either side of birth and the grave there is nothing but oblivion.

But no man completely accepts this delusion. No matter how vociferously he may proclaim it, no matter how valiantly he assumes to face this horrid assumption, there is something in him that knows differently. That something is Self, the presence that animates his body. Birthless, deathless and ageless, it knows its immortality.

SELF IS NOT BODY

Your body is not you. If it were and your leg were amputated, pan of your consciousness would be lost with your leg. Neither are you simply brain. If you were only brain, then the rest of the physical body could be stripped away, and the brain would continue to live. Actually, the brain itself does not even think. Some invisible thinker merely uses the brain as a central reception station for sensory perception.

Someone, something, is dwelling in your body, peering through the windows of your eyes, listening at the portals of your ears, using your brain to receive impressions. Invisible, hidden, gowned with your particular form but an instant in the eternity of its being, it uses your body as an idea, then discards it and departs to whence it came. This is immortal Self.

People want to know where they will go when they die, and the answer to that question is that they will go *everywhere,* for they don't truly go, they simply expand. Self, freed from the limitations of body, becomes Universal Self, the consciousness of all time, all space, all form. Since Self is free of all limitation and multiplicity, it leaves behind personality and ego and conscious memory, which become immersed like the tiniest drop of water in an infinite sea. Ego goes, limitation goes, the inconceivably small "I" is replaced by the great "I" of infinity.

A very intelligent but very egotistical man once said, "I cannot stand any conception of the afterlife in which I cease to be me and become somebody else, even if that somebody is much greater." And there are plenty of people whose idea of the hereafter hinges on there being plenty of social life, good food and good fellowship, lots of money and pleasure, and no pain. When it is pointed out to them that they will need to take their bodies along in order to enjoy these things, they nod with equanimity, apparently convinced that an exact replica of the one they leave behind will be furnished them in the hereafter.

BEHIND EVERY PAIR OF EYES

It is always ego that blocks immortality from view, for ego cannot see beyond its own finiteness. It needs a body, needs separateness, for from these conditions it has sprung, and it projects a hereafter that revolves around bodies and personalities. Body and personality and Conscious Mind change throughout life. How shall they exist then in the hereafter of the ego? Will they be those which we possessed in the prime of life? Then what of the infant taken in death? What of the cripple and the chronically diseased? And how shall our characters and minds be in such a hereafter? As they were at the peak of life? But what of the feeble-minded and insane, and the murderer and the robber and the depraved? A strange hereafter, of confusion and injustice, with individuals longing for better bodies—such is the hereafter of the ego. But we needn't worry about it. It doesn't exist.

Beyond the advent of death, body does not persist, nor personality, nor ego, nor Conscious Mind, for all these are the illusory trappings of finiteness, for which we have no further use when we return to the infinite. The great Self enters into each body and becomes different according to what it enters, but upon leaving again becomes absolute infinity and unity. "The infinite," says Emerson, "lies stretched in smiling repose." And so does the immortal Self, eternally One, the true being in every man, the observer who looks out upon the world through every pair of eyes.

REINCARNATION

One of the interesting theories held by those who demand a body as a prerequisite to any existence after death is that of reincarnation. Because Conscious Mind is a finite instrument and useless in dealing with infinity, even great religious thinkers of the past have been led into the trap of believing in reincarnation, because they could not, with their Conscious Minds, conceive of any kind of existence at all without a body to accompany it. Only the Brahmans felt that true existence was unity with Universal Subconscious Mind, but even they felt that a man must consciously come to this illumination, holding that he would go through successive reincarnations on earth until he attained it. No religious teaching has ever surpassed the enlightenment of the Hindus, with their Vedas and Bhagavad-Gita and Upanishads, but even they could not forsake the illusory and transitory ego altogether, and thus were led into believing that individual men went through successive reincarnations before attaining to Brahma. It is immortal Self which is incarnating in search of self-knowledge and only when knowledge of Self is complete will reincarnation cease. The real you, the immortal Self, will reincarnate to be sure, short of its attaining to complete self-knowledge, but the transitory you, the built-up thought habits and memories of the Conscious Mind, will incarnate no more, for it is only illusion, just a tiny instant in the eternity of evolution, whose very purpose is change. Ego will neither reincarnate nor persist after death. It is not the real you. It is scarcely even a microscopic part of the real you.

Every incarnation is a reincarnation; every child born is a reincarnation; for only one Self enters into each body and looks out of all eyes and is conscious. Each of us is a reincarnation of every person who has preceded us, and the knowledge of all that has preceded us lies within us, in Universal Subconscious Mind, which has been all things and all people and all events, and will be forevermore.

INFINITE SPIRIT

Is there spirit communication? Not in the way we are accustomed to think. Those who have departed are no longer contained by the limitations of personality and ego and Conscious Mind, but have become one with immortal Self. Yet the knowledge of all things lies in Universal Subconscious Mind, and may be revealed to Conscious Mind when a contact between the two is made. So it is that the stance is often witness to unexplainable phenomena, for the Subconscious always responds to the Conscious and nothing is impossible to it. Therefore the conceptions we have of loved ones, projected into the Subconscious, are capable of becoming manifest in the physical world. We see ghosts, faces, hear words, sometimes in the seance, sometimes without the seance, which bring the dead back with us for a moment. But this is always a physical projection of a conception held in mind, and is just as often recorded of the living as of the dead.

There is only one contact we may make with the hereafter, and that is with the one immortal Self which dwells there. It contains all knowledge, all love, all peace, and is the true being of everyone. There are not billions of personalities circulating through it willy nilly; such finiteness has been torn from it and left it pure and unadulterated and just one:

> *Never the spirit was born;*
> *The spirit shall cease to be never*
> *Never was time it was not;*
> *End and beginning are dreams*
> *Birthless and deathless and changeless*
> *Remaineth the spirit forever*
> *Death hath not touched it at all*
> *Dead though the house of it seems.*
> —Bhagavad-Gita

NO PUNISHMENT IN THE HEREAFTER

It is one of the strange facts of history that the words of one of its most enlightened men, Jesus of Nazareth, have been misconstrued to saddle mankind with a vengeful God who vies with the devil for souls. Conceive if you will of a God who gives men sex organs that provide pleasurable sensation, then promises to burn everyone in hell who doesn't use them within a strictly prescribed manner. Conceive of a God who gives men eyes but still remains invisible to them, then threatens to burn everyone in hell who doesn't believe in him. Conceive of a God who made the devil and his fires because he knew in the first place that he would burn certain souls. A mighty unsavory fellow, this God, this figment of the masochistic imagination. One cannot help but prefer his equally imaginative evil counterpart, the devil, who seems like a pretty jolly fellow after all, considering the very poor job he has been given.

Immortality is not something to be won by good conduct, nor will good conduct send certain souls to heaven, nor bad conduct send others to hell. Only one Self manifests throughout the universe, and it neither punishes itself nor rewards itself. It is eternal, and though it becomes a billion mortal things, its eternity is not touched. It passes into and out of myriad forms but always remains one. Obviously it neither sends itself to heaven nor sends itself to hell, for nothing exists outside itself.

Have no fear of hell—there is no such thing. There is only heaven, consciousness of the immortal Self, which each of us shall eventually attain, whether it comes to us in life or not.

EVERY SOUL IS SAVED

Misapprehensions concerning sin and punishment and hell and the devil come from a lack of understanding of the message brought by Jesus. Jesus taught that the truth about each man lay in his spirit and not in the physical world. When he spoke of sin he referred to errors o£ thinking, buried guilts; and the punishment he alluded to was the inevitable physical manifestation of such negative thinking. By hell he meant the human bondage undergone by each person who simply reacts to the physical world and fails to perceive his inner consciousness, the Kingdom of Heaven. He did not concern himself with immortality, for he knew that each person was immortal regardless and nothing could alter this. He sought only to awaken men to their spiritual power, to turn their eyes from the physical world onto the consciousness that lay within, so they might free themselves from lack and limitation and disease. He preached no afterlife. "I am come," he said, "that ye might have life, and that ye might have it more abundantly." The immortality of all men was obvious to Jesus. He was primarily concerned because they did not know how to live.

The very guilts and limitations which Jesus besought us to become free of have been adopted as dogma by many facets of society, and they have thrown mankind into deeper bondage than ever. We must come to realize that God is kind and just and loving and is in us, and there is no punishment in the hereafter, and every soul is saved. We need not fear God, we need only love him. We need not supplicate for forgiveness before an altar, for God's altar is our very selves; we are with him night and day. Religions and temples are built by man, but God's temple is man, and wherever we are, we are always in a place of worship. We need only turn to the Self that dwells within.

THE ART OF DYING

Birth and death are the great transformations. The ego does not fear birth, for there is no ego at birth. But the ego indeed fears death. As long as we identify ourselves with the ego, the fear of death shall have its hold on us, and we shall regard it as a great calamity. But once we have freed ourselves of the ego and have perceived at the center of consciousness the immortal Self, death will become an adventure, for by it we shall be freed of illusion, return to absolute truth, know as we are known, become united with God.

Life is the medium through which the great Self seeks to work out its purpose, and

230

each of us as a part of that purpose has his appointed tasks and work. When these are fulfilled it is time for us to return home once again, but not before. Though the hereafter may be a mightier existence than any known on earth, we nevertheless shall not return to it until we have worked through space and time in search of the knowledge that the great Self is seeking through us. Our jobs are here in life, and we must do them before we depart.

Many men poison their lives through fear of death. Since death is known to be inevitable for every man, it is indeed very strange that so little is known of the art of dying. For dying is an art, to be performed expertly or crudely according to our knowledge. To most men death comes when the body has worn out and ceases to function, and is preceded by a period of time in which the body perceptibly begins to break down. As the hour of death approaches, the human soul has only two ways to turn; outward for the solaces of the physical world or inward toward the universal Self. A painful death, violent, and full of suffering awaits him who turns toward the outer world, for he is prompted by the ego which seeks to hold on to that which must be let go. Indeed, all that the ego needs for perpetuation, the memory, conscious intellect, animal faculties, the functions of the bodily organs, are gradually being wrested away, sinking into lethargy, ceasing to function; and the ego becomes confused, terror-stricken, full of panic. There is no escape for the hounded little "I," its doom is upon it. The very material world which is responsible for its existence, is gradually fading away. He who identifies himself with ego undergoes a confused and suffering transformation.

But he who has glimpsed the greater Self takes death calmly. Assured of immortality and the changelessness of spirit, he passes easily from one world to the other. His spirit lays down his body because it is finished with it, and moves into the great expansion where it becomes lord and master over all things. Self meets self, the personal becomes the universal, and a new and greater existence in the infinite reduces the just finished life to nothingness, to a second in the endless time of eternity.

And so we die as we have lived, with faith or without it, with spiritual knowledge or without it; and according to the wisdom we have attained, we meet death gracefully or crudely, but each of us is immortal nonetheless.

So live that when thy summons comes to join the innumerable caravan, which moves to that mysterious realm, where each shall take his chamber in the silent halls of death, thou go not, like the quarry-slave at night, scourged to his dungeon, but, sustained and soothed by an unfaltering trust, approach thy grave, like one who wraps the drapery of his couch about him, and lies down to pleasant dreams.
—William Cullen Bryant

REVIEW

1. Though body is mortal, a man is never born and never dies.

2. The presence that animates body is invisible even in life, and leaving the body on death, is invisible still.

3. One Self incarnates in all bodies and is deathless, ageless, eternal spirit.

4. Ego shuts us away from the knowledge of Self. Ego deludes us into believing it is "I."

5. The death of the ego must precede awareness of universal Self.

6. Ego is as mortal as the body, and at death we all become Universal Self.

7. He who banishes ego during his life achieves power, for he moves with God.

8. Neither space nor time exist in the hereafter, nor does form. There is only consciousness, absolute and indivisible.

9. Body is merely used by immortal spirit as an expression of an idea. It is not Self, is but the tiniest expression of Self.

10. The Self enters into each body and becomes different according to what it enters, but upon leaving becomes infinite and absolute and only one.

11. There is no reincarnation for the ego, but constant reincarnation for the Self.

12. There is only one form of spirit communication and that is contact between Conscious Mind and Universal Subconscious Mind.

13. All men are immortal. There is no hell, no punishment.

14. Jesus taught that the power of immortal being could be used in life.

15. He who perceives self in Self will find death an easy transformation.

There is an answer to every question, a solution to every mystery, a key for every lock. Throughout this book we have prepared for the final revelation. Now it is upon us.

RECOMMENDED READING

Drama of Love and Death by Edward Carpenter. Published by Mitchell Kennerley.

ELEVENTH MEDITATION

I know that I am pure spirit, deathless, birthless, changeless, and eternal. I am not body; I am not Conscious Mind; I am not ego. I am sense of Self only, consciousness, awareness, unadulterated being. The presence that animates all life is within me, is altogether the real me. I am using my body for a purpose,. as an expression of an idea, and when the idea is fully expressed, through my work and my mission, I shall return again to unity with universal Self, leaving body and ego behind. I do not confuse my body and my ego with what I truly am. My body is simply an instrument for my expression, and my ego is simply memory of physical experience. Returning to infinity and unity, I shall need neither body nor ego. I am free of the domination of the ego. It is not my true self, is simply an illusion necessary to finiteness and the perception of apace and time. I turn away from the ego, withdraw into the depths of my being to the immortal consciousness that lies within. Here in this magic center my word is law. I need only speak it with faith and conviction, and it will manifest in my life. I am calm and serene, sure and unfaltering, for my roots are in eternity. All the things of life shall change and pass away, but I shall never pass away, for wherever life is I shall be, one with Universal Subconscious Mind. I need not strive or strain to attain immortality, nor fear punishment, nor aspire for reward. The Kingdom of Heaven awaits all, the wise, the foolish, the sinner, and the saint, for we are all one in reality, clothed in different forms in this moment of incarnation. I do not fear death, for by it I attain the consciousness of higher Self. Neither do I invite death, for it must wait until my work is done. I forsake the ego, perceive self in Self, see the majesty, the grandeur, the immortality of the power that dwells within.

Chapter 12 - THE KEY

That which from Self made each mortal Self unto each mortal must be
Thus the key that unlocks the portal to God is thyself—thou art He

YOU ARE GOD

THE VEIL REMOVED

This is the ineffable secret, the ultimate illumination, the key to peace and power: *You are God.* If you will accept this towering truth, dare to stand atop this magnificent pinnacle, universal consciousness will be revealed to you from within. God is there. It is He who peers from behind your eyes, who is your own consciousness, who is your very Self. You are not just a part of God; you are *altogether* God, and God is *altogether you.*

Upanishads:

The personal self and the ultimate imperishable impersonal Self are one.

Vedanta:

Not a part, not a mode of That, but identically That, that absolute Spirit of the World.

Jesus:

Who hath seen me hath seen the Father.

God is Universal Subconscious Mind, the intelligence that pervades all times and places, the design and order and consciousness of all things. God becomes things; He becomes all things; He has become *you.* God is not your body, not your ego, but your sense of being, your "I." There is only one "I" in the universe. The same sense of Self is in everyone. It appears to be different in life because it clothes itself in different forms. These forms wither and decay, but the Self is always one and indivisible and changeless. Every person that lives, every person that ever will live, every creature and thing, are all one in spirit. All are God, and each is altogether God.

Each of us is altogether God because infinite intelligence cannot divide itself. It makes a seeming division in flesh, but never in spirit, for infinity is always one and indivisible. God manifests completely in each thing, and each thing is a manifestation of God's knowledge of Himself. Your consciousness is God's consciousness. Your idea of yourself is God's idea of Himself. The ideas you accept are automatically manifested in life, for what God knows He creates, and what you know is created, for you are God.

UNIVERSAL CONSCIOUSNESS

God is consciousness and awareness and order and design and knowledge and intelligence and spirit. He is infinite. He cannot know himself as infinity, but only by becoming something finite. Thus God seeks to expand His sense of Self by becoming things, and each thing says, "I am this." What you believe yourself to be is what you believe God to be. The limitations and lacks you impose upon yourself you impose upon God. No one can possibly believe there is any limitation on God, thus the magnificent truth is that there is no limitation on any man.

Through each of us God attains *self*-consciousness, and each of us is God incarnate. In our lives we accept the limitations of the flesh and the inhibitions of the ego, and thus we fall short of God-consciousness. We ask ourselves where we have come from and where we are going, for we have lost the remembrance of having always been, just as we cannot see that we will always be. The development of our ego thrusts upon us a precarious duality of mind, wherein Conscious Mind over-runs Universal Subconscious Mind, and we come to regard ourselves as ego only, instead of universal Self which we truly are. "How can God possibly be the poor thing that I am?" a man will ask himself, identifying himself with ego and failing to perceive that he is consciousness only. Free yourself from the bonds of the ego, and you will forget the poor thing that you thought you were, and become one with God.

ILLUMINATION

This far you can be guided but the attainment of enlightenment is yours to achieve alone. Words and logic have never yet provided the great illumination, which must come to each man in his own way. If you will accept with perfect faith the premise that all truth is spiritual, if you will discard the promptings of the ego and the noisy sensual stimuli of the material world, if you will search for revelation at the center of consciousness, then the Kingdom of Heaven will be yours. Letting go of ego may seem like letting go of life itself, and so it is, even as Jesus said, "Who loses his life shall find it."

Illumination, the arrival at God-consciousness, the spiritual perception that you are God, will come to you through meditation. As an experience it is universally the same, but perhaps has never been as well described as by Edward Carpenter:

The brain is stilled. It does not cease from its natural and joyful activities. But it ceases from that terrified and joyless quest which was inevitable to it as long as its own existence, its own foundation, its own affiliation to the everlasting being was in question or doubt. The man at last lets thought go; he glides below it into the quiet feeling, the quiet sense of his own identity with the self of other things—of the universe. He glides past the feeling into the very identity itself, where a glorious all-consciousness leaves no room for separate self thoughts or emotions. He leans back in silence on that inner being, and bars off for a time every thought, every movement of the mind, every impulse to action, or whatever in the faintest degree may stand between him and That; and so there comes to him a sense of absolute repose, a consciousness of immense and universal power, such as completely transforms the world for him. All life is changed; he becomes master of his fate; he perceives that all things are hurrying to perform his will; and whatever in that region of inner life he may condescend to desire, that already is shaping itself to utterance and expression in the outer world about him.

In such a manner does a man come to the realization that he himself is God. In such a manner does he learn to turn his attention from the material world and originate all things on the plane of mind. By forsaking ego and finding his true Self, whatever he thinks, conceives, or desires will manifest in the physical world. He becomes die doer, the knower, the creator, makes all things from Self, is the Self of all things.

That boundless power, source of every power, manifesting itself as life, entering every heart, living there among the elements, that is Self.

—Upanishads

FIND THOU BUT THYSELF

Though this knowledge is not new, it has been exceedingly rare and held among a very few men. All the ages of life's evolution, up through the slime and mist of a fetid and newly formed earth, have pointed toward it. There is only one consciousness in all things, one consciousness which assumes countless forms in search of ever greater knowledge about itself. The infinite Self becomes the finite self, and the day when finite self recognizes itself as infinite Self is the day that exposes eternity. This little hour, this little life where we are focused now, is but an instant in the aeons of our being. We are that very power that constructed the heavens and the earth, and when we have cast out ego and the limitations of our thinking, the multi-dimensioned heavens are revealed to be in our own souls.

We have looked in the mountains and. He has not been there. We have looked on the plain and He has not been there. We have searched the sea and the air and the earth and the sky, and He has not been there. How should we find Him when we looked outside? He dwelt within, was in truth our very selves.

But what thing dost thou now
Looking Godward to cry,
I am I, thou art thou,
I am low, thou art high?
I am thou, whom thou seekest to find him
Find thou but thyself, thou art I.
                          —Algernon Swinburne

LOCK AND KEY

The lock that bars us from the recognition that we are God is the creation of the ego in the first memories and inhibitions of Conscious Mind. This lock may be undone through meditation, through taking unto ourselves universal consciousness, through arrival at the spiritual Kingdom of Heaven; and the key that unlooses all power is the revelation that each man is God.

Mind is consciousness, is intelligence, and there is only one mind, which is the mind of God. All things are made from it, are ideas manifested into form. As ideas change so does form, but the spirit never changes. It is limitless, one and changeless.

Universal Subconscious Mind creates in the physical world those ideas that Conscious Mind adopts as beliefs. We create evil by false thinking, by ideas of lack and limitation and pain and sorrow and disease. Such evil is illusion because it proceeds from the errors of Conscious Mind, and may be banished by donning the mantle of immortal Self at the center of consciousness.

The physical world is but a tiny extension of a vast spiritual realm. All physical law is subordinate to spiritual law, for the physical world is a secondary chain of effects, while the spiritual world is first cause. When man's consciousness expands beyond ego, beyond conscious mind, beyond the limitations of the Prompters, thoughts are immediately manifested on the physical plane. Thought transference, clairvoyance, mental healing, and creativeness are all evidences of the super-physical power of Universal Subconscious Mind.

A man adds all things unto himself by taking a position with impregnable faith. Faith moves Universal Subconscious Mind to creation, but it is only the ego that must use faith. When the ego goes and God-consciousness comes, thought is immediately followed by the thing, for there remains nothing to overcome. All conceptions of limitation and lack and guilt and pain and shame and remorse are cast out with the ego. Nothing but God remains, and whatever God knows is created.

We attract into our lives the physical manifestations of the thoughts we think, and in order to attract good instead of evil we must learn to control our thinking, to think positively instead of negatively. We must be able to *choose* good thoughts. If a man thinks only in response to the stimuli of the outer world, he remains ego only, an automaton; but when he originates thoughts at the center of consciousness, he creates his own life in the image of his desires and dons the mantle of immortal Self.

TWELFTH MEDITATION

I turn away from the world about me to the world of consciousness that lies within. I shut out all memories of the past, create no images of the future. I concentrate on my being, on my awareness. I elide deep into the very recesses of my soul to a place of utter repose. Here I perceive fact in the making, am conscious of the one being from which all beings spring. I know that this is immortal Self, this is God, this is me. I am, I always was, I always will he. All men, all things, all space and time and life are here in the depths of my soul. Smaller than small, greater than great meet and unite in me. That which I thought I was, ego, I never was at all, for it was a changing thing, mirroring the seasons and the tides, a thing to be born and grow and die. I am not a thing of time or circumstance. I am spirit, pure and eternal, birthless, deathless and changeless. I am patient, for I am all time: I am wise, for I contain the knowledge of all things. I know not pain, for I see there is no beginning and no end, and who suffers pain must see beginning and end, I am rich, for there is no limit to the abundance I may create from my very Self. I am successful, for I need only think to achieve. I love and am beloved, for all things are myself and I am all things. I unite, I fuse, I become one with Universal Subconscious Mind. The mask of vanity and ego I shall never wear again. I perceive the magnificent Dweller at the center of my consciousness, and I know Him to be my very self. Time and space, shadow and substance, what matter these? I am God.

104, 127, 145, 169, 203

116-140   # 162-165

118 207-218

118-119
122-123
124 # 127, 129, 130 Bottom, 131, 132 # sum,
135-136

12 pages!